CHURCHILL AND STRATEGIC DILEMMAS
BEFORE THE WORLD WARS

CHURCHILL
and
STRATEGIC DILEMMAS
before the
WORLD WARS

Essays in Honor of Michael I. Handel

Editor

JOHN H. MAURER
US Naval War College

LONDON AND NEW YORK

First published in 2003 by
FRANK CASS PUBLISHERS

This edition published 2013 by Routledge
2 Park Square, Milton Park, Abingdon, Oxfordshire OX14 4RN
711 Third Avenue, New York, NY 10017

First issued in paperback 2014

Routledge is an imprint of the Taylor & Francis Group, an informa business

British Library Cataloguing in Publication Data

Churchill and strategic dilemmas before the world wars:
essays in honor of Michael I. Handel
  1. Churchill, Winston, Sir, 1874–1965 – Views on military strategy – Congresses.
  2. Churchill, Winston, Sir, 1874–1965 – Views on Germany – Congresses 3. Churchill,
  Winston, Sir, 1874–1965 – Views on Japan – Congresses 4. Churchill, Winston, Sir,
  1874–1965 – Views on technology and war – Congresses 5. Great Britain – Foreign
  relations – Germany Congresses 6. Germany – Foreign relations – Germany Congresses
  6. Germany – Foreign relations – Great Britain – Congresses 7. Great Britain – Foreign
  relations – Japan – Congresses 8. Japan – Foreign relations – Great Britain – Congresses
  9. Great Britain – Foreign relations – 1901–1936 – Congresses 10. Great Britain –
  Foreign relations – 1936–1945 – Congresses I. Maurer, John H. II. Handel, Michael I.
  327.4'1043'092

ISBN 13: 978-0-7146-5468-3 (hbk)
ISBN 13: 978-0-415-76142-0 (pbk)

Library of Congress Cataloging-in-Publication Data

Churchill and strategic dilemmas before the World Wars: essays in honor of Michael I.
  Handel / editor, John H. Maurer.
    p.   cm.
  Includes bibliographical references and index.
  ISBN 0-7146-5468-X (cloth) – ISBN 0-7146-8374-4 (paper)
  1. Great Britain – Military policy. 2. Great Britain – Foreign relations – 20th century.
  3. Churchill, Winston, Sir, 1874–1965 – Contributions in strategy. 4. Strategy –
  History – 20th century. 5. National security – Great Britain – History – 20th century.
  I. Handel, Michael I. II. Maurer, John H.

UA647.C564 2003
355'.033541'09041–dc21

2003051450

Typeset in 10.5/12pt Times NR MT by Servis Filmsetting Ltd, Manchester

Contents

Notes on Contributors

Christopher M. Bell is an associate professor of history at Dalhousie University, Halifax, Nova Scotia. He is the author of *The Royal Navy, Seapower and Strategy Between the Wars* (2000) and co-editor of *Naval Mutinies of the Twentieth Century: An International Perspective* (Frank Cass, 2003). He has written articles on British strategy and war plans, and is currently working on a book on Winston Churchill and British sea power.

David Jablonsky (Colonel, Infantry, ret.) is the professor of national security affairs in the Department of National Security and Strategy at the US Army War College, Carlisle, Pennsylvania. A graduate of Dartmouth College and the US Army War College, he received a MA from Boston University in international relations, and holds MA and PhD degrees in European history from Kansas University. He has held the Elihu Root Chair of Strategy and the George C. Marshall Chair of Military Studies at the Army War College, and currently holds the Dwight D. Eisenhower Chair of National Security Studies. He is the author of five books dealing with European history and international relations.

Brian McKercher is professor of history, Royal Military College of Canada. He is the author of *The Second Baldwin Government and the United States, 1924–1929: Attitudes and Diplomacy* (1984), *Esme Howard: A Diplomatic Biography* (1989), and *Transition of Power: Britain's Loss of Global Pre-eminence to the United States, 1930–1945* (1999). In addition to being the author of numerous articles, he has edited (with L. Aronsen) *The North Atlantic Triangle in a Changing World: Anglo-American-Canadian Relations, 1903–1956* (1996), (with Michael Dockrill) *Diplomacy and World Power: Studies in British Foreign Policy, 1890–1951* (1996), *Anglo-American Relations in the 1920s: The Struggle for Supremacy* (1991), and *Arms Limitation and Disarmament, 1899–1939* (1992). With Keith Neilson, he is the general editor of the Praeger Series on Foreign Policy in the Interwar Period; he is also general editor of the Praeger Series on Diplomacy and Strategic Thought.

John H. Maurer is professor of policy and strategy at the US Naval War College in Newport, Rhode Island. He is the author of *The Outbreak* *of the First World War* (1996), and has published books about great-power military interventions in the developing world and naval arms control between the two world wars. He is also associate editor of the journal *Diplomacy & Statecraft*. Before joining the faculty of the Naval War College, he served as executive editor of *Orbis: A Journal of World Affairs* and held the position of senior research fellow at the Foreign Policy Research Institute. He is currently writing a book on Winston Churchill and Great Britain's decline as a world power.

Acknowledgements

The essays in this volume were written for an international strategy conference held in honor of the late Michael I. Handel during November 2001, at the United States Naval War College in Newport, Rhode Island. Michael Handel taught during the last decade of his life in the Naval War College's Strategy and Policy Department. He was our esteemed colleague and close friend. When Michael discovered in early 2001 that he was seriously ill and had only a short time to live, we wanted to find some way to express our admiration for his life's work and our gratitude to him for the way he enriched our lives. One of the traditional ways to honor a distinguished scholar, of course, is for his colleagues and students to join together in presenting him with a book of essays. We thought that this tribute would be a fitting way for our department to honor Michael, who has made such a valuable contribution to the study of strategy through his writings, lectures, teaching, and conferences. When we approached Michael about our plans, he embraced the entire project, and during his final illness played a major role in organizing the effort. Michael liked to encourage the study of strategy by bringing together scholars for gatherings marked by the lively exchange of ideas. His whole-hearted enthusiasm for this project was a tonic for those of us who deeply admired his work and would soon mourn his passing. The conference and this volume, by his involvement in their conception, bear Michael's direct imprint. Our first debt in producing this volume, then, is to Michael Handel himself, whose teaching, scholarship, and intellectual rigor provided a model to us all.

At the Naval War College, the administration gave their complete support to Michael and us in carrying out this enterprise. The then Dean of Academics, Charles P. Neimeyer, the then Provost, Rear Admiral (ret.) Barbara McGann, and the President of the Naval War College Foundation, Rear Admiral (ret.) Joseph C. Strasser, provided generous funding and administrative support for the conference. Later, Alberto Coll, Dean of the Naval War College's Center for Naval Warfare Studies, gave additional funding, without which the conference could not have taken place. Michael's friend, Mary Estabrooks, working in the office of the Dean of Academics, made the wheels of the administrative bureaucracy turn for us. Anita Rousseau, also in the Dean's office, ably assisted us in making this conference a reality. Meanwhile, William Spain, the Assistant Dean of Academics, oversaw the smooth running of the conference. The President of the Naval War College, Rear Admiral Rodney Rempt, presided over the conference's proceedings and graciously welcomed its participants to his home.

George Baer, then chair of the Strategy and Policy Department, supplied ever-useful advice for orchestrating the conference and gave his full backing for the project. The current chair, Tom Nichols, has also supported this major effort by the Department to honor Michael. From within the Strategy and Policy Department, Carol Keelty helped in the daunting task of bringing together for the conference scholars from Europe, Israel, Canada, Australia, and across the United States.

The response to our invitation from Michael's friends was overwhelming, with the result that they have produced three volumes instead of one in honor of Michael's memory. These three volumes reflect some of the diverse interests and themes of Michael's work. John Maurer of the Strategy and Policy Department edited the present volume. Michael's longtime friend, Richard Betts of Columbia University, and Thomas Mahnken, from the Strategy and Policy Department, edited *Paradoxes of Strategic Intelligence*. Bradford Lee and Karl Walling, also from the Strategy and Policy Department, edited *Strategic Logic and Political Rationality*.

Credit, too, for bringing these volumes to print belongs to Michael's publisher of longstanding, Frank Cass, and to his son Stewart Cass. Michael himself had approached Frank and Stewart Cass, wanting them to publish these volumes. Stewart took the time to attend the conference, and his sound guidance and enthusiastic backing have greatly assisted us in our work. No authors could ask for a more congenial publisher.

Finally, Michael's partner in life, his wife Jill, helped us at every stage of this project. Jill faced the adversity afflicting her family with courage and constancy, caring for Michael during his final illness while tending to the needs of their four children. The presence of Jill and her older children at the conference lifted the spirits of its participants, and she has supported us in the subsequent preparation of these volumes for publication. These volumes, then, represent not only a tribute to Michael and his life's work but to Jill's bravery.

Introduction

John H. Maurer

Michael I. Handel, to whom the authors of the following essays dedicate this volume, had a longstanding interest in Sir Winston S. Churchill. This interest is hardly surprising. As a leading scholar in the field of strategy, Michael Handel examined some of the most important strategic decision makers and thinkers – whom he called 'masters of war' – who lived over the long span of human history from ancient Greece and China to the twenty-first century. In the twentieth century, very few individuals occupy as prominent a place for both high leadership in wartime and a writer on politics and strategy as Winston Churchill does. Churchill is today perhaps best remembered for his leadership role during the Second World War. Of course, he played a leading role in directing Great Britain's policy and strategy during the entire period of the two world wars and the opening decade of the Cold War. Churchill wrote at length on war and politics throughout his life. His voluminous writings provide an incredibly rich source for the study of strategic and political decision making. Michael Handel avidly read what Churchill wrote about the difficulties he experienced in trying to fashion a coherent strategy and ensure that the conduct of military operations adhered to it.

In his extensive studies on intelligence, politics, strategy, and war, Michael Handel made considerable reference to Churchill's writings and actions in wartime. Michael Handel, however, wanted to write more on Churchill. On several occasions, he mentioned to me how he would like to write a book about Winston Churchill as a strategist. At one point, we even considered collaborating in writing a book or holding a conference on the topic. Michael Handel also thought about including additional chapters on Churchill in some future edition of *Masters of War*, his outstanding examination of the strategic thought of Carl von Clausewitz, Sir Julian Corbett, Baron Antoine-Henri Jomini, Mao Tse-tung, and Sun Tzu. In what would have been an important addition to that study,

Michael Handel intended to explore how Churchill as a strategist sought to find a competitive advantage in wartime, and thereby hold down the cost of winning. One key aspect of Churchill's strategic outlook that especially interested Michael Handel was the importance assigned to intelligence by the British leader. Churchill avidly sought and consumed intelligence about the political and strategic environment in which he operated. Intelligence could provide information about the makeup of the enemy's forces and intentions. Churchill, too, saw deception as providing a cloak for one's own actions, helping to confer strategic surprise. Michael Handel wrote extensively about intelligence matters, and his works stand out in their importance in the field of strategic studies. The high value that Churchill assigned to the use of intelligence in strategy made him an important subject of enquiry.

Another topic that interested Michael Handel was how Churchill accorded great importance to technological innovation and military transformation in fighting wars. Neither Churchill nor Handel thought technology provided a panacea to difficult strategic problems. A competent enemy, in their view, might find ways in their strategy to counter any technological innovation. Nonetheless, both saw how military transformations can still confer important strategic and operational advantages to one side in a conflict. Churchill's backing of the tank during the First World War impressed Michael Handel as an example of how wise political leadership can encourage transformation in a military organization.

A third aspect of Churchill's strategic makeup that Michael Handel wanted to write about more extensively was his advocacy of indirect strategies for winning in war. Of course, Churchill played a well-known role as one of the sponsors of the ill-fated Dardanelles campaign during the First World War. In the Second World War, Churchill supported the campaigns in North Africa and the Mediterranean. Michael Handel wanted to explore the controversies surrounding these campaigns. While hardly uncritical of Churchill, Michael Handel nonetheless viewed the British leader as a master of war. He hoped to provide a systematic treatment of Churchill as a strategist, offering a synthesis of what made this British leader stand out as a strategic theorist and war leader.

The essays in this volume cannot substitute for the work that Michael Handel intended to write about Churchill. Instead, what we have done in these essays is explore how Churchill assessed the changes taking place in the international environment during the first half of the twentieth century. In particular, we have examined how Britain and its empire faced major threats from the rising challengers of Germany and Japan, and how technological changes also posed new dangers to its security. These challenges led to the two costly world wars. Even though Britain emerged on the winning side in both struggles, the cost of victory in these struggles undermined Britain's position as a global power. Our essays, then, examine Churchill's assessments of Britain's strategic predicament in a rapidly changing and increasingly more dangerous world.

In the first chapter, I examine how the rise of imperial Germany as a naval power threatened British security, and what Churchill thought Britain needed to do to manage this danger. Churchill became First Lord of the Admiralty in the autumn of 1911, in the immediate aftermath of an international crisis that threatened to engulf Britain in a war with Germany. At the Admiralty, Churchill aimed to ensure Britain's security against the increasing menace posed by German naval power. The German navy posed an immediate threat to Britain's security. Churchill called the development of Germany's navy an 'ever-present danger' to Britain. In response to the buildup of the German navy, Churchill adopted a program of naval construction that would keep Britain stronger at sea than Germany. This aim required that Churchill build a domestic political consensus behind his naval program. Domestic political considerations, then, loomed large in Churchill's formulation of British naval policy. By ensuring domestic political support for the Admiralty's naval buildup, Churchill maintained a commanding lead over Germany in the naval competition. Although Churchill presided over a major buildup in the British navy's strength, he abhorred the naval competition between Britain and Germany and the resulting deterioration in relations between the two countries. He wanted to end this competition by bringing about a negotiated settlement of the naval rivalry. To Churchill's great disappointment, however, Germany's leaders did not want to negotiate an arms-control pact with Britain. Even if Germany could not overtake Britain in their naval competition, German decision makers refused to consider any arms-control proposal that curtailed their naval shipbuilding program. Churchill's arms-control proposals, in the view of Germany's leaders, appeared as nothing more than clever attempts to upset their naval plans. Consequently, Britain faced an open-ended and expensive arms competition with Germany. This outcome was far from what Churchill wanted; nonetheless, he was determined to keep Britain ahead of Germany in this competition. When Germany's leaders converted an international showdown over the Balkans into a world war, Britain was at least strong at sea and prepared to fight against this German bid for mastery in Europe.

The second chapter, by Christopher Bell, explores Churchill's assessment of the threat posed by Japan to Britain's imperial position in East Asia before the Second World War. Bell argues that Churchill showed a remarkable consistency in his strategic appreciation of the threat posed by Japan during the period between the two world wars. Churchill did not see

Japan by itself as posing the greatest danger to British security. Instead, Churchill feared that Japan might act as a jackal state, attacking Britain when it was already embroiled in another war. Bell maintains in his essay that to Churchill 'Germany clearly posed a "mortal peril" to Britain; Japan did not.' If Japan attacked while Britain was tied down in a conflict elsewhere, the British Empire could not hope to cope with so many serious, simultaneous threats. Churchill understood that, in these circumstances, Britain would find it very difficult to meet the danger emanating from Japan. Even a cursory examination of what Churchill wrote about Britain's strategic predicament in East Asia shows just how alive he was to the daunting strategic problems that the British Empire would face in fighting a war against Japan. Further, a full generation before the outbreak of the Pacific War, Churchill understood that Britain's security in Asia rested on the support of the United States. Churchill urged that Britain align itself with the United States and attempt to create a powerful bloc in the Pacific to contain Japanese expansion. The combined power of the British Empire and the United States, in Churchill's estimation, ought to make Japanese decision makers more cautious and deter Japan from attacking in a bid to seize hegemony in East Asia. Churchill clung to this assessment even though he also knew that Japanese militarists had taken Japan on to a path of confrontation with Britain and the United States. Unlike Neville Chamberlain, who hoped to reach an accommodation with Japan, even if that antagonized the United States, Churchill saw Britain's safety in the Pacific as resting in attempts to combine American and British power. Churchill, consequently, gave too much credit to Japanese decision makers, thinking that they would show greater prudence and restraint in their actions than they did, because he expected that they would seek ultimately to avoid a ruinous war with Britain and the United States. Nonetheless, he did grasp the importance of American power in defending British interests and stopping Japan from gaining hegemony in East Asia. Churchill was painfully aware of the limits of British power, and understood that Britain won its wars by working with powerful allies.

Brian McKercher examines in this volume's third chapter Churchill's assessment of Britain's strategic predicament before the Second World War and his policy prescriptions for dealing with the dangers that emerged to threaten the British Empire during the 1930s. Churchill, in McKercher's view, was a politician 'on the make' during this period, trying to promote himself on the domestic political scene and take over the reins of power. The criticisms about rearmaments and foreign policy leveled by Churchill at the National government that led Britain during this period were part of a campaign to make him Prime Minister. This controversial view of Churchill's actions serves an important purpose in highlighting the role domestic political decisions play in the making of strategy and policy. Strategic decision making does not occur in a domestic political vacuum. McKercher's assessment is that Churchill did not offer a realistic strategic alternative to appeasement. Churchill instead meant his criticism of the defense effort and foreign policy of the government to embarrass Stanley Baldwin and later Neville Chamberlain, to weaken their grip on power, and to promote himself. Churchill's strategic prescriptions, calling for Britain to rearm at a faster pace and to form a coalition to contain Germany, seem unrealistic in McKercher's estimation. This provocative view, while not likely to convince those who see Churchill's strategic alternative as superior to the line adopted by the National government, nonetheless does draw attention to just how bad Britain's strategic choices were during the 1930s. Britain faced an extremely dangerous international environment, challenged simultaneously in Europe and Asia by expansionist, predatory regimes in Hitler's Germany, Fascist Italy, and militaristic Japan. The buildup of German air power and Japanese naval power, creating two formidable instruments for offensive war, made the British Empire increasingly vulnerable to attack. The failure of the National government to make adequate pre-war preparations against either of these growing dangers ensured that Britain would initially fight at a great disadvantage when war finally arrived.

The final chapter, by David Jablonsky, provides an assessment of Churchill's attempts to harness technological innovation to gain strategic advantages for Britain. Churchill gave close attention to how technological innovation might transform the strategic environment. Technological innovation and military transformation were key elements of Churchill's strategic outlook. Churchill wanted to dominate war's interactive nature, and technology provided him with one way to seize the strategic initiative. By gaining surprise, technology could enable Britain to defeat it enemies while holding down the costs of winning. Signals intelligence received the priority it did from Churchill because the insight it provided enabled him to anticipate and counter the enemy's moves. Churchill considered it an imperative duty that a country's highest leaders provide direction and impetus to spur the development and use of technology. Churchill was also alive to the difficult trade-offs that occur in making decisions about the employment of new technologies. Against a first-class opponent, able to adapt quickly and imitate, an initial technological advantage might only turn around to cause even greater damage on the innovator. Decisions on the employment of new technologies thus needed to take into account the enemy's likely reaction. Churchill understood the importance of assessing which side in a conflict might derive the greater strategic benefit from innovation before plunging ahead with the employment of new technologies. In this essay, Jablonsky examines how Churchill presided over a contentious debate about the use of 'Window' to reduce the losses suffered by Bomber Command in its offensive over Germany. Before giving permission to proceed with the employment of Window, Churchill wanted to consider the costs to Britain if Germany reacted by copying the British lead and reopened a major bomber offensive. In addition, Churchill recognized that new weapons by themselves do not guarantee success in war. Military transformation must be rooted in a larger strategic framework, linking new weapons and doctrines for their employment to the achievement of the larger political purpose served by fighting. Churchill, for example, castigated Germany's military leadership during the First World War for how it pioneered a transformation in naval warfare by using submarines in a campaign to destroy British commerce. Germany's military operators, blinded by the appeal of immediate operational success, committed a major strategic error. The German submarine campaign, while inflicting heavy losses on the merchant shipping of their enemies, strategically backfired by triggering the United States' entry into the war. Germany's leaders thus contributed to their own defeat. Military transformation, in other words, does not automatically translate into overall success in wartime. Despite Churchill's fascination with the details of new technologies and weapons designs, as well as his sponsorship of innovations with dubious operational merits, he did not lose sight of how the true measure of effectiveness for any military transformation is whether it serves a country's larger policy and strategic purpose. This assessment about strategic effectiveness was too important for the armed services to decide for themselves. In Churchill's view, the political leadership needed to guide and ultimately decide.

The authors of this volume deeply regret that our friend Michael Handel did not live long enough to write more about Churchill as a strategist. We are all the poorer because of his untimely passing. Before Michael Handel's death, we all talked with him about the essays that we proposed writing as a tribute to him. In what were some of our last conversations with him, he gave us suggestions about our topics and, most importantly, encouraged us to complete these essays as a book. We owe Michael Handel a great deal: his scholarship, his brilliant conceptual insights into the complicated issues in strategy and international affairs, his willingness to help others in their work, and his friendship. It is the last that we miss the most, and we offer this book of essays as a tribute to his memory.

1

The 'Ever-Present Danger':
Winston Churchill's Assessment of
the German Naval Challenge
before the First World War

John H. Maurer

Introduction

Winston Churchill became First Lord of the Admiralty during the autumn of 1911 at a time when the rise of German naval power posed an immense threat to Great Britain's security. The previous summer, when Germany provoked an international showdown with France over Morocco – the so-called 'Agadir (or Second Moroccan) Crisis' – Britain's leaders had even feared that at one point in the confrontation a war might erupt with the German navy launching a surprise attack on the British fleet, scattered at its peacetime bases in home waters. As First Lord of the Admiralty, the civilian head of the Royal Navy, the government minister responsible for supervising Britain's naval defense efforts, Churchill was determined to prevent Germany from defeating Britain at sea. 'Of all the dangers that menaced the British Empire', Churchill would later write, 'none was comparable to a surprise of the Fleet. If the Fleet or any vital part of it were caught unawares or unready and our naval preponderance destroyed, we had lost the war, and there was no limit to the evils which might have been inflicted upon us.' In Churchill's estimation, Germany's battle fleet, concentrated in German home waters just across the North Sea from Britain, poised to launch a first-strike surprise attack, represented an 'ever-present danger'.[1]

Churchill's determination to ensure Britain's naval preparedness for war did not mean that he considered a conflict between Britain and Germany as inevitable. 'I do not believe', he told a political associate, 'in the theory of inevitable wars.'[2] Churchill held the firm conviction that war would serve neither country's best interests. In a speech delivered in 1908, he derided the notion that the rivalry between the two countries pointed toward a clash of arms. 'I think it is greatly to be deprecated', he stated, that persons should try to spread the belief in this country that war between Great Britain and Germany is inevitable. It is all nonsense . . . there is no collision of primary interests – big, important interests – between Great Britain and Germany in any quarter of the globe . . . Look at it from any point of view you like, and I say you will come to the conclusion in regard to relations between England and Germany, that there is no real cause of difference between them, and . . . these two great people have nothing to fight about, have no prize to fight for, and have no place to fight in.[3]

Instead of impending conflict, Churchill looked forward to 'the peaceful development of European politics in the next twenty years'. This period of peace was the result of 'the blessed intercourse of trade and commerce [which] is binding the nations together against their wills, in spite of their wills, unconsciously, irresistibly, and unceasingly weaving them together into one solid interdependent mass'. What Churchill called 'the prosaic bonds of commerce' were dampening international crises, promoting the peaceful settlement of disputes between 'civilized and commercial States'. The danger of international economic collapse, he contended, imposed 'an effective caution and restraint even upon the most reckless and the most intemperate of statesmen'. To buttress his point of view, Churchill could point to the fact that during the previous 40 years 'no two highly-organized commercial Powers have drawn the sword upon one another'.[4] Before becoming First Lord of the Admiralty, Churchill downplayed the likelihood of a war between Britain and Germany.

Throughout this period, too, Churchill repeatedly expressed deep admiration for the achievements of the German people in the fields of education, government administration, science, and technology. Germany, in particular, served as the model for the social reforms that Churchill wanted to see enacted by a Liberal government in Britain. 'The Minister who will apply to this country the successful experiences of Germany in social organisation', he wrote to the Prime Minister, H. H. Asquith, 'may or may not be supported at the polls, but he will at least have left a memorial which time will not deface of his administration.'[5] Churchill wanted Britain to emulate Germany's accomplishments by providing a social-welfare net and in adopting government measures to promote employment.

The ability of Britain's Liberal government to carry out an ambitious program of social reform appeared in jeopardy, however, because of the growing rivalry with Germany in naval armaments. In conversations with German leaders, Churchill forcefully called this 'armaments competition to be madness'.[6] Not surprisingly, then, when David Lloyd George, the Chancellor of the Exchequer, attempted to negotiate a settlement of the emerging naval rivalry with Germany and improve relations between the two countries during the summer of 1908, Churchill backed his colleague's initiative. This support for Lloyd George earned Churchill a rebuke from *The Times*, which thundered: 'The foreign policy of Great Britain is too gravely vital a matter to be taken out of the high plane of statesmanlike guidance by inexperienced politicians in a hurry.'[7] Rather than being viewed as holding an anti-German foreign policy stance, Churchill had acquired a reputation for wanting to restrain British naval spending in favor of emulating German social-reform efforts.

Realities of international politics and military power, however, tempered Churchill's willingness to accommodate Germany. On two occasions he traveled to Germany at the invitation of Kaiser Wilhelm to attend German army maneuvers. Churchill held a deep respect for German military prowess. While attending the German army's maneuvers in the autumn of 1909, he wrote to his wife: 'This army is a terrible engine. It marches sometimes 35 miles in a day. It is in number as the sands of the sea – & with all the modern conveniences.'[8] At the outset of a major European war, the German army, Churchill predicted, would launch a massive onslaught against France, striking through neutral Belgium, attempting to win quickly by crushing French military power and seizing Paris. A powerful German offensive strike through Belgium, in Churchill's estimation, stood a good chance of obtaining a rapid decision over France.[9] Germany, in other words, possessed the armed strength to overthrow the balance of power on the European continent.

Germany's arms programs and foreign policy actions, too, increasingly troubled Churchill. The bullying behavior exhibited by the German government during the Agadir Crisis, in particular, galvanized Churchill to consider the strategic contours of the opening stages of a war started by Germany to defeat France in a lightning campaign. When Germany initiated the great-power confrontation over Morocco during the summer of 1911, Churchill wanted Britain to align itself alongside that of France. To prevent the German army from quickly winning a major European war, French forces required immediate British military assistance.[10] 'It is not for Morocco, nor indeed for Belgium, that I w[oul]d take part in this terrible business', Churchill wrote to Lloyd George. 'One cause alone c[oul]d justify our participation – to prevent France from being trampled down & looted by the Prussian junkers – a disaster ruinous to the world, & swiftly fatal to our country.'[11] Germany's rulers, then, threatened a terrible struggle in which nothing less would be at stake than the domination of Europe by a triumphant German superpower. In response, Churchill urged a tougher foreign policy stance by Britain toward Germany and a higher level of military preparedness.

In addition to the threat posed by the German army to France, the relentless buildup of the German battle fleet, along with Berlin's rude unwillingness to reduce its naval program, led Churchill reluctantly to conclude that the ambitions harbored by Germany's leaders did indeed pose a serious threat to the peace of Europe. Churchill thought: 'The determination of the greatest military Power on the [European] Continent to become at the same time at least the second naval Power was an event of first magnitude in world affairs.'[12] Churchill bluntly expressed these views at the time in conversations with the German ambassador. 'It was no good shutting ones eyes to facts', he stated, 'and that however hard Governments and individuals worked to make a spirit of real trust and confidence between two countries they would make very little headway while there was a continually booming naval policy in Germany.'[13] The buildup of a German battle fleet, consciously designed by Germany's leaders to undermine Britain's security, stood as a major obstacle to international cooperation between the two countries. Germany could remove this obstacle, reducing the danger of war and improving relations with Britain, by dropping its naval buildup.

This chapter examines Churchill's views about Germany's naval buildup and how he thought Britain needed to respond to this German challenge. Churchill wanted to ensure that Germany did not overtake Britain in their naval competition. At the same time, he wanted to avoid a mutually ruinous war between the two countries. While Churchill was determined to prevent Germany from gaining an opportunity to defeat Britain at sea, he also sought negotiations between the two countries to reduce their naval rivalry. Churchill was far from an implacable enemy of Germany. Before the outbreak of the First World War, he never dropped his interest in trying to diminish the armaments and geopolitical competition, from which neither country in his view derived benefit. Churchill considered these two tasks, ensuring Britain's naval safety and taking steps to improve relations with Germany, as inextricably linked together. In Churchill's estimation, keeping Britain ahead of Germany's naval challenge provided a precondition for negotiations and increased the likelihood of their success. That a negotiated settlement to reduce the Anglo-German naval rivalry failed to occur was not due to any want of effort on Churchill's part; instead, this failure came about because of the single-minded determination of Germany's leaders to build a navy that directly threatened Britain's security.

Defeating the German Naval Challenge: 'We Shall . . . Break these Fellows Hearts in Peace, or their Necks in War'[14]

Churchill became First Lord of the Admiralty as part of a government shakeup in Britain triggered by the Agadir Crisis. The prospect of an imminent war with Germany led British decision makers to undertake high-level discussions that examined Britain's strategic options if the crisis led to fighting. These political and strategic deliberations revealed a fundamental disagreement between the leaders of the army and navy about what strategy Britain ought to follow in case of war. The two armed services could not agree on a common strategy. At the beginning of a war with Germany, the army intended to deploy the bulk of its strength to France and wanted the navy to safeguard its movement across the Channel onto the continent. The navy's leadership disagreed with the army's strategic plan and refused to cooperate: they wanted to follow a maritime strategy that included using the army to seize forward bases along the German coastline. Since the service chiefs of the army and navy could not agree on a common strategy, the political leadership needed to decide. The consensus that emerged among senior members of the British government, including the Prime Minister, was to back the strategy proposed by the army for the initial period of war. In Asquith's view, the navy's "plan" can only be described as puerile, and I have dismissed it at once as wholly impracticable'.[15] Further, the Prime Minister concluded from the poor showing made by the navy's leadership in presenting their strategic plans and in responding to the threat of war during the crisis that sweeping changes needed to occur at the Admiralty. Asquith's lack of confidence in the navy's leadership led to Churchill going to the Admiralty.

A number of daunting challenges faced Churchill when he took up his position as First Lord of the Admiralty. His tenure at the Admiralty is rightly considered an important era of reform.[16] A top priority was the creation of a war staff for the navy. Churchill also pushed technological innovation. Battleships shifted from coal to oil, creating a new demand for that fuel, and the development of aircraft and submarines received impetus from Churchill. In addition, he promoted efforts to improve conditions for the navy's enlisted personnel, the so-called 'lower deck'. This ambitious agenda of reform, along with Churchill's driving, questioning style of management, caused considerable controversy and provoked tension between him and some of the service's uniformed leaders. When the First Sea Lord, Admiral Sir Arthur Wilson, pointedly refused to establish a war staff for the navy, Churchill showed no hesitation and received the government's backing to remove him.

Churchill initially hoped when he went to the Admiralty that he could also stabilize or even curtail spending on the Royal Navy. The navy's estimates had increased by over £10,000,000 (or over 30 per cent) during the previous four years,[17] largely in response to the major increase in Germany's warship construction. Beginning in 1908, Germany's tempo of large surface warship construction – the number of battleships and battle cruisers started each year – increased to four. This tempo of four large warships a year was scheduled to drop to two beginning in 1912. German construction of battleships and battle cruisers, if Germany did not amend its navy law, would remain limited to two for a six-year period. This drop in Germany's construction of large surface warships, Churchill thought, should enable him to trim British shipbuilding and hold down naval spending. What soon became clear to Churchill, however, was that Germany intended to make additions to its existing program of naval construction, and expectations of reduced spending on the navy were unrealistic.

In Germany, the Agadir Crisis spurred the Imperial Navy Office to press for major increases in warship construction and combat readiness. The architect of Germany's naval buildup was Admiral Alfred von Tirpitz. Picked by the Kaiser in 1897 to head the German navy, Tirpitz was ambitious, forceful, and proficient. His life's ambition was to make Germany into a naval power that could rival Britain on the seas. Germany emerged during Tirpitz's tenure of office as Britain's most serious opponent in the high-stakes competition for naval mastery. In the aftermath of the Agadir Crisis, Tirpitz saw an opportunity to strengthen the German navy. The German government's handling of the crisis had been inept: Berlin had provoked a confrontation with France and then appeared to back down under British pressure. As a consequence, ardent German nationalists sought to portray the crisis and subsequent negotiations as a major diplomatic defeat for Germany. In the opinion of the Navy Office, Germany needed to embark on a substantial arms buildup to overcome the humiliation suffered at the hands of Britain and France.[18]

The Navy Office's proposal for increased shipbuilding, however, ran into tough political opposition from within the German government.[19] Germany's Chancellor, Theobald von Bethmann Hollweg, vehemently opposed an amendment to the navy law that called for the construction of additional capital ships. One of the cardinal goals of Bethmann Hollweg's foreign policy was to improve relations with Britain to the point where it would not intervene against Germany in case of a major European war. The Navy Office's shipbuilding proposal would destroy Bethmann Hollweg's efforts to obtain Britain's neutrality. Furthermore, Bethmann Hollweg thought that Germany must give priority to the army in the allocation of defense resources. Increased military preparations made by France and Russia called into question Germany's dominance on land.

Quite simply, Germany could not afford to compete with the Dual Alliance of France and Russia on land and, at the same time, with Britain on the seas. The Chancellor received support in his contest with the Navy Office from the Treasury Minister Adolf Wermuth, who argued that the imperial government could not afford the spending requests of both the army and navy.

The political struggle within the German government over a new amendment to Germany's navy law was fought out through the autumn of 1911 and early 1912. Both sides employed every bureaucratic weapon at their disposal: threatened resignations, press leaks, calculated foot dragging, efforts to find bureaucratic allies, and the manufacture of detailed position papers. Kaiser Wilhelm, caught in the middle of this domestic political tussle within the German government, could not make a clear decision on the issue of naval increases. His instinct was to support Tirpitz and go ahead with the Navy Office's program of making additions to Germany's warship-construction program. Wilhelm wanted more battleships, armed with the most powerful weapons, and he was infuriated with those who sought to curtail the navy's proposed increases. At the same time, Wilhelm felt unable to pay the political price of sacking his Chancellor Bethmann Hollweg. Wilhelm, Bethmann Hollweg, and Tirpitz eventually reached an uneasy compromise, embodied in an amendment to the navy law, which called for Germany to start 15 capital ships (instead of 12) during the period 1912–17. In addition, the German navy was to obtain funding for major increases in combat readiness. This compromise fell short of the annual three-tempo of capital ship construction requested by Tirpitz; nonetheless, the German Navy Office had achieved quite a great deal of what it wanted in maintaining the development of Germany's naval strength and increasing the fleet's combat readiness.

While Germany's leaders fought amongst themselves over the question of naval armaments, British decision makers considered how to respond if the German navy increased its level of effort. To British 'hawks', the proper response to Germany's naval program was clear: Britain should maintain a decisive superiority over the German battle fleet. The rallying cry of those intent on staying ahead of Germany was the so-called 'two-keels-to-one' standard, whereby Britain would build two capital ships for every one started by Germany. As Admiral Sir John ('Jackie') Fisher, Britain's flamboyant First Sea Lord between 1904 and 1910, put it: 'Germany keeps her whole fleet always concentrated within a few hours of England. We must therefore keep a fleet twice as powerful as that of Germany always concentrated within a few hours of Germany.'[20] This view was frequently echoed by commentators, publicists, opposition politicians, and government officials determined to prevent Germany from upsetting the balance of power in Europe and threatening Britain's sea lines of communication.[21]

Responding to Germany's naval buildup by undertaking a large British effort, however, dismayed many Liberals, who wanted a more constructive approach to managing Britain's foreign affairs and security policies. In the view of these Liberals, major increases in British battleship building programs actually undermined Britain's security. Britain's actions, as much as any undertaken by Germany, in their view, spurred the arms competition. Lloyd George, for instance, railed against British naval policy – in particular, the introduction of the all-big-gun battleship, the *Dreadnought* – because he believed it provoked other countries to compete against Britain. 'We started it [that is, the naval competition]', Lloyd George declared. 'We had an overwhelming preponderance at sea which would have secured us against any conceivable enemy, but we were not satisfied. We said, "Let there be Dreadnoughts." What for? We did not require them.'[22] Liberal political leaders and commentators frequently voiced the view that a two keels-to-one standard would only stimulate the naval competition. The Liberals subscribed to what a later generation of scholars and policy analysts during the Soviet–American Cold War would dub the action–reaction phenomenon. The Liberals, too, had come to power with a view to carrying out a substantial progressive political agenda for social reform at home and the reduction of international tensions. Germany's naval buildup jeopardized both of these goals by causing a worsening in Anglo-German relations and a concomitant increase in defense expenditures, which many Liberals would rather devote to expanded social programs.[23] Quite simply, Britain's last Liberal government wanted to avoid a naval arms race with Germany.

Given the Liberal belief in the action–reaction dogma, some Liberals thought that Britain could reduce the naval competition by taking unilateral steps to cut British shipbuilding. British restraint, so it was thought, would induce a slow-down in shipbuilding by the other powers. When the Liberals came into office, they curtailed the shipbuilding program that they inherited from the preceding Conservative government by cutting one battleship from the first year's naval estimates and eliminating two others from the following year's program. The new Liberal government hoped that these unilateral cuts would set the stage for a general reduction in naval shipbuilding. These hopes, however, were dashed when Germany curtly refused to curtail its naval program and then even added to it. British restraint did not translate into a reduction in German shipbuilding. Churchill would later write: 'No one could run his eyes down the series of figures of British and German construction for the first three years of the Liberal Administration, without feeling in the presence of a dangerous, if not a malignant, design.' Since Germany's warship construction increased as the Liberal government cut back its building of large armored ships, Britain's lead was narrowing. Germany's battle fleet posed a direct threat to Britain's security. In Churchill's view, Britain had 'been made to feel that hands were being laid upon the very foundation of her existence. Swiftly, surely, methodically, a German Navy was coming into being at our doors which must expose us to dangers only to be warded off by strenuous exertions, and by a vigilance almost as tense as that of actual war.'[24]

In responding to the German naval challenge, Churchill sought a middle ground between the two extremes represented by the champions of British naval supremacy advocated by die-hard Tories and the unilateral arms-control proposals of radical Liberals. He wanted to forge a domestic political consensus behind a framework for managing the naval rivalry with Germany and guiding Britain's response to German shipbuilding. His goal was to dampen the naval rivalry and thereby improve relations between the two countries. Given the attitude of the German Navy Office, Churchill faced what amounted to an impossible task: Tirpitz wanted to exploit the German domestic political scene to achieve further increases in naval strength, even if this entailed a downturn in relations with Britain. For his part, Churchill wanted to make clear to German decision makers that any increases on their part would result only in British counter-measures, leaving Germany further behind in the naval competition. The programs espoused by Tirpitz and Churchill thus threatened to increase the rivalry rather than curtail it.

Churchill proposed that Britain undertake a long-term program of naval construction that was explicitly pegged to Germany's shipbuilding. Since the existing German navy law called for the construction of 12 capital ships between 1912 and 1917, Churchill proposed a program to provide a superiority of 60 per cent in the number of British battleships built during the same period.[25] In addition, if Germany increased its ship-building program, Britain would respond to any extra German capital ships by building at a rate of two-to-one. For example, if Germany added three capital ships to its program, Britain would respond by building six additional capital ships. In calling for a two-to-one response to German additions, Churchill was following a policy advocated by British hawks, defusing their criticism of the Liberal government's naval defense efforts.

In trying to shape the future behavior of Germany's leaders, Churchill had the support of Lloyd George. With Lloyd George as an ally on naval policy, Churchill could hope to withstand any challenges from radicals within the Liberal Party who sought to undertake unilateral cuts in British shipbuilding. 'Germany had to learn', Lloyd George said, 'firstly that we intended to maintain the supremacy of our Navy at whatever cost, and secondly that we did not propose to allow her to "bully" whomsoever she pleased on the continent of Europe.'[26] Lloyd George had already suggested that Britain undertake a long-term program of construction as a response to Germany's shipbuilding in 1909, during the famous naval panic of that year.[27] Churchill thus helped ensure Lloyd George's support by following his lead.

Churchill's shipbuilding plan exploited Britain's economic strengths, its armaments and shipbuilding industries, and financial strength. In a speech delivered in Glasgow in February 1912, Churchill first publicly presented his strategy of escalating punishments.

> If there are to be [naval] increases upon the Continent of Europe, we shall have no difficulty in meeting them to the satisfaction of the country. *As naval competition becomes more acute, we shall have not only to increase the number of ships we build, but the ratio which our naval strength will have to bear to other great naval Powers*, so that our margin of superiority will become larger and not smaller as the strain grows. Thus we shall make it clear that other naval Powers, instead of overtaking us by additional efforts, will only be more outdistanced in consequence of the measures which we ourselves shall take.[28]

By adopting this strategy for the naval competition, Churchill wanted to impress upon Germany's leaders the futility of keeping up their naval challenge. 'Nothing in my opinion', Churchill wrote to Lord Fisher, 'would more surely dishearten Germany, than the certain proof that as a result of all her present and prospective efforts she will only be more hopelessly behindhand.'[29] By demonstrating British resolve and ability to stay ahead of the German naval challenge, Churchill expected that Britain could eventually induce Germany's leaders to negotiate an arms-control agreement and reach a political understanding to reduce the prospect of conflict. Churchill's plan, then, was meant as a step toward persuading Germany's leaders to drop their naval challenge and moderate their foreign-policy ambitions. In a very astute way, Churchill was promoting what the political scientist Robert Axelrod has called 'the shadow of the future'.[30]

Churchill chose a dramatic setting – the annual presentation to Parliament by the First Lord of the Admiralty of the government's naval programs and spending requirements for the upcoming year – to unveil his program of long-term naval construction that would be pegged to German shipbuilding. The choice of such a highly visible public setting ensured that Churchill's plan to outstrip the German naval program was clearly communicated to Germany's leaders.[31] In Churchill's speech, he bluntly declared that Britain's naval efforts were directed at defeating Germany's naval challenge. The British government intended to carry out a long-term program of naval construction linked to Germany's current schedule of shipbuilding. Further, in an unambiguous warning to Berlin, if the current German navy law was amended to include additional construction, Churchill stated that Britain would respond to every extra German capital ship by building two of its own. Churchill thus proclaimed the firm intention of Britain's Liberal government to keep ahead of Germany in the naval competition, even if this required building at a ratio of two-to-one against the German construction of capital ships. By explicitly linking Britain's warship construction to Germany's program, Churchill told his listeners: 'a framework and structure for events is established by which dangerous ambitions and apprehensions alike are effectively excluded and under the shelter of which all the forces of good will may work without misconception or interference'.[32]

While Churchill was laying out a plan to defeat Germany's naval challenge, an attempt was made behind the scenes to negotiate an arms-control agreement and improve relations between the two countries. The initiative for arms-control talks came from the German shipping magnate, the managing director of the Hamburg-American Line, Albert Ballin, and the financier and expatriate German Sir Ernest Cassel.[33] That the naval rivalry fueled the growing antagonism between Britain and Germany deeply troubled Ballin and Cassel, who feared it might end in war. In their view, high-level discussions needed to take place to break the deadlock that stymied a dampening of the naval rivalry and prevented any major improvement in Anglo-German relations. To jumpstart arms-control talks, they were determined to act as intermediaries between the two governments. Ballin and Cassel thought that, with Churchill at the Admiralty, an opportune moment existed to begin negotiations. If Churchill and Tirpitz engaged in direct negotiations, then Ballin hoped that the two naval leaders might produce a formula to curtail the naval rivalry. Cassel, who maintained close ties to the Churchill family, encouraged Ballin in the view that Churchill was sympathetic to Germany and would work hard for an agreement. In turn, Ballin encouraged Cassel and Churchill to believe that the German government wanted him to visit Germany for high-level talks with Tirpitz.[34]

Churchill, backed by Lloyd George, wanted to use the initiative set in motion by Ballin and Cassel to open talks. In response to Cassel's invitation, Churchill wrote that he 'sh[oul]d be honoured by being permitted to discuss the great matters wh[ich] hang in the balance'. Churchill nonetheless declined the invitation because, if the First Lord of the Admiralty traveled unexpectedly to Germany, the two governments could not conduct the negotiations behind the scenes. What Churchill preferred was some occasion, such as a royal visit, which would provide him with a cover to undertake negotiations in Germany. Churchill did not try to disguise from Cassel his view that the proposed negotiations were unlikely to succeed. '[T]ill Germany dropped the Naval challenge[,] her policy w[oul]d be continually viewed here with deepening suspicion & apprehension; but that any slackening on her part w[oul]d produce an immediate détente with much good will from all England.' While Churchill wanted to improve Anglo-German relations, he did not see Germany's leaders cutting back on their naval buildup.[35] In his estimation of German intentions, Churchill was correct.

Given that the talks were likely to fail, Churchill had good grounds for wanting to avoid undertaking a diplomatic mission to Germany. A failure of high-level talks, once their existence became public knowledge, might cause only further damage to the relations between the two countries. After Churchill declined the invitation, the German government suggested that Grey come in his place. Yet, a visit by the British Foreign Secretary posed the same problem of drawing attention to the negotiations. Grey, like Churchill, also harbored no illusions about the likely outcome of these talks: he deemed that these discussions, just like previous negotiations, would result in failure. Nonetheless, Churchill, Grey, and Lloyd George did not want to pass up this opportunity that appeared sanctioned by the highest levels of the German government. Consequently, they decided that Lord Haldane, the Minister of War, should visit Berlin. Haldane seemed a good choice to handle these negotiations: he possessed a deep knowledge of Germany and its language, a known commitment to promoting an Anglo-German understanding, as well as the standing of a senior states-man within his own government. For Haldane to go to Berlin, under the cover of a visit to learn about German educational developments, would not raise public expectations of an imminent settlement of the naval rivalry between the two countries. Further, Grey looked upon Haldane as a friend, 'who was fully in his confidence'.[36] Grey, watchful of challenges to his authority as Foreign Secretary, and under criticism from within the Liberal Party for his handling of Britain's foreign policy, could keep more control over the negotiations if Haldane took the lead rather than Churchill or Lloyd George.

Even though Churchill had stepped aside in favor of Haldane, he fully supported the opening of negotiations. From a domestic political stand-point, Churchill wanted to show that the government had made every effort to bring an end to the naval rivalry with Germany. Churchill confided that his position would 'be all the stronger in asking the Cabinet and the House of Commons for the necessary monies if I can go hand in hand with the Chancellor of the Exchequer [that is, Lloyd George] and testify that we tried our best to secure a mitigation of the naval rivalry and failed'.[37] Again, Churchill wanted to keep in step with Lloyd George and shield himself from radical Liberal criticism.

Some of Churchill's colleagues within the Liberal Party, however, were not so sure about his commitment to successful negotiations. While Haldane carried out negotiations with Germany's leadership in Berlin, Churchill gave a speech in Glasgow, stating that 'the German Navy is to them more in the nature of a luxury'. To Churchill's consternation, his colleagues were furious, thinking that his provocative language would inflame Germany's leaders and sabotage the negotiations. When Churchill asked Lloyd George for his opinion of the speech, he received an unpleasant reproach. Lloyd George confided to the newspaper magnate Sir George Riddell that, when Churchill asked 'what he thought of his speech in Glasgow . . . . I told him [that it was] most imprudent and calculated to ruin Haldane's mission to Germany, which was on a fair way to success. L[loyd] G[eorge] added, "Winston did not reply, but I could see his face."' When Riddell tried to argue that the speech might strengthen Haldane in his negotiation by 'showing that British overtures are not due to cowardice or unreadiness', Lloyd George 'would not agree to this view'.[38] Churchill himself would later write of the episode: 'I found my colleagues offended.'[39]

Churchill's public pronouncements also exasperated Germany's leaders. After Churchill presented the government's naval policy to the House of Commons, Bethmann Hollweg wrote to Ballin: 'Churchill's speech did not come up to my expectations. He really seems to be a firebrand past praying for.'[40] Churchill's speeches garnered for him among Germany's leaders a reputation as a dangerous demagogue, stirring up popular passions in Britain to support greater naval armaments, while seeking ways to curtail the German naval buildup.

Churchill's actions, however, had little impact in determining the outcome of the arms-control negotiations with Germany. Haldane's visit to Berlin and follow-up talks failed to reach agreement because Germany's leaders were not willing to make the concessions demanded of them by the British side. Britain expected an end to Germany's naval challenge, which meant reductions – not additions – to German naval strength and combat readiness. Meanwhile, the German government demanded that Britain not fight alongside France if a European war erupted. The negotiations revolved around trying to find a formula to reconcile these conflicting strategic aims. Tirpitz, in the midst of his struggle with Bethmann Hollweg about the new amendment to the navy law, opposed making any major compromise in arms control requiring cuts in Germany's naval program. He saw the Haldane mission as a cunning attempt by British diplomacy to 'disconcert us in the building of the fleet, and at the same time widen the split in the [German] government'.[41] Haldane stressed during his negotiations in Berlin that a reduction in Germany's naval program was a precondition for a wider-ranging political agreement between the two countries. He bluntly told Wilhelm and Tirpitz: 'if we were to enter into an agreement for settling differences and introducing a new spirit into our relations, that agreement would be bones without flesh if Germany began new shipbuilding immediately. Indeed, the world would laugh at the agreement, and our people would think we had been befooled.'[42] Tirpitz, however, refused to budge: he insisted that Germany needed to add more ships to the scheduled program and increase the German fleet's combat readiness. The Chancellor's only hope was to obtain the backing of Kaiser Wilhelm. This backing, in turn, depended on Bethmann Hollweg obtaining what amounted to a guarantee of British neutrality in case of a major European war. Wilhelm, unwilling to curtail his naval ambitions, refused to consider making cuts in the German navy required to buy an agreement from the British.

The failure of these talks led almost immediately to the German government going ahead with the amendment to the German navy law, which duly passed the Reichstag by a large majority on 20 May 1912. Tirpitz's amendment provided for the construction of additional capital ships over the next six years and increase in fleet readiness. By 1920, the German fleet, according to the Navy Office's plan, would number at least 20 dreadnought battleships and 11 battle cruisers. In addition, the German fleet would possess almost 50 smaller cruisers, 144 destroyers, and 72 submarines. Germany would require 101,500 naval personnel to man this fleet.[43]

Britain, in turn, promptly responded to the German naval increases. Churchill announced that the government would introduce a supplementary estimate, providing for additional naval construction and personnel. Britain would carry out Churchill's threat to stay ahead of Germany at sea by building four additional battleships over the next six years, maintaining a two-to-one advantage over the two ships added by the amendment to the German navy law. As an expedient to concentrate more naval strength in home waters against Germany, Churchill also wanted to reduce Britain's fleet in the Mediterranean.[44] These steps were meant to enhance British security in home waters in response to Germany's naval buildup.

In moving so quickly in response to the projected German increases, Churchill undercut the ability of the opposition Tories to create a naval panic over the government's defense measures, as they had in 1909. Further, by adapting the two-to-one keels standard over Germany in the building of large armored ships, making it apply to any increases in the German naval program, Churchill co-opted an important plank of the Conservatives' own naval policy. Churchill also kept Arthur J. Balfour, the former

Conservative prime minister and senior statesman, well informed about the naval situation. Germany's foreign policy and naval buildup greatly troubled Balfour, because they pointed toward a major war. After viewing 'with the deepest misgiving' assessments passed along to him, Balfour wrote to Churchill: 'A war entered upon for no other object than to restore the Germanic Empire of Charlemagne in a modern form, appears to me at once so wicked and so stupid as to be almost incredible! And yet it is almost impossible to make sense of modern German policy without crediting it with this intention.'[45] By keeping Balfour aware of the naval situation, and adopting part of the Conservative opposition's naval policy, Churchill showed considerable political skill.

Churchill, in another move to garner public support for his naval program, turned to Lord Fisher for help and guidance. Whereas Fisher, as First Sea Lord, had worked behind the scenes in 1909 to press the Liberal government for a larger warship construction program, Churchill co-opted the retired admiral, using him to avoid another naval panic. The deep mutual admiration that each man felt for the other did not stop them from attempting to play on the other's vanity. Churchill solicited and took seriously Fisher's views about how the Admiralty could increase Britain's naval strength. Fisher wanted Britain to follow a standard of building two battleships for every one started by Germany. To allay Fisher's fears about naval preparedness, Churchill unfolded his plans for staying ahead of Germany's naval program. He assured Fisher of his intention to 'announce publicly the policy of two keels to one [in capital ships] on all increases above the existing German Navy Law'.[46] Churchill, in turn, received help from Fisher in presenting the issues at stake and managing the political opposition and opinion makers. Fisher pressed Churchill to keep J. L. Garvin, the influential newspaper editor, closely informed about the naval situation. Garvin, supplied with inside information from Fisher, had played a major role in stirring up the 1909 naval scare. Fisher wrote that Churchill 'might rely upon [Garvin] as a Patriot before Party as regards the Navy . . . I hope you will seize an early opportunity of fore-gathering with you.' Meanwhile, Fisher wrote to Garvin: 'Winston is now saturated and is diabolically clever at exposition so I am happy and look forward to bigger and better things . . . [While] Winston is weak on the 2 Keels to 1, but perhaps I am also to blame there in putting forward less to gain more! So the "Islanders", the Navy League, you and Stead and Alan Burgoyne and Fiennes are alright in hammering away at the 2 Keels to 1, as it strengthens and backs up Winston in his own camp!'[47]

Churchill, heeding Fisher's advice, wrote to reassure Garvin about the naval situation created by the new amendment to the German navy law.

There really is no need for anxiety so far as the relative strength of the German and British fleets is concerned. A steady overhauling process has now begun and will operate from 1915 onwards. In this and the next five programmes, Germany proposes to build 14 capital ships and we 25 . . . You must remember also that the power of the unit is continually increasing, and that the great fleet of Dreadnoughts which the Germans have already built will soon be outclassed by the preponderance of later British ships over later German ships.

Britain was, in effect, staying ahead of Germany at a pace of almost two-to-one in the number of modern large battleships, as many in the opposition Conservative ranks wanted. Further, Britain was spending on the navy twice the amount that Germany allocated. This expenditure ensured the readiness of the navy for war. 'This letter', Churchill wrote Garvin, 'is for your private eyes alone, and I write it because you are a patriot and deserve to be reassured. As long as we do not relax our exertions, and proceed on the sober lines I have laid down, we shall – in the absence of any new development – break these fellows hearts in peace, or their necks in war.'[48] Churchill's public statements and behind-the-scenes lobbying helped to avert a panic reaction in Britain to Germany's naval buildup. The government's program, as forcefully presented by Churchill, appeared to provide for the country's security against the growing German threat. Only the extreme right, represented by Leo Maxse's *National Review*, for example, found Churchill incorrigible and blasted his program as totally inadequate in meeting Britain's defense requirements. By Churchill's management of his own party, the opposition, and opinion makers, he had formed a consensus in the center of the political spectrum about how to stay ahead of Germany in the naval arms race.

The grim determination of Britain's leaders to stay ahead of Germany in the naval competition was captured in the parliamentary debates during July 1912 over Churchill's request for supplementary funds and imperial defense. No fewer than five future First Lords, in addition to Churchill, spoke in these debates about Britain's strategic predicament and the nature of the German threat.[49] Churchill led the debate by giving a masterful presentation on the new amendment to the German navy law, its strategic implications, and how the government intended to respond. In addition to the German shipbuilding increases, Churchill underscored the improvement that would take place in the combat readiness of Germany's battle fleet. Instead of keeping only two squadrons (or 17 battleships) ready for service without the prior mobilization, the 1912 amendment to the German navy law increased the number of ready battleships to 25. This 50 per cent increase in combat readiness greatly improved Germany's ability to fight at sea at short notice and increased the danger of a German surprise first-strike. 'Taking a general view', Churchill told the House of Commons, 'the effect of the Law will be that nearly four-fifths of the entire German Navy will be maintained in permanent full commission – that is to say, instantly and constantly ready for war. Such a proportion is remarkable, and, so far as I am aware, finds no example in the previous practice of modern naval Powers.' The message delivered by Churchill was that no quick fixes or panic effort on Britain's part could address the strategic problem posed by Germany's naval buildup. Instead, Churchill envisioned an open-ended competition, calling for a long-term buildup of British naval power as a response. 'Cool, steady, methodical preparation, prolonged over a succession of years', Churchill stated, 'can alone raise the margin of naval power . . . The strain we have to bear will be long and slow, and no relief will be obtained by impulsive or erratic action. We ought to learn from our German neighbours, whose policy marches unswervingly towards its goal across the lifetime of a whole generation.'[50] The German naval buildup confronted Britain's leaders and people with a high-stakes choice over whether they wanted to resist Germany's bid to supplant them as a world power. Churchill did not minimize the costs or dangers inherent in defeating the German naval challenge. Britain, however, could maintain its preponderance at sea over Germany so long as it mustered the political will to follow Churchill's program. Whether Germany's leaders would see that their actions were counterproductive and did not serve their country's interests was another matter.

A Naval Understanding with Germany

While Churchill was unwavering in wanting to defeat the German naval challenge, he abhorred the prospect of a protracted, expensive competition with Germany in naval armaments. Even as Churchill sought to frustrate Germany's foreign-policy ambitions by keeping Britain ahead in the naval competition, he also aimed to make Berlin more amenable to arms-control negotiations. Churchill, when he took up his position at the Admiralty, hoped that Britain could induce Germany to slow down its rate of warship construction. During the winter of 1911–12, the Admiralty estimated that Germany intended to start 15 capital ships over the next six years. Churchill proposed that Germany spread this program over 12 years instead of six. In return for this slowdown, Churchill was even willing to consider a reduction in Britain's construction of battleships. If Berlin agreed to slowing down the rate of German warship construction, that would be tantamount, in Churchill's estimation, to Germany's giving up its naval challenge.[51] As he pointed out to Lord Fisher, the program of naval construction that he publicly outlined 'will be capable both of expansion and of diminution, of retardation and acceleration . . . it would always be open within certain limits for England and Germany to agree upon proportionate reductions'.[52] During his first months in office, then, Churchill was developing arms-control proposals designed to end the naval competition with Germany and bring about an improvement in Anglo-German relations.

These initial arms-control schemes evolved into Churchill's proposal that the major naval powers join Britain in taking a 'holiday' from their competitive building of battleships. Churchill publicly appealed for a holiday in the construction of warships on three separate occasions before 1914. In Churchill's presentation of navy estimates on 18 March 1912, when he put forward his plan to peg British warship construction to defeat the German shipbuilding program, he proposed for the first time a naval holiday. To break the competition in shipbuilding, Churchill called for the introduction of 'a blank page in the book of misunderstanding' between Britain and Germany. 'Any retardation or reduction in German construction', he declared, 'will . . . be promptly followed here . . . by large and fully proportioned reductions.' In the year 1913, for instance, the British Admiralty anticipated that Germany would start construction of three capital ships. If Germany dropped this annual contingent of ships from its program, Churchill declared that Britain would 'blot out' the corresponding five capital ships it planned to start that year. 'The three ships that she [Germany] did not build', Churchill told the House of Commons, 'would therefore automatically wipe out no fewer than five British potential super-"Dreadnoughts" [that is, the latest class of battleships], and that is more than I expect them to hope to do in a brilliant naval action.' By taking a holiday from building for a year or even two, Germany would also obtain substantial savings in naval spending. Churchill concluded: 'Here, then, is a perfectly plain and simple plan of arrangement whereby without diplomatic negotiation, without any bargaining, without the slightest restriction upon the sovereign freedom of either Power, this keen and costly naval rivalry can be at any time abated.'[53]

Germany's leaders found no merit whatsoever in Churchill's arms-control initiative. The Kaiser sent Churchill a 'courteous message . . . expressing his great regret' that the naval holiday proposal 'would only be possible between allies'.[54] To his intimates, however, Wilhelm was much less courteous: he branded Churchill's speech as 'arrogant'.[55] Germany's leaders simply refused to consider the holiday proposal as a serious arms-control initiative.

Churchill was not put off, however, by the cold water poured on his proposal by Germany's leaders, and continued to see the holiday scheme as a means of dampening the naval competition. Intelligence reaching the Admiralty at the end of 1912, indicating that Germany intended to introduce another amendment to its navy law during the coming year, increasing yet again the annual rate of German battleship construction, gave Churchill a further reason to renew the offer for a naval holiday.[56] Churchill wanted to avoid the additional increases in naval spending that would be required if Germany did go ahead with this amendment. Consequently, he repeated the proposal on two separate occasions during 1913. On 26 March 1913, once again in his presentation of navy estimates to Parliament, Churchill offered to drop the four battleships Britain intended to begin during the upcoming year if Germany would cancel or delay the two capital ships it was scheduled to start. It was Churchill's opinion that under these circumstances a 'mutual cessation [of battleship building] could clearly be no disadvantage to the relative position' of Germany.[57]

Germany's rulers did not share Churchill's assessment of the relative naval position of the two countries. The German government officially responded in a polite way to Churchill's scheme, with Bethmann Hollweg telling the Reichstag that Germany was waiting for formal proposals. The holiday, put forward publicly in speeches, was not considered by Germany's leaders a genuine plan for negotiations. In their estimation, it was a propaganda stunt. Behind the scenes, Germany's leaders worked to bury the idea. They tried to discourage a formal arms-control proposal based on the holiday scheme.[58] The German ambassador Prince Karl Max Lichnowsky, for example, made clear in private discussions that Berlin did not welcome further public mention of the holiday proposal.[59] Tirpitz went even further by trying to play upon British fears that Anglo-German relations might deteriorate as a consequence of British arms-control efforts. He instructed the German naval attaché in London to say that 'Churchill can now only injure the tender plant of a German–English détente by his holiday proposal'.[60] Germany's leaders wanted to plant the notion that the holiday proposal would prove counterproductive, and only hurt the prospects for improved relations between the two countries. When the German naval attaché reported in the spring of 1913 that Churchill intended to renew the holiday offer despite clear indications from Berlin that it would be unwelcome, Germany's leaders braced themselves to reject it. Wilhelm wrote on the attaché's dispatch: 'We are on our guard!'[61]

The report of the German naval attaché proved accurate. On 18 October 1913, in a speech given in Manchester, Churchill repeated the holiday proposal. Churchill insisted on making the proposal again despite considerable opposition from within the British government. Some of

Churchill's colleagues fell into line with Berlin in not wanting to antagonize Germany's leaders. Grey, however, backed Churchill. In his speech,
Churchill gave the fullest public exposition of what he meant by the
'holiday' proposal. He observed that during the upcoming year Britain
would begin building four new battleships for the Royal Navy. Meanwhile,
Germany was scheduled to begin two capital ships during the same year.
If Germany dropped the two capital ships in its program, Britain would
delete four battleships. According to Churchill's calculations, Britain
would save £12,000,000 and Germany £6,000,000 over the following three
years if these ships were never built.[62]

The repetition of the holiday proposal provoked a storm of protest in
Germany. Goschen reported from Berlin that Churchill's offer had
attracted coverage 'in all the more important German newspapers and has
been received with almost universal disapproval'. In the assessment of the
British embassy, the only difference between German newspapers 'lies in
the varying degrees of politeness or rudeness with which they refuse even
to consider the holiday year suggestion'. Count Ernst von Reventlow, the
prominent foreign affairs editor of the conservative *Deutsche Tageszeitung*,
for example, blasted Churchill by saying that Britain's First Lord should
take a holiday from making speeches.[63]

Churchill's proposal was also attacked by opponents at home.
Advocates of British naval supremacy derided the holiday proposal as
unworkable and counterproductive. At one extreme of the political spectrum, the *National Review* thought it 'really stupefying' that the government appeared obsessed with 'the Disarmament craze', and it poured
scorn on 'the mountebank at the Admiralty' (that is, Churchill) for his
'platform performances [which] are as idiotic to us as they are offensive to
Germany, and play into the hands of the vast army of Anglophobes who
preach a *jehad* against this country. Politicians of this calibre will say anything to get themselves reported.'[64] Arthur Lee, the principal Conservative
opposition spokesman in Parliament, offered a more responsible criticism
of the holiday proposal, saying that 'almost insuperable obstacles [stood]
in the way of any attempt to carry that into practice'.[65] In addition, critics
pointed out that, if a 'holiday' occurred during a year when Britain
intended to build four and Germany only two capital ships, it would
undercut Churchill's pledge to meet any additional German battleship
construction on a two-to-one basis.[66] Other critics of the plan thought it
undignified for Britain to repeat an offer that Germany had already
spurned. By repeating the offer, Churchill would only encourage
Germany's leaders into thinking that Britain might tire of the naval competition. Goschen in Berlin argued: 'one cannot help thinking that a determined execution of what [Churchill] outlined in 1912 would have a far

greater effect upon German shipbuilding than what he has now done'. In Goschen's opinion, 'the best way of taking the wind out of the sails of the Big Navy Party in Germany is to state frankly that if threatened with further efforts to reduce our supremacy we shall make a big effort, by loan if necessary, to render that supremacy unassailable'.[67] The Foreign Office agreed with Goschen's appraisal. Arms-control negotiations with Germany, the Foreign Office feared, might weaken Britain's standing with France. In the view of the Foreign Office, Britain should move arms control to the sidelines in Anglo-German relations.

Despite the objections raised on all sides to the holiday proposal, Churchill remained committed to finding a way to moderate the naval rivalry. He asserted that Britain 'ought never to allow the discussion of this vital question to be stifled just because it is unwelcome to the ruling classes in Germany, or still less because France for obvious reasons wants the naval strain to continue'. In return for Germany's agreement to a naval holiday, Churchill was even willing to give up the prospect of starting in 1914 the three battleships that the Admiralty hoped Canada would contribute, as well as the four battleships scheduled for the British program.[68] The opposition to the holiday proposal forced Churchill, however, to avoid renewing it in his presentation of navy estimates in March 1914.

While Germany had consistently and pointedly refused to consider the holiday scheme, the German government nonetheless seemed to shift its position toward arms control in early February 1914. In an appearance before the Budget Committee of the Reichstag, Tirpitz and the German Foreign Secretary Gottlieb von Jagow unexpectedly stated that the German government awaited proposals from Britain about how to curtail the naval rivalry. The Berlin correspondent of *The Times*, in covering their statements before the Reichstag, reported Tirpitz as saying that 'positive [arms-control] proposals had not yet reached Germany. If they did they would certainly be examined with good will.'[69] Tirpitz showed an interest in proposals that established 'a ratio of strength between the English and German navies of about 16 to 10 [in battleships]'. This ratio he wanted to express in squadrons, each consisting of eight battleships, with Germany permitted five and Britain eight. With this ratio and force levels established by an agreement, Germany would build toward a navy possessing 41 battleships and Britain could maintain 65. These force levels, Tirpitz suggested, could be obtained if Germany started each year the construction of two battleships while Britain limited itself to building three. Tirpitz also floated a proposal for limiting the size of capital ships. After testifying that Germany had not forced the pace in increasing the size of battleships, since the German navy only followed Britain's lead, Tirpitz stated: 'if a general reduction of displacement were to set in he would welcome it'.[70] Jagow added that the relationship between Britain and Germany 'could be described as a really good one [*recht gut*]'. Both governments, in Jagow's estimation, possessed 'thorough mutual confidence' in the other, and public opinion in Britain and Germany exhibited the 'feeling that they [that is, the two countries] could cooperate and work side by side on many points and in many questions, and that their interest met in many respects'.[71]

Churchill's calls for a holiday in naval shipbuilding, however, did not receive any encouragement from Tirpitz and Jagow, who made clear that the German government did not consider the proposal as serious or open for negotiation. Tirpitz labeled Churchill's holiday proposal as 'an election speech'. As Tirpitz put it to the Reichstag deputies, he had read about the holiday proposal 'in the newspapers, for I have received no further intimation of the matter'. Jagow added that '"official proposals" for a holiday year in shipbuilding have not reached the German government'. A Reichstag deputy on the Budget Committee agreed, saying: 'the utterances of a British Minister on a festive occasion did not supply a sufficient basis for a discussion'. Tirpitz made it plain that, if the British government officially put forward the holiday plan as the basis for arms-control negotiations, Berlin would reject it. A number of objections, in Tirpitz's opinion, stood in the way of implementing the holiday scheme. For example, it was unclear to Tirpitz whether ships dropped in any given 'holiday' year could be made up in subsequent years or were permanently dropped from each country's program of construction. Since Tirpitz maintained that Germany's building program called only for the construction of new warships to replace older vessels, ships permanently dropped would reduce the overall size of the German battle fleet. The German Navy Secretary also objected that the holiday plan would disorder Germany's government finances, upset its shipbuilding yards, and thereby disrupt the orderly long-range plan of the Navy Office for naval construction. Meanwhile, Tirpitz maintained that British shipyards would not suffer the same amount of disruption because they were building warships for other countries. Finally, the question remained as to whether other countries, such as France and Russia, would go along with this plan. Tirpitz underscored the point that neither the Russian nor the French government had 'given any indication of their agreement with the suggestion'.[72] The Berlin correspondent of *The Times* noted: 'None of the speakers [in the Reichstag meeting] . . . said a single word in favour of the holiday year idea.'[73] Although Tirpitz and Jagow rejected Churchill's holiday proposal, they had nonetheless appeared to open the door for renewed negotiations about the naval competition. The German government, in these public pronouncements, also indicated that it wanted a rapprochement with Britain. If Britain took the initiative and put forward concrete arms-control proposals, Berlin would begin serious negotiations.

The newspaper reports about the presentations made by Jagow and Tirpitz stung Grey into action. The British Foreign Secretary wanted to find out if the German government actually wanted to open serious negotiations about the naval question. Grey requested more information from Berlin about whether the German government genuinely wanted arms-control proposals from Britain. Part of Grey's motivation in approaching the German government was to answer critics from within his party, who viewed his foreign-policy stance as standing in the way of better Anglo-German relations. Only a few days before, Grey had delivered a major speech on the naval competition, in which he had maintained that no progress in arms-control negotiations was feasible because the German government did not want to explore the issue. 'The ships which Germany is laying down', Grey told his listeners, 'are being laid down under a Naval Law which cannot be altered by anything we can do . . . It is no good making to them proposals which they will not welcome and are not prepared to receive.'[74] No sooner had Grey delivered this somber message, than Berlin had publicly showed an interest in negotiations. Grey was thus in danger of looking out of touch with a genuine desire on the part of the German government to cooperate on the naval issue and to produce an overall improvement in Anglo-German relations. The Foreign Secretary could not politically afford to leave unanswered any public initiative by the German government for a reduction in the arms competition. The Foreign Office consequently instructed Goschen to ask Jagow for a clarification of Tirpitz's public remarks.

The response from the German government to Grey's enquiry was hardly encouraging: Berlin repeated Tirpitz's released statement that he would consider a British proposal permitting Germany to complete its naval program and establishing a ratio of eight-to-five in squadrons of eight battleships each. From the British perspective, this was hardly a serious proposal. What Tirpitz wanted was for the British government to accept that Germany should carry out its full program of warship construction. The German Navy Secretary was not proposing any reduction whatsoever in Germany's shipbuilding program. Consequently, no savings in arms spending would occur. Germany's leaders also remained completely opposed to any suggestion of Churchill's naval holiday. Eyre Crowe at the Foreign Office noted on Tirpitz's reply: 'The German government continue to speak with two tongues. I feel confident that if we make a "definite proposal" we shall not be treated straight-forwardly in the negotiation, and I regard any such negotiation with so unscrupulous an adversary as highly dangerous.'[75] In the view of the British Foreign Office, then, negotiations would not produce any worthwhile results and might even prove counterproductive. What Germany's leaders stated publicly and what they said behind the scenes seemed greatly at variance and did not inspire confidence in the British Foreign Office about the prospect of successful negotiations.

Churchill, however, was not put off by Tirpitz or the opinion of the Foreign Office. His determination to defeat the German naval challenge did not preclude negotiations. Quite the contrary, Churchill was eager to explore opportunities to dampen the naval rivalry between the two countries and improve relations. The previous December, for instance, Churchill had prompted Grey to talk to the German ambassador about the concentration of the two countries' battle fleets in home waters. Two of Germany's most powerful battleships were leaving for a cruise of two months' duration in the Atlantic. While these powerful German warships were away, the Admiralty could afford to send four British battleships for a cruise to the Mediterranean without jeopardizing Britain's naval superiority over Germany in home waters. 'The fact that the Germans are sending these ships for a cruise relieves the undue concentration in Home Waters', Churchill wrote to Grey, 'and we wish to meet it by a similar movement on our part which will show how promptly we respond to anything which makes for a naval détente.'[76] By what a later generation would call tacit bargaining, Churchill thus hoped to promote cooperation between the two countries in the arena of arms control.

Furthermore, a conversation between Tirpitz and the British naval attaché seemed to indicate that the German government, despite their uncompromising response to Grey's enquiry, did not close off completely the prospect of talks between the two countries' naval leaders. Tirpitz, according to the British naval attaché, 'was anxious . . . to understand the real feeling of the British Admiralty on the shipbuilding question'. In speaking about Germany's naval program, the German Navy Secretary protested that he 'had been as frank as he knew how'. Nonetheless, Tirpitz continued: 'He was rather afraid that he was still somewhat misunderstood in England.' Tirpitz even went so far as to suggest (in an uncharacteristically cooperative way): 'His own view was that nothing could be more desirable than that both Admiralties should know each other's feelings. These could not be discovered from a study of the estimates of either country. It was also impossible to get at the real feeling by reading Ministerial speeches or press leaders.' Tirpitz went on to reproach what he considered as biased reporting in the British press. 'Anglo-German relations would undoubtedly be sweetened', Tirpitz stated, 'if the British press would leave Germany alone for a bit.'[77] While Tirpitz offered no concrete proposal for high-level talks, his statements, as recorded by the British naval attaché, seemed to encourage the notion that negotiations might help to clear away misunderstandings and lead to an improvement in relations between the two countries.

An occasion for the resumption of face-to-face talks soon presented itself. The Royal Navy, with the Foreign Office's approval, intended to send a squadron of British battleships to Kiel in June as part of that city's annual regatta. This goodwill visit by British warships to Germany would offer an opportunity for Churchill to meet with the German leadership, who would take part in the festivities at Kiel. Albert Ballin, acting as an intermediary, sought to obtain an invitation for Churchill to accompany the British squadron. Although Ballin's previous initiatives to bring about meetings between the two countries' leaders had failed to bring any nego-tiated settlement of the naval rivalry, this did not in the least deter him from trying again. Ballin, according to his devoted lieutenant and biogra-pher Huldermann, 'clung to his favourite idea that the naval experts of both countries should come to an understanding'.[78] Working once again behind the scenes with Cassel, Ballin wanted to bring about a meeting between Churchill and Tirpitz. The origins of this arms-control initiative thus bears a striking resemblance to the failed Haldane Mission of two years before. As in the previous attempt, Ballin and Cassel tried to jump-start negotiations by arranging for Churchill to visit Germany. Both men knew that Churchill would welcome the opportunity to take part in nego-tiations designed to moderate the naval rivalry and thereby strengthen the emerging détente between the two countries. While Churchill had backed out of going to Germany on the previous occasion in favor of Haldane, he did not want to take a backseat when the possibility of high-level negoti-ations again emerged in the spring of 1914. When Churchill questioned 'whether Tirpitz really wanted to see me and have a talk', Cassel assured him that 'this was so'.[79] Encouraged by Ballin and Cassel, Churchill wanted to seize this opportunity for opening direct, high-level talks with Germany's leaders.

Yet, despite Tirpitz's remarks to the British naval attaché, as well as the assurances of Ballin and Cassel, the German government showed no genuine enthusiasm for renewed negotiations. That Churchill might use the occasion of the Kiel festivities as an opportunity to visit Germany had already occurred to German leaders. In 1913 the Kaiser feared that, even without a formal invitation, Churchill might show up at the Kiel week cel-ebrations. The Kaiser, in a brutally frank conversation with the British naval attaché, 'remarked very decidedly that he [Wilhelm] had *not* asked the First Lord to the Kiel regatta, but that the First Lord seemed to have a habit of turning up uninvited, as he had done at the Kaiser Manoeuvres [in 1909]'. The British naval attaché also duly recorded: 'The Emperor remarked that he did not know how to take the First Lord, what he said to him he thought Mr Churchill transposed later. He was a man who could not be trusted.' Wilhelm went on to describe as a 'fiasco' the previous visit by Lord Haldane.[80] Wilhelm's remarks stopped cold any notion that Churchill might use the Kiel festivities as an opportunity to visit Germany during 1913. In the spring of 1914, however, the prospective arrival of British battleships – a visit the German government wanted – made it difficult for the Kaiser to reject out-of-hand a proposal that Churchill come along as well. 'An invitation would not be opportune', the Kaiser instructed the German Foreign Office, 'but he [that is, Wilhelm] is convinced that an official enquiry by the British as to whether Mr Churchill and his colleagues in the Admiralty would be welcome . . . would be received with pleasure.'[81] The Kaiser, apparently making a virtue out of necessity, even offered an invitation through his brother, Prince Henry, to Churchill. 'The Emperor wishes it to be understood', Prince Henry told the British ambassador in Berlin, 'that he has invited the First Lord of the Admiralty and the Sea Lord to Kiel officially, and that he hoped that at all events both Mr Churchill and Prince Louis of Battenberg would be present during the Kiel week.'[82] Through the efforts of Ballin and Cassel, then, Churchill received his invitation to Germany.

To guide negotiations during a visit to Kiel, Churchill worked up a four-point arms-control agenda. At the top of his list was a discussion of the holiday proposal. Churchill also thought that room for agreement might exist with regard to limitations in the size of capital ships. These two proposals – a holiday in building and limits on the size of capital ships – ended up as major elements of the famous naval arms control agreement reached at the Washington Conference of 1921–22. In addition, Churchill wanted to explore ways to reduce the danger of surprise attack. One proposal he wanted to explore was to reduce 'the unwholesome concentration of fleets in Home Waters'. A reduction in concentration would remove some of the danger inherent in the Anglo-German naval rivalry. Another topic for discussion was the development of confidence-building measures – that is, formal procedures for mutual inspections – that 'would go a long way to stopping the espionage on both sides which is the continued cause of suspicion and ill-feeling'. Churchill would later write that these topics, if discussed and 'agreed upon, would make for easement and stability'.[83]

Churchill's agenda for arms-control talks, however, would have encountered strong opposition in Germany. Tirpitz's soothing words to the British naval attaché did not reflect accurately either his own views or that of the German government. There existed no genuine willingness on the part of Wilhelm or Tirpitz to reduce the German naval program. Quite the reverse was actually the case, since both Wilhelm and Tirpitz wanted to make additions to German naval preparations during the spring of 1914. Wilhelm, for instance, pressed to start the extra battleship called for in the 1912 amendment to the German navy law. Meanwhile, Tirpitz's staff wanted to increase the readiness of the German fleet so that it could carry out a 'lightning-fast offensive'. To increase the combat power of German ships and the fleet's readiness, Tirpitz asked for an extra 150–200 million marks over what was already scheduled for spending. Bethmann Hollweg, citing both diplomatic and financial reasons, fended off these requests for further naval increases.[84] Nonetheless, what these discussions among German decision makers clearly show, neither Wilhelm nor Tirpitz looked to slacken the pace of the competition or seek an accommodation on the naval rivalry that would meet the desires of Britain's Liberal government. Both merely were waiting for a suitable occasion, when they could beat down Bethmann Hollweg's objections and obstructions, to make further increases in the threat posed by the German fleet to Britain.

In addition, Germany's leaders had already rejected the holiday proposal, and they deeply resented Churchill's repeated public calls for it. On every occasion that the holiday proposal was broached by Churchill or British officials, the German leaders made unmistakably clear (even to the point of rudeness) their view that this arms-control initiative was non-negotiable. Kaiser Wilhelm and Tirpitz saw Churchill's efforts as an attempt to wreck the German naval program. During the previous year, when the German government became aware that Churchill intended to renew the holiday offer, they worked strenuously behind the scenes to deter it from happening. The Kaiser bluntly made it known that he took personal affront to the holiday scheme and did not want it raised again. The British ambassador in Berlin reported: 'The Emperor said that he did not wish to make a fuss, but that he wished his words repeated quietly and privately in the proper quarter.'[85] By going ahead with a public appeal for the holiday proposal in October 1913, Churchill showed a blatant disregard for the expressed opinion of the Kaiser and the German government. Nothing had happened since the previous autumn that would indicate a change in attitude of Germany's leaders. The Kaiser wrote to Bethmann Hollweg in the spring of 1914 stating once again his firm opposition to further arms control talks. 'I wish to see the whole endless and dangerous subject of limitation of armaments', Wilhelm wrote, 'rolled up and put away for good. What it comes to finally is that England is protesting against my right to decide on the sea power required by Germany, in fact an attempt to break down the Naval Law.'[86] Germany's Foreign Secretary, Jagow, bluntly told Goschen: 'the [naval holiday] idea is Utopian and unworkable'. Goschen held the view that 'Winston Churchill's proposal that there should be a "year's inactivity in Naval construction" for everybody is not liked here – ostensibly because the idea is unworkable – but really I expect, because it is an offer which they can't very well accept – and which may make them liable to be told later by us – "We have made you an offer and you wouldn't accept it.'"[87] Goschen correctly concluded that the German government had no real intention of considering the holiday proposal as the basis for negotiation.

The German ambassador, Lichnowsky, reporting back to his government about the prospect of Churchill's visit to Kiel, also opposed a renewal of arms-control discussions in any upcoming talks. On 10 May 1914, Lichnowsky reported that Churchill 'now seems inclined' to visit Kiel, 'and will probably come on board his yacht, accompanied by a few Sea Lords and his beautiful and charming wife'. Lichnowsky warned his superiors: 'Churchill is an exceedingly crafty fox and is sure to try to spring some proposal or other on us . . . As a politician he is somewhat fantastic and unreliable.'[88] At the end of May, when it seemed increasingly unlikely that Churchill would visit Kiel, Lichnowsky offered the view that if the First Lord did at the last moment 'go to Kiel after all, I cannot imagine that it would do any harm, unless we start discussing unnecessary stuff with him'. By 'unnecessary stuff', Lichnowsky meant negotiations about the naval arms rivalry. Lichnowsky volunteered to warn Churchill 'that it would be better for him not to refer to the naval holiday or other nonsense of that kind'.[89] One can imagine Churchill's response to Lichnowsky's characterization of his holiday proposal – the number one item on his agenda for talks with German leaders – as 'nonsense'. In addition, Lichnowsky did not speak only for himself: his opinion accurately reflected the views of the German government in their determined opposition to any high-level discussions designed to reduce the two countries' warship-building programs.

Churchill, while wanting to begin a constructive negotiation with Germany's leaders, harbored few illusions about the reception that he was likely to receive when he presented to them once again the holiday proposal. 'I do not expect', he admitted, 'any agreement on these [holiday proposals], but I would like to strip the subject of the misrepresentation and misunderstanding with which it has been surrounded, and put it on a clear basis in case circumstances should ever render it admissible.' It is difficult to see, however, when the holiday plan would ever gain a favorable hearing from Germany's rulers. Nonetheless, if Churchill could not move Germany's leaders to agreement, he could still use a German refusal to negotiate seriously about arms control to his benefit in deflating the opposition at home to the Admiralty's spending requests. The struggle over the navy's budget the previous winter made it imperative in Churchill's estimation that he undertake some arms-control initiative. 'I hope', Churchill wrote to Asquith and Grey, 'in view of the very strong feeling there is about naval expenditure and the great difficulties I have to face, my wish to put these points to Admiral Tirpitz . . . may not be dismissed.'[90] If Churchill could not induce Germany's rulers to cut back on warship construction, then perhaps he could at least placate the radical Liberals who wanted to reduce British naval spending.

Grey, however, opposed any high-level negotiations between the two governments. Although Grey had been informed of the back-channel attempt by Ballin and Cassel to open talks, and he approved of the visit of the British battle squadron to Kiel, the Foreign Secretary was taken aback when Goschen's telegram arrived with the invitation from the Kaiser (through Prince Henry) that Churchill would travel along as well to Germany. 'This will never do at the present moment', Grey noted on Goschen's telegram, 'and there was so I understood no question of the First Lord and the First Sea Lord going with the fleet.'[91] Only two weeks before, Grey had received a note from Churchill, saying that a visit by him to Germany during the Kiel festivities was 'impracticable'.[92] Grey quickly moved to put the brakes on negotiations led by Churchill. Instead of a summit at Kiel, Grey suggested that the two sides explore ways to reduce the naval rivalry by opening talks at a much lower level, involving the naval attachés in London and Berlin. If these negotiations showed promise, then Grey thought that follow-up higher level meetings could take place. Grey, then, did not so much veto the possibility of talks, but advocated a more cautious step-by-step negotiation, testing the German side and exploring the prospect for agreements. After all, the beginning of these talks resembled the opening of the Haldane Mission, which had signally failed to produce a naval understanding. Grey no doubt saw nothing to indicate that Churchill's visit would produce any different outcome. Quite the contrary, the brief flurry of discussions with Jagow and Tirpitz only three months before had indicated that the German government lacked any interest in serious talks. In opposing Churchill's initiative, Grey had the backing of his advisers at the Foreign Office, who looked upon negotiations about naval limitations as counterproductive. The Foreign Office feared that a visit by Churchill would result in questions about Britain's entente relationships with France and Russia, and Grey wanted to avoid this contentious topic. Perhaps, too, Grey saw this initiative as a challenge to his control of Britain's foreign policy. Grey resented anything that gave the appearance of interference in the running of his department. Despite several challenges to his position and views on foreign policy, Grey had showed himself a shrewd bureaucratic turf fighter, holding onto the reins of power for over eight years. Churchill's attempt to engineer negotiations might have appeared to Grey as similar to previous efforts to get around him.[93] In replying to Churchill's arms-control proposal, a glimmer of Grey's testiness about trespassing on the departmental responsibilities of a colleague appears: 'I put this [alternative approach of beginning arms control negotiations with talks between naval attachés] forward with diffidence as it is out of my sphere.' Asquith backed Grey in rejecting a visit by Churchill to Germany.[94] Goschen was thus duly instructed to inform the German government that Churchill would not accompany the British battleship squadron to Kiel.[95]

Despite Grey's objections and Asquith's veto, Churchill apparently persisted in his effort to meet with the German leaders. Even though Goschen diplomatically gave word that Churchill could not accept the Kaiser's invitation, the German government still remained unsure whether a visit might occur. According to Ballin, 'Churchill sent word that, if Tirpitz really wanted to see him, he would find [a] means to bring about such a meeting.' A last-minute visit by Churchill thus remained a distinct possibility, with the Germans even reserving a mooring spot for the Admiralty yacht *Enchantress* in case the First Lord crossed over the North Sea.[96] Since the Kaiser and Tirpitz did not really want to open negotiations about naval matters, the German government made no further effort to entice Churchill into visiting Kiel. Grey and the Foreign Office staff were no doubt correct in their assessment that negotiations of the naval issue with the German government would likely lead nowhere. The efforts of Ballin, Cassel, and Churchill to bring about serious negotiations thus came to naught. The outbreak of war that summer meant that Britain and Germany would settle their naval rivalry by fighting and not by negotiation.

Conclusion

Even before the outbreak of war in the summer of 1914, Churchill considered Britain and Germany to be engaged in a high-stakes contest for naval mastery and over the European balance of power. Churchill went to the Admiralty with the clear aim of defeating Germany's naval challenge. This aim entailed that Britain build more ships than Germany, man them, and keep the British fleet in constant readiness for war, thereby staying ahead of the German navy in the naval competition. Closing off Germany's ability to win a major battle at sea also led Churchill to push for the concentration of British naval power in home waters. He would later write: 'Germany made a bold bid for naval supremacy, and we had to face this mighty power across the narrow North Sea with every feeling that our national existence was at stake.'[97] Churchill did this out of the strategic conviction that naval concentration in home waters – staying superior to the naval forces massed by Germany in the North Sea – was key to Britain's security.

To acquire the ships, men, and supplies needed to maintain British naval superiority over Germany confronted Churchill with a difficult domestic political problem. He wanted to avoid any panic, such as had occurred in early 1909, spurred by a perception that Germany was on the verge of catching up or surpassing Britain in the naval competition. A public outcry about Britain's naval security could aid politically the opposition Conservatives and hurt the Liberal government. Churchill acted to pre-empt attempts by the Conservative opposition to stir up a public outcry on British naval security. His naval program, as well as the way Churchill publicly presented it, for the most part satisfied the Conservative opposition, and the issue of naval security lost a great deal of its partisan rancor. The Conservatives could not credibly manufacture a scare about Britain's naval security during Churchill's tenure as First Lord.

While Churchill disarmed his Conservative critics, he provided ammunition to left-wing critics. His success in muting the Conservative opposition came at the cost of galvanizing hostility from within his own party. Liberals opposed to large expenditure on naval armaments grew increasingly frustrated with Churchill and the apparent unwillingness of their own party's leaders to rein in the navy's budget. This frustration expressed itself in the sharp criticism of Churchill and his leadership of the navy by government colleagues and from the Liberal party's rank-and-file during the winter of 1913–14. To Churchill's dismay, his opponents within the Liberal Party exhibited a marked determination to force him from the government, and the struggle within the government over naval spending was a close-run contest. Only Asquith's fabled political skills, as well as Lloyd George's reluctance to push the controversy to the point of actual resignations, prevented the government from breaking up on the issue of the navy's spending. Churchill's ability to occupy the middle ground on the debate about naval preparedness – placating (while not completely satisfying) both the Conservatives and the Liberals – is a testament to his political skills in forging a consensus on a critically important and potentially divisive policy issue. This consensus was a key element in ensuring that Britain kept ahead of Germany in their naval rivalry.

Preserving Britain's naval predominance, however, did not translate into arms-control negotiations with Germany or promote an international understanding between the two countries. Churchill had hoped that his steps to ensure Britain's naval security would eventually result in an improvement in Anglo-German relations. In Churchill's estimation, Germany's leaders would conclude that their naval effort had failed to gain them any important strategic advantage once Britain demonstrated its clear determination to stay ahead in the naval competition. Germany's leaders, Churchill thought, would want to open negotiations, seeking an accommodation with Britain about naval armaments. By 1914, Churchill considered Germany close to wanting serious discussions about ways to settle the naval rivalry. 'The personalities who expressed the foreign policy of Germany', Churchill would later write, 'seemed for the first time to be men to whom we could talk and with whom common action was possible.' The ability of Britain and Germany to cooperate in settling the Balkan crises of the previous year encouraged the belief that both countries might go even further in strengthening the détente in their relations. Churchill reflected on the opportunity for cooperation: 'There seemed also to be a prospect that the personal goodwill and mutual respect which had grown up between the principal people on both sides might play a useful part in the future; and some there were who looked forward to a wider combination in which Great Britain and Germany, without prejudice to their respective friendships or alliances, might together bring the two opposing European systems into harmony and give to all the anxious nations solid assurances of safety and fair-play.'[98] Anglo-German relations, in other words, held the key to the peace of Europe. When, during the 1930s, Churchill's political opponents labeled him a warmonger, he tried to defend himself by pointing out how much he wanted to find a negotiated settlement of the naval rivalry with Germany. In answer to critics, he maintained: 'You have heard me described as a war monger. That is a lie. I have laboured for peace before the Great War, and if the naval holiday had been adopted the course of history might have been different.'[99] Churchill thought that defeating the German naval challenge would provide the basis for arms-control talks, contributing in turn to a stable relationship between Britain and Germany and to the peace of Europe.

Germany's leaders in 1914, however, remained quite far removed from wanting to negotiate meaningful reductions in naval forces. The German leadership did not possess 'the personal goodwill or mutual respect' that Churchill imagined. Churchill, along with other leaders of Britain's Liberal government, such as Grey, Haldane, and Lloyd George, thought that a 'peace party' existed in Berlin. St Loe Strachey, editor of the Spectator, recalled that British leaders 'believed that there was a powerful peace party in Germany, or rather, that a party which called itself a peace party would remain in being, would grow in strength, and would ultimately control the situation if we refrained from upsetting the pacific applecart'. The notion of a German peace party received encouragement from Bethmann Hollweg, who thought that he could better secure concessions from the British in negotiations between the two countries if they feared a shift within Germany's leadership to a more bellicose foreign policy adopted by a war party. This British misperception about Germany's rulers contributed to the view that relations between the two countries were steadily improving and on the verge of a breakthrough. Unfortunately, as Michael Ekstein has observed, 'there were no "doves" in Berlin in July 1914'.[100]

In attempting to arrange a naval arms-control agreement, Churchill faced an implacable enemy in Tirpitz. Tirpitz and the Imperial Navy Office showed no interest whatsoever in Churchill's holiday proposal, except to find ways to defeat it. The holiday plan threatened Tirpitz's goal of carrying out a long-term, orderly warship-building program, leading one day to the acquisition of a fleet that would rival that possessed by Britain. Tirpitz's armaments plan required long-term stability in the construction of warships, both as a way to hold down the cost of Germany's naval buildup and to shield the navy from parliamentary pressures and interference.[101] The holiday proposal would derail the Navy Office's strategy, upsetting timetables for warship construction, escalating their costs, and increasing the likelihood of political confrontations within the German government and with the Reichstag over defense spending.

Tirpitz, consequently, wanted nothing to do with any arms-control initiative that curtailed his planned naval buildup. At every opportunity, Tirpitz worked to prevent serious arms-control talks, heaping scorn upon those who promoted negotiations. Because Cassel sought to arrange high-level arms-control negotiations, Tirpitz branded him 'a Jewish renegade in whose house the Anglo-French entente was sealed'. Haldane, after meeting Tirpitz, quite correctly described him as 'a dangerous man'.[102] This view was shared by others. Goschen, the British ambassador, held the

> firm opinion that if Lord Haldane had talked to him [Tirpitz] till Doomsday he could not have persuaded him to diminish the number of ships for which he has applied and which there is but little doubt the Reichstag will sanction. Even to spread their construction over a number of years, as Lord Haldane suggested will be . . . gall and wormwood to him, and I feel certain that nothing more favourable to our views can be obtained.[103]

When Colonel Edward House, President Woodrow Wilson's confidant and emissary, traveled to Europe in the spring of 1914, attempting to improve great-power relations, he found no support for arms control among Germany's leaders. Tirpitz, in particular, stood out against a reduction in arms programs. House thought that Tirpitz 'evidenced a decided dislike for the British, a dislike that almost amounted to hatred'.[104] This deep-seated opposition evinced by Tirpitz toward British arms-control initiatives meant that he was hardly a suitable partner for negotiations. Arms control threatened Tirpitz's life's work of building a fleet to challenge Britain.

When Tirpitz floated his own arms-control proposals, it was always with a mind either to justify his own program of shipbuilding or to attempt a slowdown of British warship construction. While Tirpitz complained that Churchill only floated arms-control initiatives that were one-sided and self-serving, the very same could be said for him. The notion of a compromise settlement, which would include a reduction in German shipbuilding, found no favor with him. Instead of reducing the German naval effort, Tirpitz never wavered in wanting to build a navy that posed a dangerous threat to Britain and undermined its position as a world power.

In rejecting the holiday plan, Tirpitz held the view that in the long run the naval balance of power was shifting against Britain. The construction of a powerful battle fleet, he maintained, would require a generation or more to complete, and he consistently took a long-range view of the naval competition with Britain. The gap in naval strength between Britain and Germany, in his estimation, would narrow, since the British navy could never maintain a crushing superiority over the large battle fleet that he intended to build. In the autumn of 1911, when Churchill took up his position at the Admiralty, hoping that he could hold down British naval spending, Tirpitz was looking forward to further increases in the German battle fleet and the coming end of Britain's naval mastery. Tirpitz envisioned 'that once 60 [German] capital ships of some 25,000 tons [displacement] are available and ready for war', Britain would require no less than '90 capital ships, *based in home waters*', to maintain a three-to-two superiority in battle-fleet strength over Germany.[105] An assessment completed by the German Navy Office during the summer of 1913 agreed, stating that 'the English are at the limit of their strength in finances, politics, and naval technology'.[106] The German navy's leadership identified several factors that were hurting Britain's ability to keep ahead of Germany. The Navy Office, quite correctly, concluded that Lloyd George would oppose further increases in naval spending with an election pending. Britain's Liberal government, in the German view, courted political disaster if it raised taxes. The British Admiralty, then, could not look forward to constant increases in naval spending. Manpower constraints would also prevent major additions to the British fleet. As a consequence of these financial and manpower constraints on British naval strength, Captain Müller argued: 'Four to five capital ships a year represent the highest possible financial effort of Great Britain over a long period . . . If a normal "three-tempo" [that is, the start of three capital ships each year] were the established rule in Germany, the military distance between England and Germany would diminish.'[107] In addition, Britain needed to find naval forces for service outside home waters. Tirpitz argued in his memoirs that every 'warship constructed anywhere in the world except in England was ultimately an advantage for us because it helped adjust the balance of power at sea'.[108] Germany's diplomacy could accelerate this decline of Britain's naval position by finding coalition partners. Finally, no revolutionary new weapons system was likely to appear that would transform the naval balance dramatically in Britain's favor. In arms-control negotiations, Tirpitz thus preferred a diplomatic deadlock, which would permit this gradual shift of the naval balance of power in Germany's favor.

That naval construction around the world might only lead Britain to forge a coalition of its own to defeat Germany's naval ambitions did not lead Tirpitz to reassess his plan to build up German naval power. Tirpitz would not relent in wanting a fleet to rival that of Britain, regardless of the consequences for Anglo-German relations. In *The World Crisis*, Churchill offers a damning judgment of Tirpitz, assessing the consequences of his naval policy. Tirpitz, in Churchill's view, was a 'sincere, wrong-headed, purblind old Prussian [who] firmly believed that the growth of his beloved navy was inducing in British minds an increasing fear of war, whereas it simply produced naval rejoinders and diplomatic reactions which strengthened the forces and closed the ranks of the Entente'.[109] Tirpitz was a poor strategist, more interested in building weapons than in understanding the larger national purpose that they served and how others might react to them. Bethmann Hollweg remarked: 'For Tirpitz the Navy is an end in itself.'[110]

Tirpitz's shortcomings as a strategist, of course, reflect a larger failure on the part of imperial Germany's rulers to set realistic and coherent political aims, matched by supporting strategies. Tirpitz was not alone amongst German decision makers in wanting to challenge Britain's naval predominance. Behind Tirpitz stood Kaiser Wilhelm. The German naval buildup was Wilhelm's creation. A powerful navy was the settled ambition of Wilhelm, and he showed considerable rudeness to anyone who wanted to curtail it. Within Germany's ruling oligarchy, Wilhelm consistently sided with Tirpitz when disagreements occurred over armaments programs, strategy, and foreign policy. He even pushed for the building of additional warships in the spring of 1914 after Tirpitz had concluded that further construction would prove counterproductive, only strengthening Churchill's ability to forge a domestic political consensus in Britain to stay ahead of Germany. Whereas Tirpitz's departmental responsibilities and advocacy contributed to his blindness, Wilhelm had no such excuse. Wilhelm, despite considerable evidence and advice to the contrary, discounted the baneful effects of the German naval buildup for the deterioration of Germany's strategic predicament. Churchill, consequently, would not have found a willing negotiating partner in Wilhelm.

In addition, Churchill's speeches as First Lord particularly infuriated Wilhelm. Among Germany's leaders, Churchill had acquired the reputation of a bully. The German naval attaché, Captain Erich von Müller, reporting on Churchill's presentation of the Admiralty's spending requests to the House of Commons in March 1914, commented: 'Mr Churchill departed from his former habit, and in his speech this year avoided making hostile remarks about the German Navy.' Müller thought that Churchill had only changed his tone because he 'realizes that his former habit of "plain speaking" resulted in the opposite of the intimidation that he hoped for'. In Müller's assessment, Churchill now wanted to avoid in his speeches provoking Germany into the construction of additional warships, permitting Britain to take advantage of the slower rate of German naval building.[111] Müller's report illustrates how Germany's leaders viewed Churchill as habitual in his rudeness when speaking about the German navy, and only able to break this habit when he intended some deception. Given this view of Churchill in German ruling circles, a visit by him to Germany stood no chance of leading to constructive arms control negotiations.

Since no domestic political change within Germany pointed toward an arms-control agreement, Britain faced instead the prospect of an open-ended arms competition, with the German navy continuing to pose a dangerous threat to British security. Germany's leaders, despite their straitened financial circumstances, still thought that the best way to obtain a settlement with Britain was by going ahead with their naval program. Some of Germany's leaders even harbored the illusion that the German naval buildup had already paralyzed Britain's foreign policy, deterring the British government from intervening on the side of France in a war on the European continent. Jagow, the German foreign secretary, doubted that Britain would take part in a struggle between Germany and France. 'We have not built our fleet in vain', Jagow maintained, 'and in my opinion, people in England will seriously ask themselves whether it will be just that simple and without danger to play the role of France's guardian angel against us.'[112] Staying ahead of Germany in the naval competition, then, did not translate into deterring Germany from unleashing a war to gain hegemony in Europe.

Germany's military leaders, too, still considered themselves to have a good chance of crushing French military power in a relatively short campaign. Britain's pre-war naval preparations could not confer on France safety from a German invasion. By defeating the French army and imposing a harsh settlement on France, Germany could overturn the European balance of power and undermine Britain's security. When Germany's leaders, for instance, thought at the end of August and early September 1914 that the French army was as good as beaten, they considered how to use the defeat of France as a springboard for a further round of fighting against Britain. If Britain did not make peace after France's defeat, the German government intended to make a substantial increase in the navy, helping to finance this naval buildup by using the indemnities that Germany would have imposed on the French and the Belgians. This naval buildup, along with the use of newly acquired bases in France and Belgium, would enable Germany 'to lay siege to Britain and so . . . compel England to recognize the situation created by Germany on the Continent'.[113] The fighting of the First World War would show British leaders just how difficult a task they faced in preventing Germany from inflicting humiliating defeats on Britain's coalition partners. In a war fought to prevent Germany's domination of Europe, Britain could lose on land as well as at sea.

The naval competition between Britain and Germany thus formed a part of a larger rivalry between the two countries. Britain's goal in this rivalry was to contain Germany, upholding a balance of power and pre-venting a German hegemony in Europe. Meanwhile, Germany's leaders resented the very notion of a balance of power that aimed at containing and limiting their ambitions. Britain's balance-of-power diplomacy appeared to them as an encircling coalition, which they wanted to disrupt. Bethmann Hollweg, by trying to reduce the naval rivalry, sought to improve relations with Britain and break apart the coalition that sought to contain Germany. Bethmann Hollweg's efforts, however, did not go nearly far enough. The German leadership refused to consider a drastic curtailment in their naval program. Further, they escalated the naval rivalry by attempting to increase the combat readiness of the German fleet. In addition, Berlin demanded nothing less than Britain's promise of unconditional neutrality in case of a European war, even if Germany started the war with a massive offensive strike against France. A neut-rality agreement such as that proposed by Berlin would isolate France and Russia from British support, destroying the very notion of a balance of power. While Churchill sought to improve relations with Germany, he could not abide the price demanded by Berlin. No British government – Liberal or Conservative – was willing to concede to Germany such a free hand in Europe.[114] The inability of Britain and Germany, then, to settle by negotiation their naval rivalry was inextricably linked to this larger strug-gle over the European balance of power.

The outbreak of war in the summer of 1914, in Churchill's judgment provoked by Germany's leaders, involved Britain in a desperate struggle for the mastery of Europe. Churchill maintained 'that the war was started and it was being maintained by the Prussian military aristocracy, which set no limits to its ambition of world-wide predominance . . . In a word, it is the old struggle of 100 years ago against Napoleon . . . We are at grips with Prussian militarism.'[115] A recent assessment on the origins of the First World War by the historian Michael Howard takes a similar view:

A German hegemony offered nothing except a rule based on military power, exercised by a caste concerned only to preserve and extend its dominance, and, in Eastern Europe at least, based on an explicit doctrine not only of territorial conquest, but of racial superiority. This creed was to be labeled by Allied propagandists 'Prussianism,' . . . a creed that despised the liberal democracy of the West, elevated service to the state as the highest virtue, and glorified military values above all others. Such sentiments can be found elsewhere in Europe, not least in Britain, but nowhere did they exist in so ferocious a combination. There can be no doubt that a military victory would have strengthened rather than eroded them.[116]

In the war with Germany, then, Britain was fighting for nothing less than the highest stakes.

While Churchill rejected the view that war between Britain and Germany was inevitable, Germany's foreign policy and weapons programs nonetheless pointed toward conflict. Churchill considered:

The very rapid growth of the German Navy, stimulated year after year by successive expansions of their Fleet Law, constitutes the main preoccupation in the minds of those responsible for the security of the country. The union of a Navy of such great power with the largest Army in Europe will be a most sinister and disquieting fact, especially when we consider that these gigantic engines of destruction will be wielded by a Government in Germany which can be said to be in any real sense a democratic Government, with Ministers responsible to Parliament, but by a military and bureaucratic oligarchy.

Germany's naval arms buildup prevented Britain from reducing its own defense efforts. This competition, in turn, stood in the way of a genuine détente in the relations between the two countries. Churchill hoped 'that the democratic forces in Germany will again have greater control of their own Government'. In the meantime, Britain needed to stay ahead of Germany in the naval competition and work with France and Russia to prevent German aggression.[117] Churchill thought that Germany's leaders, if faced with the choice between accommodation and war, would rein in their ambitions, and reject a high-risk gamble to overthrow Europe's balance of power. The outbreak of war showed instead the recklessness of Germany's rulers. Churchill would return after the war to this theme of how Germany's behavior brought great ruin on their country and the world. It seemed to Churchill that 'Germany . . . had rushed with head down and settled resolve to her own undoing'.[118] Before the war, Churchill had spoken out about the folly of thinking that either Britain or Germany would benefit from a trial of strength. Neither country would find in a war with the other a prize worth fighting for. The horrendous struggle unleashed by Germany's leaders confirmed the wisdom of Churchill's judgment.

NOTES

1 Winston S. Churchill, *The World Crisis, 1911–1914* (London: Thorton Butterworth, 1923), pp. 72, 148.
2 Churchill to William Royle, 20 December 1911, in Randolph S. Churchill, *Winston S. Churchill*, vol. II, Companion Part 2, *1907–1911* (London: Heinemann, 1969), pp. 1360–1. (Hereafter referred to as Churchill, *Companion*.)
3 'Government Policy and the Foreign Situation', 14 August 1908, Robert Rhodes James, ed., *Winston S. Churchill: His Complete Speeches, 1897–1963*, vol. II: *1908–1913* (London: Chelsea House, 1974), pp. 1082–7. (Hereafter referred to as Rhodes James, ed., *Speeches*.)
4 'Free Trade', 4 August 1908, in Rhodes James, ed., *Speeches*, vol. II, p. 1081–2.
5 Churchill to Asquith, 29 December 1908, in Churchill, *Companion*, p. 863.
6 Report by Captain von Müller, 20 June 1913, in E. T. S. Dugdale, *German Diplomatic Documents*, vol. IV: *The Descent to the Abyss, 1911–1914* (London: Methuen, 1931), p. 287.
7 'Mr Churchill at Swansea', *The Times*, 17 August 1908. *The Times* labeled Churchill's speech as 'vituperative rhetoric', exhibiting 'careless violence of expression'.
8 Churchill to Clementine Churchill, 15 September 1909, in Mary Soames, ed., *Speaking for Themselves: The Personal Letters of Winston and Clementine Churchill* (New York: Doubleday, 1998), p. 30.
9 Churchill presented a masterful strategic analysis of how the initial campaign in a war between France and Germany might unfold. See *World Crisis*, pp. 60–4.
10 Ibid.
11 Churchill to Lloyd George, 31 August 1911, Churchill, *Companion*, vol. II, part 2, pp. 1118–19.
12 Churchill, *World Crisis*, pp. 20–1.
13 Churchill to Grey, 9 September 1909, enclosing a note about a conversation with the German ambassador, Churchill, *Companion*, vol. II, part 2, pp. 958–61.
14 Churchill to J. L. Garvin, 10 August 1912, Garvin Papers, Harry Ransom Humanities Center, University of Texas at Austin.
15 See the judicious account of these deliberations offered by Samuel R. Williamson, *The Politics of Grand Strategy: Britain and France Prepare for War, 1904–1911* (Cambridge, MA: Harvard University Press, 1969), pp. 167–204.
16 See, for example, Arthur J. Marder, *From the Dreadnought to Scapa Flow: The Royal Navy in the Fisher Era, 1904–1919*, vol. I: *The Road to War, 1904–1914* (London: Oxford University Press, 1961), 252–71.
17 Jon Tetsuro Sumida, *In Defence of Naval Supremacy: Finance, Technology and British Naval Policy, 1889–1914* (Boston, MA: Unwin Hyman, 1989), Table 3.
18 See A. von Tirpitz, *Politische Dokumente*, vol. I: *Der Aufbau der deutschen Weltmacht* (Stuttgart and Berlin: J. G. Cotta'sche Buchhandlung, 1924), pp. 203–7. (Hereafter cited as Tirpitz, *Aufbau*.)

19 On the struggle over German naval spending during the winter of 1911–12, I have drawn upon Michael Epkenhans, *Die wilhelminische Flottenrüstung, 1908–1914: Weltmachtstreben, industrieller Fortschritt, und soziale Integration* (Munich: Oldenbourg Verlag, 1991), pp. 93–142; Volker R. Berghahn, *Germany and the Approach of War in 1914* (New York: St Martin's Press, 1973), pp. 107–24; Fritz Fischer, *War of Illusions: German Politics from 1911 to 1914* (New York: Norton, 1975), pp. 112–40; and Walther Hubatsch, *Die Ära Tirpitz* (Gottingen: Musterschmidt, 1955), pp. 90–105.

20 From a letter quoted in Arthur J. Marder, ed., *Fear God and Dread Nought*, vol. II: *Years of Power, 1904–1914* (London: Jonathan Cape, 1956), p. 103.

21 On the Conservative opposition to the Liberal government's naval policy, see A. J. A. Morris, *The Scaremongers* (London: Routledge & Kegan Paul, 1984).

22 'Mr Lloyd-George at Queen's Hall', *The Times*, 29 July 1908.

23 On the attitudes of the Liberal Party's left wing on the naval arms competition, see Howard Weinroth, 'Left-wing Opposition to Naval Armaments in Britain before 1914', *Journal of Contemporary History*, no. 4 (1971), pp. 93–120; and A. J. Anthony Morris, *Radicalism against War, 1906–1914* (Totowa, NJ: Rowman & Littlefield, 1972).

24 Churchill, *World Crisis*, pp. 38, 41.

25 Admiralty 116/1294B.

26 F. W. Wiemann, 'Lloyd George and the Struggle for the Navy Estimates of 1914', in A. J. P. Taylor, ed., *Lloyd George: Twelve Essays* (New York: Atheneum, 1971), p. 73.

27 Michael G. Fry, *Lloyd George and Foreign Policy*, vol. I: *The Education of a Statesman: 1890–1916* (Montreal: McGill-Queen's University Press, 1977), pp. 111–12.

28 Churchill, *World Crisis*, p. 101. Emphasis in the original.

29 Churchill to Fisher, 19 February 1912, in Churchill, *World Crisis*, p. 105.

30 Robert Axelrod, *The Evolution of Cooperation* (New York: Basic Books, 1984), pp. 124–32.

31 On the importance of communicating threats, see the classic study by Thomas C. Schelling, *The Strategy of Conflict* (Cambridge, MA: Harvard University Press, 1960), pp. 146–50.

32 For the debates about naval estimates in March 1912, see *Parliamentary Debates* (Commons), Fifth Series, vol. 35, cols 1549–654.

33 Lamar Cecil, *Albert Ballin: Business and Politics in Imperial Germany, 1888–1918* (Princeton, NJ: Princeton University Press, 1967), pp. 180–99.

34 See Randolph S. Churchill, *Winston S. Churchill*, vol. II: *Young Statesman, 1901–1914* (London: Heinemann, 1967), pp. 559–61. (Hereafter cited as Churchill, *Young Statesman*.)

35 Churchill to Cassel, 7 January 1912, in Churchill, *Young Statesman*, pp. 560–1.

36 George Macaulay Trevelyan, *Grey of Falloden* (London: Longmans, 1937), p. 228.

37 Stephen Koss, *Asquith* (London: Allen Lane, 1976), pp. 148–9.

38 Diary entry, 10 February 1912, in J. M. McEwen, ed., *The Riddell Diaries, 1908–1923* (London: Athlone Press, 1986), p. 32. Lord Fisher agreed that Churchill's speech did more good than harm. Fisher wrote Churchill: 'your Glasgow speech was as straight as a die. It said *We'll fight to the finish and mean to win – make no d–d mistake, dear friends.*' Fisher to Churchill, 5 March 1912, in Marder, ed., *Fear God*, vol. II, pp. 435–6. Churchill also received support from the Prime Minister. 'Asquith did not join in the hue and cry against Mr Churchill,

whom he considered to have made "a plain statement of an obvious truth", even though the word "luxury" might not have been happily chosen.' J. A. Spender and Cyril Asquith, *Life of Herbert Henry Asquith, Lord Oxford and Asquith* (London: Hutchinson, 1932,) vol. II, p. 68.

39 Churchill, *World Crisis*, pp. 100–1.

40 Marder, *Dreadnought to Scapa Flow*, vol. I, p. 285.

41 Grand-Admiral [Alfred] von Tirpitz, *My Memoirs* (London: Hurst & Blackett, 1919) vol. I, p. 215.

42 For Haldane's account of his negotiation in Berlin, see his diary published in G. P. Gooch and Harold Temperley, eds, *British Documents on the Origins of the War, 1898–1914* (London: His Majesty's Stationery Office, 1930), vol. VI, no. 506, pp. 676–85. (Hereafter cited as *B.D.*)

43 Holger Herwig, *'Luxury' Fleet: The Imperial German Navy 1888–1918* (London: George Allen & Unwin, 1980), pp. 77–8.

44 Churchill's proposal to concentrate naval forces in home waters and withdraw warships from the Mediterranean infuriated Kaiser Wilhelm, who considered this step tantamount to a British mobilization against Germany and a declaration of war. Wilhelm informed Metternich: 'If England withdraws her ships from the Mediterranean home to the North Sea, it will be taken here as a threat of war and be answered by a strengthened Supplementary Law – triple tempo – and eventual mobilization.' See Wilhelm to Metternich, 5 March 1912, *G.P.*, vol. 31, no. 156.

45 Balfour to Churchill, 22 March 1912, Churchill, *Companion*, vol. II, part 3, pp. 1530–1.

46 Churchill to Fisher, 9 March 1912, Churchill, *Companion*, vol. II, part 3, pp. 1526–7.

47 Quoted in Morris, *Scaremongers*, p. 316.

48 Churchill to J. L. Garvin, 10 August 1912, Garvin Papers.

49 The five future First Lords were Arthur Balfour, Walter Long, Arthur Lee, Leo Amery, and Eyres Monsell.

50 For the debates about the supplementary naval spending request and imperial defense that were held during July 1912, see *Parliamentary Debates* (Commons), Fifth Series, vol. 41, columns 835–946, 1197–308, 1384–498.

51 Churchill, *Companion*, vol. II, part 3, pp. 1504–5.

52 Churchill to Fisher, 19 February 1912, in Churchill, *World Crisis*, p. 105.

53 *Parliamentary Debates* (Commons), fifth series, vol. 34, cols. 1340–1.

54 Churchill, *World Crisis*, p. 111.

55 Quoted in Marder, *Dreadnought to Scapa Flow*, vol. I, p. 285.

56 Churchill, 'Memorandum on Naval Estimates 1913–14', 24 December 1912, ADM 116/1294B.

57 *Parliamentary Debates* (Commons), fifth series, vol. 50, cols. 1749–91.

58 See Grey to Goschen, 5 March 1913, *B.D.*, vol. X, part 2, no. 465, pp. 687–8.

59 Lichnowsky to Bethmann Hollweg, 23 June 1913, *G.P.*, vol. 39, p. 48.

60 Tirpitz, *Aufbau*, vol. I, p. 396.

61 Report of Captain Müller, 20 June 1913, *G.P.*, vol. 39, pp. 39–46.

62 Rhodes James, *Speeches*, pp. 2173–6; and 'Mr Churchill in Manchester', *The Times*, 20 October 1913.

63 Goschen to Grey, 22 October 1913, *B.D.*, vol. X, part 2, no. 485, p. 719.

64 *National Review*, vol. 62, no. 369 (November 1913), p. 368.

65 Lee's views reported in *The Times*, 28 March 1913.

66 See *The Times*, 21 October 1913.

67 Goschen to Nicolson, 24 October 1913, *B.D.*, vol. X, part 2, no. 486, p. 720.
68 Churchill to Grey, 24 October 1913, *B.D.*, vol. X, part 2, no. 487, p. 721.
69 'The German Navy', *The Times*, 5 February 1914. Several days later, Tirpitz's statement was changed to say that, if Britain put forward concrete arms-control proposals, 'I have no doubt that such proposals would be examined most minutely [*auf das Eingehendste*].' See the article labeled 'A Corrected Edition' by *The Times*' Berlin correspondent, 'Sixteen to Ten', *The Times*, 9 February 1914.
70 Quoted in 'Sixteen to Ten', *The Times*, 9 February 1914.
71 Quoted in 'The German Navy', *The Times*, 5 February 1914.
72 See *B.D.*, vol. X, part 2, no. 502, enclosure 2, pp. 739.
73 'The German Navy', *The Times*, 5 February 1914.
74 Grey delivered this speech in Manchester on 3 February 1914, and it is quoted extensively in Woodward, *Britain and the German Navy*, pp. 426–7.
75 Goschen to Grey, February 10, 1914, *B.D.*, vol. X, part 2, no. 501, pp. 736–7. In addition, see *B.D.*, vol. X, part 2: Grey to Goschen, 5 February 1914, no. 498, pp. 734–5; Goschen to Grey, 6 February 1914, no. 499, p. 735; Goschen to Nicolson, 6 February 1914, no. 500, p. 736; Goschen to Grey, 11 February 1914, no. 502, pp. 737–9.
76 Churchill to Grey, 4 December 1913, CHAR 13/22B.
77 Captain Henderson's report on a meeting with Tirpitz, 21 March 1914, enclosure in Goschen to Grey, same date, *B.D.*, vol. X, part 2, no. 503, pp. 740–1.
78 Huldermann, *Ballin*, p. 192.
79 Churchill to Grey, 8 May 1914, Churchill, *Companion*, vol. II, part 3, p. 1977.
80 Watson to Goschen, 'Remarks of His Majesty the Emperor to Naval Attaché', 12 May 1913, *B.D.*, vol. X, part 2, no. 475, p. 701. (Emphasis in the original.) Despite the Kaiser's assertion to the contrary, Churchill received an invitation to the German army's manuevers in 1909. See Churchill to his mother, Lady Randolph Churchill, 4 August 1909, Churchill, *Companion*, vol. II, part 2, p 903. In his memoirs, Wilhelm admits that Churchill attended German army maneuvers on both occasions as his guest. See Churchill, *World Crisis*, p. 98.
81 Treutler to German Foreign Office, 27 April 1914, *G.P.*, vol. 39, p. 100.
82 Goschen to Grey, 18 May 1914, in *B.D.*, vol. X, part 2, no. 509, pp. 744–5.
83 Churchill to Asquith and Grey, 20 May 1914, Churchill, *Companion*, vol. II, part 3, pp. 1978–80.
84 On German armaments policy, see the very fine account offered by David Stevenson, *Armaments and the Coming of War: Europe, 1904–1914* (Oxford: Clarendon Press, 1996), pp. 339–40.
85 Goschen to Grey, 3 July 1913, *B.D.*, vol. X, part 2, no. 480, pp. 705–6. In Goschen's opinion, Churchill should not renew the holiday proposal. King George agreed, adding to Goschen's report: '*I entirely agree with the hope expressed by the Emperor.*' Both Asquith and Morley, as a consequence, wanted to shelve the holiday proposal. Grey, however, sided with Churchill, and his support cleared the way for a renewed offer for a naval holiday. See 'Minute by Mr Winston Churchill', 8 July 1913, ibid, no. 481, pp. 706–7. For Grey's support, see Grey to Goschen, 28 October 1913, ibid, no. 488, p. 722.
86 Wilhelm to Bethmann Hollweg, 9 February 1914, *German Documents*, vol. IV, p. 320.
87 Goschen diary entry, 26 March 1914, *Goschen Diary*, p. 268.
88 Lichnowsky to Jagow, 10 May 1914, in Lichnowsky, *Reminiscences*, pp. 346–8.
89 Lichnowsky to Jagow, 26 May 1914, in ibid., pp. 346–7.

90 Churchill to Asquith and Grey, 20 May 1914, Churchill, *Companion*, vol. II, part 3, pp. 1978–80.
91 Minute by Grey on Goschen to Grey, 18 May 1914, *B.D.*, vol. X, part 2, no. 509, p. 745.
92 Churchill to Grey, 8 May 1914, Churchill, *Companion*, vol. II, part 3, p. 1977.
93 Lloyd George, for example, when he visited Germany during the summer of 1908, had sought high-level negotiations with German decision makers. Grey, in response, complained to Asquith about this interference in the running of British foreign policy. The interview given by Lloyd George and published on New Year's Day 1914 had also elicited a response by Grey. Since Lloyd George supported Churchill's visit to Kiel, Grey might have seen this initiative as yet another challenge to his authority. On the relationship between Lloyd George and Grey over the making of British foreign policy, see Fry, *Lloyd George and Foreign Policy*.
94 Memorandum by Grey, 25 May 1914, *B.D.*, vol. X, part 2, no. 512, pp. 748–9.
95 Since no formal invitation was sent by the German government – only the statement of Prince Henry to Goschen – there was some confusion over whether Churchill had actually been invited after all to visit Germany and over how to respond. The German embassy in Britain, for example, was confused about the visit, not apparently knowing about Prince Henry's invitation. Lichnowsky told Churchill's mother at a dinner party that, while the German government 'had not invited him [Churchill], but that should he decide to come, he might be sure of a cordial reception'. Lichnowsky to Jagow, 26 May 1914, in Lichnowsky, *Reminiscences*, pp. 346–7. Goschen, consequently, tactfully used the occasion of a state luncheon to talk directly to the Kaiser about the matter. First, however, Goschen ascertained that Wilhelm had indeed instructed Prince Henry to offer a verbal invitation. The British ambassador then informed the Kaiser – no doubt to his great relief – that Churchill would be unable to visit Kiel. 'His Majesty quite understood the situation and expressed his regret that they [Churchill and Battenberg] could not come in the most friendly manner.' Goschen to Grey, 3 June 1914, *B.D.*, vol. X, part 2, no. 515, p. 750.
96 Quoted in Huldermann, *Ballin*, p. 192.
97 Churchill to Stanley Baldwin, 5 December 1924, in Martin Gilbert, *Winston S. Churchill*, vol. V, companion part 1: *The Exchequer Years, 1922–1929* (Boston, MA: Houghton Mifflin, 1981), p. 306.
98 Churchill, *World Crisis*, pp. 178–9.
99 Quoted in Martin Gilbert, *Winston S. Churchill*, vol. V: *1922–1939: The Prophet of Truth* (Boston, MA: Houghton Mifflin, 1977), p. 494.
100 Michael Ekstein, 'Sir Edward Grey and Imperial Germany in 1914', *Journal of Contemporary History*, vol. 6, no. 3 (1971), pp. 123–4, 131.
101 A long-term building program, by providing stability in weapons purchases, can offer substantial budgetary advantages. Jacques Gansler, in his studies on defense procurement, estimates that 'the overall cost of program instability is somewhere around 10–15 per cent'. See his *Affording Defense* (Cambridge, MA: MIT Press, 1989), p. 133.
102 Quoted in Herwig, *'Luxury' Fleet*, p. 76.
103 Goschen to Nicolson, 9 February 1912, Nicolson MSS, FO 800/353.
104 Diary entry for 23 May 1914, Edward House Papers, Sterling Memorial Library, Yale University.
105 Quoted in Berghahn, *Germany and Approach of War*, p. 107.

106 Quoted in Ivo Nikolai Lambi, *The Navy and German Power Politics, 1862–1914* (Boston, MA: Allen & Unwin, 1984), pp. 379–80.

107 Quoted in Woodward, *Britain and the German Navy*, p. 421.

108 Tirpitz, *My Memoirs*, vol. I, p. 178.

109 See Churchill, *World Crisis*, pp. 114–15.

110 Quoted in David E. Kaiser, 'Germany and the Origins of the First World War', *Journal of Modern History*, vol. 55, no. 3 (September 1983), p. 457, note 46.

111 Report of Captain Müller, 30 March 1914, *G.P.*, vol. 39, pp. 86–99.

112 Imanuel Geiss, ed., *July 1914: The Outbreak of the First World War: Selected Documents* (New York: Norton, 1974), p. 25.

113 Fritz Fischer, *Germany's Aims in the First World War* (New York: Norton, 1967), p. 100.

114 John Charmley – in *Splendid Isolation? Britain, the Balance of Power and the Origins of the First World War* (London: Hodder & Stoughton, 1999) – contends that the Conservatives would have pursued a more conciliatory line toward Germany than Grey and the Foreign Office. This judgment, however, ignores too much evidence to the contrary. The Conservative leaders, if you take seriously their views, expressed both publicly and behind the scenes, were even more willing than the Liberals to confront Germany and to spend more on defense. A useful corrective to Charmley's account is provided by Morris' *Scaremongers*. Further, the Conservative opposition showed no hesitation in supporting a tough line against Germany during the July Crisis that precipitated the war. Germany's leaders at the time considered that a Conservative government would adopt a more anti-German line than the Liberals. Bülow held the view that a 'Conservative government in England would represent a very real war danger for us . . . and we should do all in our power to keep the Liberal party, to which all peace-loving elements in England adhere, at the helm'.

115 'Mr Churchill on the War', *The Times*, 30 August 1914. In this interview, Churchill told his American interviewer: 'You know I am half American myself.'

116 Michael Howard, 'The Great War: Mystery or Error', *National Interest*, no. 64 (Summer 2001), p. 83.

117 Churchill to William Royle, 20 December 1911, Churchill, *Companion*, vol. II, part 2, pp. 1360–1.

118 Churchill, *World Crisis*, pp. 41, 228.

2

Winston Churchill, Pacific Security, and the Limits of British Power, 1921–41

Christopher M. Bell

In February 1928, Britain's Chancellor of the Exchequer, Winston Churchill, informed a cabinet committee that a 'great story' was being told in Whitehall about 'how Japan was preparing and was going to spring out upon us and attack us on all our lines of Eastern communications right up to Aden and even up to Suez, and was going to dominate the whole of the Pacific and Indian Oceans and cut the British Empire into shreds'. This story was, in his opinion, 'utter nonsense. The Japanese war bogey leaves me completely cold', he claimed. 'I am not in the least upset by it. It is, of all the wars in the world, the least likely to happen.'[1]

This was not one of Churchill's better prophecies. In December 1941, fewer than 14 years later, Japan did choose the path of war with Britain. Within days, two British capital ships, the *Prince of Wales* and *Repulse*, were destroyed by Japanese torpedo-bombers in the South China Sea. Two months later, British and imperial forces defending Singapore surrendered to a smaller enemy force. Almost overnight, the Japanese 'bogey' had cut the British Empire into shreds.

Churchill played a central role in these events. He was the driving force behind the dispatch of capital ships to Singapore in 1941, and he had deliberately starved the British garrison in Malaysia of resources prior to the Japanese attack. 'If we have handled our resources wrongly, no one is so much to blame as me', he told Parliament in January 1942. 'If we have not got large modern air forces and tanks in Burma and Malaya tonight, no one is more accountable than I am.'[2] But Churchill never regretted this disposition of British forces, or the low priority assigned to the defense of Malaya. 'I would do exactly the same again', he told one colleague.[3] 'The decision was taken', he explained, 'to make our contribution to Russia, to try to beat Rommel, and to form a stronger front from the Levant to the Caspian. It followed from that decision that it was in our power only to make a moderate and partial provision in the Far East against the hypothetical danger of a Japanese onslaught.'[4]

Churchill's casual dismissal of the threat from Japan during the 1920s is difficult to reconcile with his clear warnings about Nazi Germany and urgent calls for rearmament during the 1930s. A popular explanation has been that Churchill was so committed to furthering his departmental objectives as Chancellor that he lost sight of all other considerations. He belittled the Japanese threat, it is suggested, not from conviction but as a means to balance the budget. However, this argument ignores the remarkable consistency of Churchill's views on British security in the Pacific between 1924 and 1941. The danger from Japan was always a low priority for Churchill, whether he was at the Treasury, the Admiralty, or Downing Street. He often misread Japan's intentions during this period, just as he systematically underrated its military capabilities. But these mistakes, though serious, do not provide a full explanation for the disasters Britain suffered in 1941–42. Churchill's path to war in the Pacific was neither direct nor simple. In the two decades leading to the outbreak of war, his policies were also shaped by his views on the importance of the Far East to Britain's security, his willingness to sacrifice secondary interests in order to concentrate on the most immediate and potentially serious threats, and a growing reliance on the United States to underwrite British interests in this region. When these factors are also taken into consideration, Churchill's abilities as a strategist begin to emerge in a better light.

In the spring of 1921, Winston Churchill hoped that British security in the Pacific would be safeguarded through a continuation of the Anglo-Japanese Alliance, now nearly 20 years old. However, like his colleagues in the Lloyd George coalition, he was alarmed about the possible emergence of a US challenge to British maritime supremacy. British leaders hoped to prevent an expensive naval arms race by reaching an accommodation with the United States, even if this meant formally accepting naval parity. Unfortunately, the unpopularity of the Anglo-Japanese alliance in the United States appeared to threaten any accord on naval armaments. Failure to renew the alliance, however, would offend Japan and potentially weaken Britain's strategic position in the Far East.

Churchill entered the debate in early July 1921 with a lengthy cabinet memorandum. While reluctant to alienate Japan by terminating the alliance, he was also opposed to any course that would endanger Anglo-American relations. Most importantly, he insisted that Britain's position in the Far East would be better protected in the long run by alignment with the United States than alliance with Japan. The only real danger to Australia and New Zealand, he warned, was the 'danger from Japan'. There was, in his view, no reason to suppose that the continuation of the Anglo-Japanese Alliance would act as a restraint upon Japanese behaviour. 'An alliance between the British Empire and Japan for the purpose of protecting Australia and New Zealand against Japan is meaningless', he argued.

> We should stand entirely on the basis of Japanese goodwill and good faith. They would fulfil their bargain by the simple process of holding themselves in check. So long as they did not molest us we should be their debtors and we should have to pay our dues, but if at any time we were not punctual in our payments or if they changed their minds, our security would vanish and it would vanish simultaneously with the apparition of the very danger against which it was devised. Getting Japan to protect you against Japan is like drinking salt water to slake thirst.

The right course for Britain in the long term, he held, was to establish a 'great unity of interests' with the United States, which would leave Japan 'so hopelessly outmatched that there can be no war, and the rivalries in armaments which are the precursors of war would have no purpose. The combatants will be too unequal for the question even to arise.' In a statement that might have been written 20 years later, he asserted that war with both the United States and Britain would be a 'hopeless proposition for Japan. A giant and a boy may fight a bigger giant, but if the two giants get together the boy has got to be content with innocent pleasures.'[5]

The Washington Conference of 1921–22 temporarily resolved the interconnected problems of naval-arms limitations and stability in east Asia. The Anglo-Japanese Alliance was superseded by a new four-power treaty in which Britain, the United States, Japan, and France pledged to respect each other's 'insular possessions and insular dominions' in the Pacific. A nine-power treaty, to which Italy, Netherlands, Belgium, Portugal, and China also adhered, agreed to preserve the independence and integrity of China and maintain an 'open door' there for all trading nations. Arms limitations were imposed by a five-power treaty establishing qualitative and quantitative restrictions on the navies of the United States, Britain, Japan, France, and Italy.

The British government was well satisfied with these results. As Churchill observed, Britain had successfully removed 'the Anglo-Japanese Alliance from the path of American friendship, without subjecting Japan to anything like desertion or ill-usage at our hands'.[6] Attention in London soon shifted from Anglo-American rivalry to the emerging threat from Japan. The navy was inclined to view the Japanese as an intensely nationalistic, self-sacrificing and militaristic race, dominated by a 'very Prussian minded' military caste.[7] Japan's leaders, credited with a propensity towards unscrupulous and opportunistic behavior, were not trusted to behave themselves if opportunities for expansion arose. The principal restraint on their behavior appeared to be the ability of the United States and Britain to defend their positions in the region.

Since Japan could not be trusted and US cooperation was uncertain, the Admiralty believed Britain must be fully capable of protecting its eastern interests. In 1919, Lord Jellicoe, a former First Sea Lord, recommended the permanent stationing of a large battle fleet in the Far East to deter Japanese aggression. This proved prohibitively expensive, however, and the decision was taken instead to retain the bulk of the British navy in European waters and only transfer a battle fleet to the Far East in the event of a crisis. As long as Britain possessed sufficient warships and suitable bases, the Admiralty was confident that the threat of force would not need to be carried out. As Admiral Sir Roger Keyes stated on one occasion, it would not actually be 'necessary to fight a great war in the Pacific, or "to put a battle fleet in the Pacific", but it is necessary that we should be able to send a fleet to the East capable of defeating or neutralising the Japanese fleet should the occasion arise, and this fact being known to the Japanese would at least make them discreet and check their forward policy'.[8] If force did prove to be necessary, the navy assumed that it would face a prolonged and costly struggle to inflict a decisive defeat on Japan. This would require the construction of a major naval base at Singapore and the accumulation of the oil fuel reserves required for large-scale fleet movements, programs which were endorsed by the Committee of Imperial Defence (CID) in June 1921.[9]

In early 1922, Churchill professed to be 'deeply impressed' by the navy's warnings about the potential danger from Japan. A cabinet committee he chaired on defense expenditure concluded that the 'position of Japan during the next few years will be formidable', particularly as the United States now appeared incapable of projecting its power effectively into the western Pacific. In the event of war, Britain would be in an unfavorable position:

> Unless Singapore is adequately protected before it is attacked, we cannot hold Singapore. Until oil-fuelling stations have been established there and on the route to the East at Aden and Colombo, we cannot base a fleet capable of fighting Japan on Singapore. If Singapore fell in the first two or three months of a war, the whole of the Pacific would fall under the complete supremacy of Japan, and many years might elapse before either Britain or the United States could re-enter that ocean in effective strength.

Churchill's committee endorsed the expensive programs required by the navy to wage a major campaign in the Far East, calling for 'the discreet building up of the fuelling stations and of the base at Singapore which alone can enable our fleet to offer some protection to all our interests in the Pacific, including Australia and New Zealand'.[10]

This policy was reversed by Ramsay MacDonald's Labour government when it came to power in January 1924. Committed to the cause of international disarmament, MacDonald ignored the Admiralty's objections and canceled work on the Singapore naval base entirely. Churchill, now out of office and, temporarily, without even a seat in Parliament, immediately joined in the Conservative Party's attacks on Labour's naval policies. Writing in the *Sunday Chronicle*, Churchill lamented that the navy, for the first time in its history, was powerless to protect Australia and New Zealand, 'and that the Mother Country has deliberately resolved to put it out of her power to come to their aid, whatever their need might be'.[11]

Churchill repeated this message in March 1924 when he spoke at a public meeting at Winchester House under the auspices of the Navy League.[12] Britain's moral obligation to defend Australia and New Zealand was his paramount concern. 'Disguise it as you will', he remarked, 'wrap it up in cloaks of smooth pretence, cover it with layers of excuses, hide it in a fog of technicalities, the stubborn brutal fact remains that the decision to abandon the Singapore base leaves Australia and New Zealand to whatever fate an anxious and inscrutable future may have in store.' Britain's Far Eastern Dominions, which had so recently 'spent their hearts' blood in our salvation', deserved better than to be abandoned 'even before the last dead have been gathered from the battlefields of France and Flanders into the National Cemeteries'. This, in his view, was an 'act of ungrateful desertion, it is a plain refusal without precedent in our history on the part of the Mother Country to discharge an Imperial duty'.[13]

The Conservative victory in the October 1924 general election gave the Singapore naval base a new lease on life. Churchill, who had returned to the Conservative Party earlier that year, became Chancellor of the Exchequer in the new government. The Admiralty undoubtedly expected an easier ride from the Treasury than it had become accustomed to in recent years. Churchill, after all, had been one of the navy's keenest supporters in the Lloyd George coalition, consistently backing the Admiralty's most expensive programs and praising its leaders on numerous occasions. The Treasury's relationship with the Admiralty proved, however, to be nearly as adversarial during Churchill's tenure as it had been under his predecessors.

As Chancellor, Churchill was eager to make his mark by lowering taxes and stimulating trade. He was also aware that the British public had little enthusiasm for expensive armament programs. The navy's plans to boost its estimates by nearly £10 million in the upcoming year were therefore a source of considerable alarm. Forecasting naval estimates for 1927–28 as high as £80 million (compared to £55.8 million in 1924–25), Churchill warned Stanley Baldwin, the Prime Minister, in December 1924 that increases on this scale would only 'sterilize and paralyse the whole policy of the Government. There will be nothing for the taxpayer and nothing for social reform. We shall be a Naval Parliament busily preparing our Navy for some great imminent shock.' Giving the navy all it asked for, Churchill warned, would 'not only bring the Government into ruin, but might well affect the safety of the State' by giving the Labour Party an advantage in the next general election. 'If the Socialists win in a tremendous economy wave, they will cut down and blot out all these Naval preparations so that in the end the Admiralty will not get the Navy programme for the sake of which your Government will have broken itself.'[14]

Churchill sought to undermine the navy's most expensive programs by discrediting the idea that Japan posed either a serious or immediate threat to vital British interests.[15] His opening salvo was fired in a letter of 15 December 1924 to the Prime Minister, which outlined the position he would adhere to throughout his term as Chancellor. Churchill now dismissed the possibility of war in the Far East. 'I do not believe there is the slightest chance of it in our lifetime', he insisted. His earlier concerns about Japan now gave way to a more optimistic view. 'The Japanese are our allies', he asserted.

> The Pacific is dominated by the Washington Agreement. America is far more likely to have a quarrel with Japan than we are. What question is pending between England and Japan? To what diplomatic combination do either of us belong which could involve us against each other?

There was, he asserted, 'absolutely no resemblance between our relations with Japan and those we had with Germany before the war'. But even if it turned out that Japan was disposed to attack British interests, Churchill took comfort from the fact that the Far East was a long way away. 'Japan is at the other end of the world', he reminded Baldwin.

> She cannot menace our vital security in any way. She has no reason whatever to come into collision with us. She has every reason to avoid such a collision. The only sufficient cause which could draw us into war with Japan would be if she invaded Australia. Does anybody imagine she is going to do so? Would she not be mad to do so? How

could she put an army into Australia, over 5,000 miles across the ocean and maintain it at war with the Australians and the whole British Empire[?] Nothing less than half a million Japanese would be any good, and these would have to be continually supplied and maintained. It is an absolute absurdity. Even if America stood inactive Japan would be ruined. She would never attempt it.[16]

Churchill also questioned Britain's ability to wage an offensive campaign against Japan even if the Admiralty's programs were fulfilled. A British fleet might be moved to Singapore, he admitted, but this could not prevent Hong Kong from falling early in the war.

What should we do then? We should have to send large armies (how we should raise them I do not know) to go and attack Japan in her home waters. The war would last for years. It would cost Japan very little. It would reduce us to bankruptcy. All the time it was on we should be at the mercy at home of every unfriendly power or force hostile to the British Empire. We could never do it. It would never be worth our while to do it. The only war it would be worth our while to fight with Japan would be to prevent an invasion of Australia, and that I am certain will never happen in any period, even the most remote, which we or our children need foresee. I am therefore convinced that war with Japan is not a possibility which any reasonable Government need take into account.

It would therefore be reasonable, he maintained, to instruct the Admiralty not to prepare for a major war in the Pacific. Naval leaders should be 'made to recast all their plans and scales and standards on the basis that no naval war against a first class Navy is likely to take place in the next twenty years.'[17]

Churchill's views on the likelihood of a threat emerging from Japan had clearly shifted, but his newfound optimism was shared by other leading decision makers. The Foreign Secretary, Austen Chamberlain, informed the CID on 5 January 1925 that he regarded 'the prospect of war in the Far East as very remote'. Moreover, if the 'danger of a struggle ever materialises', he predicted that the government would have 'plenty of warning'. It would therefore be 'a great mistake', he felt, 'to disquiet the Japanese and render them more nervous than they are'.[18] The only dissenting voice belonged to the navy. The Admiralty asserted that Churchill's view of Japan 'ignores history, real facts and the psychology of the [Japanese] people', but it chose not to dispute the Foreign Office's assessment of Japan's short-term intentions, realising that it would probably be futile, and possibly counterproductive, to contest this point.[19]

Long-term dangers were another matter. The Admiralty rejected the claim that there would a long warning period, and insisted that the government had a duty to make provisions for the defense of British interests in the Far East. According to the First Sea Lord, Admiral David Beatty, the lack of an immediate threat from Japan merely provided a 'breathing space in which to get out of a situation which, at the present time, is intolerable'. Japan, he warned, 'could deal us a naval blow, a maritime blow, which we are absolutely powerless to prevent and from which we should never recover'.[20]

In 1925 this was a difficult proposition to sell. Treasury officials had for years been challenging the navy's basic assumptions both about Japan and the demands of a Far Eastern war.[21] They insisted that Japan did not threaten any truly vital British interests and disparaged the forward offensive strategy contemplated by the navy. If the costs of defending Britain's eastern possessions appeared to be greater than the benefits, Treasury officials were prepared to write off that portion of the empire. They appreciated better than naval leaders the enormous national effort that would be required to achieve the decisive defeat of Japan. Churchill also weighed carefully the costs and benefits of war with Japan. He insisted that only a 'mortal peril' would justify the large expenditure and extensive preparations proposed by the Admiralty. In his opinion Japan did not constitute such a threat:

> Great as are the injuries which Japan, if she 'ran amok', could inflict upon our trade in the Northern Pacific, lamentable as would be the initial insults which she might offer to the British flag, I submit that it is beyond the power of Japan, in any period which we need now foresee, to take any action which would prevent the whole might of the British Empire being eventually brought to bear upon her.

Churchill was unwilling, however, to abandon Britain's moral commitment to its Pacific Dominions. He held that these territories could not be left at Japan's mercy and accepted that Britain must be capable of waging at least a defensive war in the region. He remained committed in principle, therefore, to the construction of a naval base at Singapore. Churchill informed the CID that he regarded this project as 'a purely defensive measure from the point of view of the British Empire'. It would be a link 'in Britain's inter-Imperial communications, and one of great guarantees we can give to our Australasian Dominions', but should not be expected to serve 'as a jumping off ground to attack Japan in her own home waters'.[22]

Churchill's position in 1925 was therefore based on a careful assessment of both domestic and strategic considerations. He rejected the Admiralty's plans to wage a prolonged and costly war to ensure Japan's decisive defeat, but he did support modest preparations for a limited, defensive war in the south Pacific. This position found broad support within the cabinet, where Churchill's efforts to limit naval expenditure were generally well received. In early 1925, the Chancellor hoped to reduce the navy's estimates for the upcoming year by deferring the construction of new cruisers. He insisted that the cruiser situation was not urgent, noting that the Royal Navy already possessed a marked superiority in this class of ship and would retain its advantage for the foreseeable future. Moreover, Britain's superior shipbuilding resources would always enable the navy to overtake Japan if it attempted to steal a lead in new construction. Lord Fisher's maxim, Churchill reminded his colleagues, was: 'Build late, build fast, each one better than the last.'[23]

With the Singapore naval base still in the early stages of construction, Churchill observed that there was no prospect of putting a large battle fleet there for at least another 10 or 11 years. 'We might as well make a virtue of necessity', he suggested, and rule out the despatch of a fleet to the Far East for the next decade. If this were done, he insisted that 'there would fall to the ground the whole expense of building and victualling ships, the submarines and destroyers and depot ships which are required to carry the main British Fleet into Far Eastern waters'. The Admiralty would, in these circumstances, require fewer cruisers to meet its obligations than it had previously calculated.[24]

When the cruiser question was considered by the CID in April 1925, the Foreign Office advised that 'aggressive action by Japan for the next ten years is not seriously to be apprehended'. The Committee agreed with Churchill that the Admiralty did not need 'to make preparations for placing at Singapore for a decisive battle in the Pacific a British battle fleet, with cruisers, flotillas, and all ancillary vessels superior in strength, or at least equal, to the sea-going Navy of Japan'. This decision effectively extended the original 'ten-year rule', adopted in 1919 as a rough guide for long-term defense planning, to cover a war with Japan until 1935. This was a significant development, as it enhanced the Treasury's ability to challenge naval programs that were based solely on the requirements of a major Far Eastern war. However, the navy's one-power standard was also recast at this time to state that the British fleet, 'wherever situated', must be 'equal to the fleet of any other nation, wherever situated, provided that arrangements are made from time to time in different parts of the world, according as the international situation requires, to enable the local naval forces to maintain the situation against vital and irreparable damage pending the arrival of the main fleet, and to give the main fleet on arrival sufficient mobility'.[25]

This was a notable victory for the Admiralty. Naval standards, like the ten-year rule, had cabinet sanction and could serve as an important bureaucratic tool in the ongoing inter-departmental struggle over defense policy. This new definition of the one-power standard would allow the navy to proceed with the construction of docking 'facilities for our latest ships at Singapore and to develop gradually the necessary oil installations on our Eastern routes'.[26]

In view of the prevailing opinion in Whitehall regarding the possibility of war against Japan, this was a significant accomplishment for the navy. On balance, this new rendering of the one-power standard represented a genuine compromise between the views of the Admiralty and the Treasury. The Cabinet accepted that the Japanese threat was sufficiently remote that immediate preparations were unnecessary, but also that the Admiralty's long-term projects could continue as a means of ensuring against this danger in the more distant future.[27]

This compromise was perfectly acceptable to Churchill, who did not share his advisers' desire to cancel the Singapore base and oil fuel programs outright. But while he took an independent position on these questions, he still hoped to achieve substantial economies by reducing the navy's new construction programs. The Admiralty only averted a complete defeat on this issue because the entire Board of Admiralty threatened to resign. Eager to avert a crisis, Baldwin proposed a compromise on 22 July 1925 that both sides were willing to accept.[28] Four new cruisers were to be laid down in the current year, but substantial savings would be achieved by starting work on these ships as late as possible. Another three cruisers were approved for the following year. In return, the Admiralty agreed to search for offsetting economies.

The following year, Churchill shifted his attack to the navy's oil-reserve program, which was referred to the CID in February 1926 for scrutiny. The Admiralty had been building up fuel supplies for several years in order to obtain a reserve equal to one year's consumption in wartime. This objective had been approved by the Cabinet in 1919 and was reaffirmed by the CID as recently as 1924. The government's Oil Fuel Board estimated that over seven million tons of fuel would be required to meet this goal, and the Admiralty intended to accumulate this amount by 1935, when the ten-year ruling of the previous year would no longer apply.

Churchill, intent on securing a reduction, insisted that this expense was extravagant. He maintained that a six-month supply of fuel would be sufficient, and could be accumulated at a slower pace than the Admiralty proposed. With the international situation becoming, 'if anything, more favourable', the Admiralty found itself isolated once again. The Prime Minister suggested a reduction in the navy's annual fuel program from 330,000 to 100,000 tons. Beatty insisted that this would threaten the mobility of the fleet in wartime and was inconsistent with the new definition of the one-power standard. The committee was intent on economy, however, and the proposal was accepted.[29]

The breakdown of the Geneva naval conference in August 1927 provided Churchill with an opportunity to re-open the cruiser question, which the Admiralty thought had been settled in 1925. The failure to reach an agreement over this class of vessel strengthened the 'big navy' lobby in the United States, and British leaders were concerned about the possibility of a massive US cruiser program. Churchill, who had taken the lead in opposing concessions to the United States over cruisers, now recommended a *reduction* in Britain's own cruiser program in order to give the Americans an opportunity to 'cool down'. On 4 August, while the First Lord was still in Geneva, the cabinet assented to a new inquiry into future naval construction.[30]

This body began its deliberations on 10 November 1927.[31] Churchill wisely emphasised the impact that dropping two cruisers from each of the 1927 and 1928 construction programs would have on the United States. He buttressed this case with assurances that his proposals would not endanger British interests. By 1931, he noted, Britain would possess more than a 25 per cent superiority over the United States and Japan combined in cruiser strength even if no new construction were undertaken.[32] When the Committee met on 1 December to reach a decision, its members unanimously backed the Chancellor.[33] Their report recommended dropping two cruisers from the current year's program and one more the following year.[34]

Having soundly defeated the navy on the cruiser question, Churchill immediately took aim at its 1928 estimates. The Admiralty had proposed a figure of £58,330,000, but the Chancellor insisted on no more than £56 million, claiming that the Admiralty had not taken full account of the favorable international situation, 'especially as regards Japan', or the government's decision that no great war 'need be anticipated for at least ten years'.[35] Bridgeman denied this charge, but there was much truth in it. The Admiralty's policies and war plans were still based on the need to prepare for a major war with Japan, while the ten-year rule, last reaffirmed in 1925, was taken to mean that the navy must be ready for such a conflict by 1935.[36] This legalistic interpretation was not unreasonable, but the Treasury had different ideas. When Captain Ernle Chatfield, the Controller, said the Admiralty had never been told anything different, Churchill insisted 'that the end of the 10 years was continually receding'.[37]

The Treasury was increasingly frustrated by the prominence of Japan in the navy's calculations despite repeated assurances on this question from the Foreign Office and the cabinet.[38] When the Naval Programme Committee discussed the oil fuel reserve in February 1928, Churchill vigorously denounced 'the great Japanese war bogey', which, he claimed, had been created by Beatty in 1920–21 'with a view to supplying the necessary stimulus on which naval estimates, naval expansion and naval supplies could be based'. Everything, he insisted, 'excludes a war between England and Japan from the sphere of reasonable probability'.[39]

The Committee rejected the Admiralty's plans to purchase 330,000 tons of oil fuel for the navy's annual reserve in 1928, and for the third consecutive year the figure was reduced to 100,000 tons.[40] Treasury officials had hoped for other reductions, however, and determined to reduce future naval expenditure by strictly enforcing their interpretation of the ten-year rule. Before the 1928 navy estimates had even been submitted to Parliament, Churchill proposed a new cabinet committee to examine the 1929 estimates.[41] The First Lord rejected the cuts suggested by the Treasury and prepared to defend the Admiralty's position when Churchill raised the matter in the cabinet.

The Chancellor now attempted to obtain a clear ruling that the ten-year rule applied at 'any given date until, or unless, a contrary decision is taken'.[42] This would make it easier for the Treasury to extract significant concessions from the Admiralty later on. The question was taken up by the CID on 5 July 1928.[43] Bridgeman and Admiral Sir Charles Madden, the new First Sea Lord, argued that Churchill's interpretation of the ten-year rule might endanger the maintenance of the one-power standard by reducing the fleet to an unacceptably low standard of readiness for a Far Eastern conflict. This argument carried little weight with the Committee. The most serious blow to the Admiralty, however, came from the Foreign Office. Austen Chamberlain provided an optimistic survey of international affairs and identified the Soviet Union as the only likely threat to British interests over the next decade. The Foreign Secretary declared that he had no objection to renewing the ten-year rule as a basis for framing the service estimates, although he cautioned that his department could not guarantee that 'war was an impossibility for any given number of years'. Once again the Chancellor had his way. The Committee agreed that the service estimates could be framed on the assumption that at any given date there would be no major war in the next ten years. This decision would be reviewed annually by the CID, and could be challenged at any time by any government department or the Dominions.[44]

Delighted Treasury officials began refining their proposals for reducing naval expenditure, but the Admiralty would not willingly abandon its practice of calculating requirements of personnel, *matériel* and stores on the basis of a Far Eastern war. As Sir Oswyn Murray, the Permanent Secretary to the Admiralty, remarked, 'the "Ten years ruling" is neither an absolute promise of peace for 10 years nor an abrogation of the principle that the Fleet must be ready for an ordinary emergency at any time'.[45] Naval leaders realised, however, that it was inadvisable to advertise this policy outside the Admiralty. It was clear that the navy had suffered a significant setback and would be more vulnerable than ever to Treasury attacks.

Churchill, determined to achieve substantial cuts, resumed his pressure on the Admiralty in late July by calling for large cuts to reserves of armaments and naval stores.[46] The First Lord was justifiably irritated by what he regarded as the Treasury's propensity 'to try to put off indefinitely even the most inevitable naval expenditure, vaguely imagining that we could redeem our position by a great intensive effort at some future time'. This policy, in his view, was 'open to strong practical objections', as it would 'inevitably lead to the disappearance of the very organisations, skilled designers and workmen whose assistance we should require in order to recover ourselves when the need arose'.[47] The Treasury, however, was unmoved. After months of bargaining, the 1929 estimates were finally settled at £55,865,000 – a figure nearly £1.5 million below the previous year, and over £4.5 million lower than 1925, Churchill's first full year as Chancellor.[48]

Churchill's attacks on the Admiralty during these years have often perplexed historians. How could the great advocate of rearmament in the 1930s have cut the navy so drastically only a few years before? How could the statesman who foresaw so clearly the dangers from Germany and, later, the Soviet Union have completely misjudged Japan? Part of the explanation for these apparent contradictions probably does lie in Churchill's tendency, as noted by J. C. C. Davidson, the Conservative Party chairman, to 'put the whole of his energy into what he believed to be the right policy of the Department over which he presided'.[49] Contemporaries, no less than historians, have found much force in this argument.[50] But while Churchill could be ruthless in pursuing his department's objectives, he always insisted on a strong voice in determining what those objectives were. Unlike other Chancellors of the period, Churchill did not accept the pure Treasury line on naval policy. He differed from his officials over a number of important issues, such as the need for a naval base at Singapore, naval competition with the United States, and the use of 'liberal' means such as arms-control agreements to protect British interests.

Churchill had other incentives to take the line he did. Most important, the mood of the electorate during the 1920s was for economy and disarmament. Churchill was under constant pressure to keep the budget balanced, make up for unexpected shortfalls, maintain social services, and implement tax reductions. He was probably right to think that heavy naval expenditure would have been unpopular and increased the likelihood of Labour's returning to power, in which event the navy might have expected even greater cuts. It should also be noted that Churchill enjoyed overwhelming support within the cabinet for his reductions in naval expenditure. During the 1920s, most informed observers – including experts at the Foreign Office – did not believe that Japan posed a serious or immediate threat to British security, something Treasury officials had been saying for years. Churchill's attacks on the Admiralty's programs during his years as Chancellor do not, therefore, represent any fundamental hostility to the navy or the pursuit of economy for its own sake.[51]

Bridgeman complained in 1928 that he did not see 'any other Ministries who do not agree with the Treasury constantly haled before a Cabinet Committee, but I have been subjected to at least three of such tribunals in the last 3 years'.[52] The navy was singled out for attack so often because its demands seemed more extravagant than those of the other services, which were not based primarily on the distant and seemingly remote threat from Japan. The navy had ample strength during the 1920s to meet any potential naval threat in Europe. If Japan was not a danger, as many outside the navy believed, the only other conceivable challenge on the seas would come from a US bid for maritime supremacy. When that possibility seemed to emerge in 1927, Churchill did not hesitate to reject the Treasury line and back the Admiralty. Paradoxically, however, protecting Britain's naval position in this instance seemed to require less rather than more naval construction, at least in the short term. This was more than just opportunism, although Churchill was undoubtedly pleased to have an excuse to put the cruiser program back on the chopping block in 1927 and later.

Churchill's struggle with the Admiralty during the 1920s was prolonged and intensified because the latter was determined to evade any restrictions the government placed on its preparations for war in the Far East. The Admiralty ignored the extension of the ten-year rule to cover such a conflict in 1925 and Churchill was left with little choice but to seek a new definition that would remove any possible loopholes. He did not do this in order to reduce naval expenditure arbitrarily, but as a means of enforcing policies and priorities decided by the cabinet. But despite the cuts that resulted, Churchill caused neither serious nor lasting damage to the navy's position during his years as Chancellor, as some of his critics have maintained.[53] Baldwin's administration spent more on the navy than the Labour governments that followed or preceded it, and authorised more new construction than any of Britain's rivals during the same period. The greatest harm to the inter-war navy was inflicted in the years after Churchill left the Treasury.[54]

In September 1931, Japan's Kwantung army opened hostilities against Chinese troops in Manchuria and quickly overran the province. This act of blatant aggression seemed to vindicate the navy's warnings about Japan, but Churchill, now out of office, initially showed little concern about these developments. In February 1933, he even expressed some sympathy towards the Japanese, who were faced on one side, he noted, by 'the dark menace of the Soviet Union' and on the other by 'the chaos of China, four or five provinces of which are now being tortured under Communist rule'.[55] With China seemingly torn between anarchy and communism, it was, he suggested, 'in the interests of the whole world' that Japan should establish law and order in China's northern provinces. At all events, there was little that could be done to reverse Japan's conquests. The League of Nations was virtually powerless to intervene. Two of the most important powers with interests in the region – the United States and the Soviet Union – were not even members. Churchill insisted that the League should avoid tasks 'beyond its strength and absolutely outside its scope', and that Britain should maintain a position of strict neutrality in the Sino-Japanese conflict.[56]

By the mid-1930s, Churchill's views had shifted significantly. Writing in 1936, he now characterized the Japanese as 'a martial race of more than sixty millions straining every nerve to arm in spite of serious financial difficulties'. Japan, he claimed, had become a 'nation imbued with dreams of war and conquest'.[57] The state was increasingly dominated by nationalist and militarist extremists in the armed forces who were determined to expand Japanese influence in East Asia at the expense of the Western powers. In earlier years, he noted in 1937, the Japanese had shown that they were a 'steady, grave and mature people; that they can be trusted to measure forces and factors with great care, and that they do not lose their heads, or plunge into mad, uncalculated adventures'. More recently, however, Japan's 'elder statesmen and their sagacious power seem to have dispersed'.[58] He concluded that the 'Mikado's government has only an imperfect authority over the naval and military warriors of Japan, and still less over their aviators'.

> The secret societies in the Japanese army and navy have very largely taken charge of the policy of their country. They have murdered so many politicians who were thought to be weaklings and backsliders that they have terrified the rest. It is painful to say it, but there are moments when we must feel ourselves in the presence of an army and navy which are running amok.[59]

By the mid-1930s, this pessimistic view of Japan was widely shared throughout Whitehall. The defense of Britain's interests in the Far East was complicated, however, by Hitler's rise to power in Germany. Naval leaders instinctively coupled the threats posed by Nazi Germany and Japan. They assumed that war with one power would inevitably lead to war with the other, and that Britain had to be capable of fighting both simultaneously.[60] The naval threat from Germany appeared manageable, however, as Britain already possessed sufficient strength to secure its essential maritime communications in a European war. As long as Britain also maintained strong defenses against a German air assault and had allies to bear the brunt of the fighting on land, the Admiralty believed Britain could defeat a continental adversary like Nazi Germany. To protect British interests in the Far East at the same time, the navy intended to dispatch a large battle fleet to the region. The size of this force would ultimately be determined by Britain's naval requirements in home waters, as the navy's first priority in wartime would always be the neutralization of any maritime threat from Germany. To meet both dangers simultaneously, the Admiralty insisted on the completion of the Singapore naval base and the formal adoption of a two-power standard of naval strength, measured against Japan and the strongest European naval power.

The strength of the Admiralty's case was recognized by the government's Defence Requirements Committee in 1935. This body, which was composed of the professional heads of the three fighting services, the Treasury, and the Foreign Office, recommended that Britain replace its outdated one-power standard – measured since 1921 against the United States – with 'a *new* standard of naval strength' equivalent to a two-power standard.[61] The government had other ideas. Britain's leaders accepted the need to rearm, but were also determined to keep defense spending to the lowest level possible, so as not to damage Britain's economic strength, on which its strategic position ultimately rested. They were also deeply conscious of the proximity of the German threat and the vulnerability of British cities to a terror bombing campaign. Germany had the power both to dominate Europe and to inflict a decisive defeat on Britain. The threat from Japan, though serious, was on an altogether lesser plane. These developments worked to the advantage of the Royal Air Force, whose share of the defense budget steadily increased during the 1930s. The navy's position perceptibly declined. In the absence of a major German naval challenge, British leaders had no incentive to increase naval spending dramatically, rather the opposite. Britain's traditional first line of defense now found itself viewed by many as an expensive luxury.

The Baldwin and Chamberlain governments were reluctant to reject the navy's 'new standard' outright, however, because that would entail at least a tacit admission that Britain's eastern interests were considered expendable. The Admiralty played its hand skillfully and managed to build warships to the limits of Britain's industrial capacity in the immediate prewar years, but it could only lay down enough ships to maintain the navy's current strength as older vessels passed out of service. When the time finally came to approve measures that would expand the fleet, the government decided that Britain could not afford the proposed 'new standard'.[62] The Admiralty, however, never questioned that its mission was to counter simultaneous threats both at home and in the Far East, and it assumed that the government would eventually be brought around to this view. In the absence of clear instructions to focus on European threats, it struggled to meet its global responsibilities with inadequate resources.

Churchill shared the government's overriding concern with Europe. 'The great danger to the world at the present time still lies', he wrote in 1937, 'not in the Far East, not in the quarrels of the yellow peoples, but in the heart of Christendom and Europe.'[63] Germany clearly posed a 'mortal peril' to Britain; Japan did not. While the two threats were obviously linked, Churchill believed that Japan was neither strong nor bold enough to embark on war unless Britain was already embroiled with Germany. Thus, if Britain could deter Hitler, Japan would probably refrain from a direct attack on British interests. But 'should Germany at any time make war in Europe', he warned that Britain could 'be sure that Japan will immediately light a second conflagration in the Far East'.[64] Everything therefore hinged on Britain's ability to preserve peace in Europe. Churchill hoped to secure Britain's position through a vigorous rearmament program and the containment of Germany through collaboration with France and other continental states. He rejected Chamberlain's policy of appeasement because he recognized that Hitler's ambitions were virtually unlimited. As long as Germany sought to dominate Europe, peaceful coexistence was clearly unattainable.

While Churchill was much less inclined than the government to recognize financial limitations on Britain's rearmament, he did share its view that Britain's most pressing requirement was a greatly enhanced air force. This appeared to offer the best means of protecting Britain from direct attack while presenting a credible deterrent to Hitler. It was the overall size of the defense budget, not its allocation between the services or focus on European dangers, that most alarmed Churchill during this period. Other than the Singapore naval base, Churchill paid little attention to deficiencies in Britain's position in the Far East. And while he welcomed the re-building of Britain's ageing battle fleet, he did not show any interest in long-term naval expansion. Nonetheless, Churchill appreciated the navy's importance in maintaining Britain's essential maritime communications. 'Nothing can be a substitute for naval strength', he stated. 'That alone can bring in our food and trade across the seas. That alone can prevent the swarming legions of the Continent being landed on our shores.'[65]

If Germany had appeared to pose a serious naval challenge, Churchill would have paid greater attention to naval rearmament. During the 1930s, however, the Royal Navy seemed to have the German threat well in hand. It possessed a crushing superiority in surface ships and was in a much stronger relative position than in 1914. Churchill also shared the navy's confidence that the combination of convoy and sonar would neutralize Germany's relatively small U-boat force, and that Britain's fleet would be able to defend itself successfully against aerial attack. The greatest threat to Britain's imports would not necessarily even be the German navy, he warned, but 'continuous air attack upon our commercial ports, warehouses, and landing stages'.[66]

The Far East posed a different set of problems. Churchill appreciated that distance would be the dominating factor in an Anglo-Japanese war. A British fleet might be able to reach Singapore, but it would still be a very long way from Japan. During the mid-1930s and earlier, naval planners hoped to overcome this obstacle by moving a fleet to Hong Kong and then improvising a series of advanced bases ever-closer to the enemy's center of power. By 1937–38, however, Britain's margin of naval strength was declining and Japan's domination of China had increased. It was no longer certain that Hong Kong could be held or recaptured, or that land and air forces would be available to support a step-by-step advance northward from Singapore. In these circumstances, the Admiralty hoped that a fleet based on Singapore would be sufficient to impose crippling economic pressure on Japan.[67]

Churchill was less optimistic. He assumed that Britain could deliver a decisive blow only by moving forces into Japan's home waters. This posed potentially insurmountable problems, however, as the strength and effectiveness of a British fleet would steadily decline the further it advanced from Singapore. Japan's position, on the other hand, would increase with proximity to its bases. Even if Britain could dispatch a numerically equal or superior fleet to the Far East, Churchill assumed that it could engage the main Japanese force in its home waters only at a disadvantage. The enemy's defensive position was thus virtually unassailable. Japan would 'always have complete supremacy in the yellow seas', Churchill concluded. 'To challenge this supremacy would be impossible and futile.'[68]

This logic cut both ways. Singapore's distance from Japan also appeared to render it relatively safe from attack. 'Consider how vain is the menace that Japan will send a fleet and army to conquer Singapore', Churchill wrote in March 1939. 'It is as far from Japan as Southampton from New York. Over these two thousand miles of salt water, Japan would have to send the bulk of her fleet, escort at least sixty thousand men in transports in order to effect a landing, and begin a siege which would only end in disaster if the Japanese sea-communications were cut at any stage.'[69]

By this reasoning, Australia was even more secure. 'Can one suppose that Japan, enjoying herself in the mastery of the Yellow Sea, would send afloat a conquering and colonizing expedition to Australia?', Churchill asked. 'It is ludicrous. More than one hundred thousand men would be needed to make any impression upon Australian manhood.'[70] Japan would never undertake such a major attack, he concluded, as long as Britain held Singapore and possessed a fleet capable of moving to the Far East.

Like most British leaders of this period, Churchill overestimated not only Britain's ability to dispatch forces to the region, but also the efficacy of sea power as a counter to any threat from Japan. At the same time, he systematically underestimated Japan's ability and willingness to project its power into South-East Asia or beyond. Britain's fleet, in his mind, was not only large enough to counter two threats simultaneously, but also possessed unmatched strategic mobility. Even if forces had to be held in Europe, there would be enough left over to deal with the Japanese. These miscalculations shaped Churchill's views right up to 1941.

He was also still inclined to regard Japan's new leaders as instinctively cautious individuals who would hesitate to attack Britain unless it had suffered crippling defeats at the hands of Germany or Italy.[71] In the meantime, Japan seemed to have more than enough to keep its hands full. After July 1937, it was embroiled in an inconclusive and costly war in China, and also had to worry about a hostile Soviet Union on its northern flank. Churchill noted with satisfaction in May 1938 that large Russian armies along the Siberian frontier were tying down nearly half a million of Japan's 'finest troops'. It was, he remarked, 'a daring adventure for Japan to try to ward off the Russian masses with her right hand while strangling this voluminous China with the other'.

> On the one side, a great bear growling low; on the other, an enormous jelly-fish stinging poisonously. Altogether a nasty job for an over-strained, none-too-contented nation to tackle. Japan is sprawled in China; Russia is crouched ready to spring in the North.

The Soviet air force, he observed, could 'inflict frightful damage upon Tokyo and other Japanese cities any fine night'.[72] The roles Churchill had assigned to the Soviet Union and Japan in 1933 were therefore reversed: it was now the Soviet Union that was rendering a valuable service 'in the Far East to civilisation and also to British and United States interests'.[73]

Japan also had to take into account the attitude of the United States, which was opposed to Japanese expansion and could place a powerful fleet on Japan's eastern flank. All of this bolstered Churchill's confidence that Britain could preserve its position in the Far East even if embroiled in a

European conflict. Racism played no important part in these calculations. Churchill certainly did not accept Japan as the equal of a first-rate European state, but he always treated Japan as a major power: it was, he wrote in 1937, a 'great nation, equipped with all the apparatus of modern industrialism and the complete armoury of mechanized war'.[74]

Churchill's ethnocentrism reinforced his inclination to view the threat from this quarter as manageable, but it did not cause him to dismiss it. In the event of war, he had no illusions about Japan's ability to 'take Hong Kong and Shanghai, and clean us out of all our interests there', but this did not diminish his confidence in Britain's ability to hold Singapore and deter a major attack on Australia. As long as Britain maintained a foothold in the region, he believed it could restore its interests in China at a later date. In a lengthy memorandum written in early 1939, Churchill warned Chamberlain against diverting forces to the Far East. Britain 'must not be drawn from our main theme by any effort to protect' minor interests in China. 'Only if the United States comes in against Japan could we supply even a squadron of cruisers to operate with them', he insisted. 'On this tableau we must bear the losses and punishment, awaiting the final result of the struggle.'[75] In the event of a multi-front war, the navy would be better employed, he insisted, in offensive operations against Germany in the Baltic and Italy in the Mediterranean.

As First Lord of the Admiralty in the early months of the Second World War, Churchill took a leading role in the formulation of British grand strategy. He was confronted almost immediately by Australian demands that Britain reaffirm its pre-war pledges to send a powerful battle fleet to Singapore in the event of war with Japan. The Australian government hesitated to dispatch its armed forces for the war against Germany without a firm commitment from Britain to Australia's defense.[76] In November 1939, S. M. Bruce, Australia's High Commissioner in London, noted that Churchill's predecessor as First Lord of the Admiralty, Lord Stanhope, had in 1938 'specifically stated that a Fleet of a definite strength, i.e. containing 7 capital ships would be sent to the Far East if Japan entered the war against us'.[77] In March 1939, Neville Chamberlain, the Prime Minister, had attempted to qualify this commitment,[78] but Casey told British ministers that his government still believed that, 'since Singapore had only sufficient resources to last out for a limited time', Britain was pledged to dispatch a fleet 'for its relief almost immediately after the outbreak of war with Japan and quite irrespective of any direct threat of invasion of Australia'.[79]

This was not at all to Churchill's liking. It would be a 'false strategy', he told representatives of the Australian and New Zealand governments in November 1939, 'to undertake to keep a Fleet at Singapore without regard to the actual naval situation. Any such undertaking would be crippling to the operation of our sea power, and would give to Japan the power to immobilise half our Fleet by a mere paper declaration of war'.[80] Churchill reassured Dominion representatives that Britain would 'never allow Singapore to fall, nor permit a serious attack on either Australia or New Zealand'. In the event of war with Germany, Italy, and Japan simultaneously, he pledged that the defense of these places would rank 'next to the mastering of the principal [i.e. German] fleet to which we are opposed, and that if the choice were presented of defending them against a serious attack, or sacrificing British interests in the Mediterranean, our duty to our kith and kin would take precedence'.[81] But he was willing to deplete British forces in European waters only in the event of a serious attempt by Japan either to capture Singapore or invade Australia; he did not intend to be drawn off by raids or feints. Until such time as a major threat developed, which he did not take as certain, Churchill maintained that Britain's proper strategy was to concentrate its naval forces in the Mediterranean to knock Italy out of the war as quickly as possible. Britain must 'use every vessel we possess to the highest possible advantage in the fighting area, and only move them to other waters when the War moved thither'.[82]

While Churchill's pledge to Australia was based on faulty calculations, it was made in good faith. He was eager to secure the release of Australian forces at this time, but there is nothing to suggest that he deliberately underestimated the Japanese threat to achieve this. The arguments he presented to Dominion representatives in November 1939 were the same ones he had rehearsed at length before the war. At this time it still seemed reasonable to expect that if the war in Europe went well, Britain would never have to make good on its pledges to Australia. Singapore, Churchill wrote, was 'a fortress armed with five 15-inch guns, and garrisoned by nearly 20,000 men. It could only be taken after a siege by an army of at least 50,000 men, who would have to be landed in the marshes and jungle of the Isthmus which connects it with the mainland.' In his opinion, 'the operation of moving a Japanese army with all its troopships and maintaining it with men and munitions during a siege would be forlorn'. If at any time Britain dispatched a fleet to relieve Singapore 'the besieging army would become prisoners of war. It is not considered possible', he concluded, 'that the Japanese, who are a prudent people . . . would embark upon such a mad enterprise.' It appeared even less likely that they would risk an invasion of Australia or New Zealand, an operation more difficult than the capture of Singapore. The most Australia would probably have to worry about, Churchill insisted, was a 'tip-and-run raid, to repel which land forces were not required'.[83]

The fall of France in June 1940 transformed the strategic landscape. The rapid collapse of Britain's only major ally, and Italy's decision to enter the war on Germany's side, put Britain's survival at stake. Faced with the threat of invasion and in danger of losing its position in the Middle East, Britain could do little to defend its interests in the Far East. Under pressure from Japan, Churchill, now Prime Minister, agreed in July to the temporary closure of the Burma Road, the principal supply route to Chiang Kai-shek's nationalist government in China, in order to play for time.[84]

But even as Britain's fortunes ebbed, Churchill remained optimistic about the situation in the Far East. Japan's energies were still seemingly absorbed in China, and it always had to worry about the intervention of either the United States or the Soviet Union. Churchill concluded that Japan's leaders would launch an expedition against Singapore only if Britain could no longer put up serious resistance. Like the Foreign Secretary, Lord Halifax, Churchill believed that there was 'a big element of bluff' in Japan's attitude.[85] 'The Japanese had shown themselves consistently reluctant to send their fleet far afield', he noted in September 1940, 'and if they were to embark on an expedition 2,000 miles from their homeland they would always have the fear of the American fleet on their flank and of the arrival of the British fleet to cut them off before they had achieved their objective of reducing the fortress.'[86]

Churchill expected Japan to adopt a more cautious strategy. Rather than risking an attack on British possessions, it would wait for a clear decision in the European war, while gradually strengthening its position in South-East Asia. In London, the greatest Far Eastern danger in the summer of 1940 appeared to be not a Japanese attack on Singapore, but the seizure of the Dutch East Indies. The best deterrent to Japanese aggression, Churchill maintained, would be the improvement of Britain's position in Europe. The correct strategy, therefore, was to concentrate Britain's limited resources in the decisive theater.

If Japan did enter the war, Churchill advocated the release of only minimal forces for the Far East until it was certain that either Singapore or Australia was directly threatened. In August 1940, for example, he thought it would be necessary to send only 'one battle cruiser and one aircraft carrier to the Indian Ocean, to be based on Ceylon, for the purpose of protecting our vital communications'.[87] Until Japan's intentions were clear, the fleet should remain concentrated in the Mediterranean in hopes of securing major victories against Italy, the weakest of Britain's enemies. If Japan did launch a major expedition against either Singapore or Australia, Churchill hoped that the United States would come to Britain's aid. But, if US support did not materialize, he maintained that 'our course was clear'.

We could never stand by and see a British Dominion overwhelmed by a yellow race, and we should at once come to the assistance of that Dominion with all the forces we could make available. For this purpose we should be prepared, if necessary, to abandon our position in the Mediterranean and the Middle East.[88]

On 11 August 1940, Churchill laid out his views in a long message to Australia's Prime Minister, Sir Robert Menzies.[89] Australian leaders accepted his assurances and continued to send troops to fight in the Middle East, but they remained uneasy about the state of Singapore's defenses and the lack of a firm commitment from London to dispatch naval forces to the Far East. In December 1940, following the successful air attack on the Italian fleet at Taranto, Menzies pressed Churchill for the transfer of three or four capital ships to Singapore from the Mediterranean fleet. This appeal was renewed when Menzies visited London in March 1941, and again in August of the same year.[90]

The idea of employing a squadron of capital ships to deter Japan also found adherents in Whitehall. In November 1940, R. A. Butler, the parliamentary under-secretary at the Foreign Office, suggested stationing a battle cruiser and an aircraft carrier at Ceylon to bolster British prestige in the region, 'hearten Australia and New Zealand', and help deter Japan.[91] Churchill, however, remained firm. He had no intention of letting valuable capital ships sit idle at Singapore while Britain was fighting for its life against Germany and Italy. As he informed Menzies in December 1940, Britain could only transfer capital ships to the Far East 'by ruining the Mediterranean situation. This I am sure you would not want to do unless or until the Japanese danger becomes far more menacing than at present.'[92]

Churchill took the same position on the critical question of air reinforcements. In 1940, British commanders in the Far East calculated that 566 aircraft would be required to defend Malaya and Singapore from a determined Japanese attack.[93] The Chiefs of Staff (COS) thought that a lesser figure would suffice. They informed Sir Robert Brooke-Popham, the Commander-in-Chief, Far East, that 'a very fair degree of security' could be achieved with only 336 aircraft, a figure they hoped to attain by the end of 1941. But this was still too much for Churchill, who denounced any large-scale 'diversions of force' to Malaya. He informed the COS in January 1941 that the 'political situation in the Far East does not seem to require, and the strength of our Air Force by no means warrants, the maintenance of such large forces in the Far East at this time'.[94] In December 1941, Malaya Command could count on only 158 aircraft, and these were mostly obsolescent models.[95] A proposal from Brooke-Popham to reinforce the British garrison at Hong Kong was also dismissed at this time. 'If Japan goes to war with us', Churchill observed, 'there is not the slightest chance of holding Hong Kong or relieving it.'

> It is most unwise to increase the loss we shall suffer there. Instead of increasing the garrison it ought to be reduced to a symbolical scale. Any trouble arising there must be dealt with at the Peace Conference after the war. We must avoid frittering away our resources on untenable positions. Japan will think long before declaring war on the British Empire, and whether there are two or six battalions at Hong Kong will make no difference to her choice.[96]

Growing US support for the British war effort over the first half of 1941 strengthened Churchill's resolve. In April, he informed the COS that it was 'very unlikely' that 'Japan will enter the war either if the United States have come in, or if Japan thinks they would come in, consequent on a Japanese declaration of war'. In his opinion, it could now be 'taken as almost certain that the entry of Japan into the war would be followed by the immediate entry of the United States on our side'. Churchill probably hoped that this assurance would stifle any debate over the allocation of resources between theaters. 'These conditions are to be accepted by the Service Departments as a guide for all plans and actions', he insisted. 'Should they cease to hold good, it will be the responsibility of Ministers to notify the Service Chiefs in good time.'[97]

The service chiefs, however, were less confident of US support and more worried about Britain's vulnerability in the Far East. In May 1941, the Chief of the Imperial General Staff, General Sir John Dill, challenged Churchill's priorities, insisting that the loss of the Middle East would not spell disaster for Britain and that the defense of Singapore should be given a higher priority. 'Egypt is not even second in order of priority', he argued, 'for it has been an accepted principle in our strategy that in the last resort the security of Singapore comes before that of Egypt. Yet the defenses of Singapore are still considerably below standard.' It was necessary, he insisted, to 'look well ahead. If we wait till emergency arises in the Far East, we shall be too late.'[98]

Churchill brusquely rejected Dill's arguments. 'I gather you would be prepared to face the loss of Egypt and the Nile Valley', he charged, 'together with the surrender or ruin of the army of half a million we have concentrated there, rather than lose Singapore. I do not take that view, nor do I think the alternative is likely to present itself.' Japan, he argued, would 'not be likely to besiege Singapore' at the beginning of a war, 'as this would be an operation far more dangerous to her and less harmful to us than spreading her cruisers and battle-cruisers on the Eastern trade routes'.[99] Until the defeat of Germany and Italy was certain, Churchill insisted that Britain would have to rely on the United States both to deter Japan and to protect British interests if deterrence failed. He also made clear that he expected the Chiefs of Staff to accept political direction on this issue.[100]

Hitler's invasion of the Soviet Union in June 1941 improved Britain's strategic position, but the diversion of British supplies to support the Soviet war effort pushed Malaya even further down Churchill's list of priorities and left Britain's position in the Far East increasingly dependent on the United States. Throughout 1941, London carefully followed Washington's lead in the Pacific in the hope of averting a new war. US leaders were determined to take a hard line with Japan, however, and their policies, though intended to prevent conflict, were increasingly provocative. The tightening of Anglo-American economic sanctions against Japan after its occupation of French Indo-China in July led to a sharp decline in relations between Japan and the Anglo-Saxon powers, and set Japan on the path to war.

The deteriorating situation in the Far East during the summer of 1941 prompted Churchill to alter course. Unwilling still to divert forces to the Far East on a large scale, he sought other means to demonstrate solidarity with the United States and impress Japan with Britain's growing strength and resolve. In these changing circumstances, the transfer of naval reinforcements to Singapore might at last serve a useful purpose. On 25 August 1941, Churchill informed the Admiralty that he hoped 'in the near future to place a deterrent squadron in the Indian Ocean'. In his view, such a force 'should consist of the smallest number of the best ships. We have only to remember all the preoccupations which are caused us by the *Tirpitz* . . . to see what an effect would be produced upon the Japanese Admiralty by the presence of a small but very powerful and fast force in Eastern waters'. Churchill therefore recommended the dispatch of a new *King George V*-class battleship to serve as the nucleus of a 'formidable, fast, high-class squadron', which he hoped to have operating in 'the triangle Aden–Singapore–Simonstown' as early as October 1941.[101]

The Admiralty had different ideas. Admiral Sir Dudley Pound, the First Sea Lord, was reluctant to risk disaster in the Far East by dispatching a small, unbalanced force to the region. Moreover, he insisted that all of Britain's modern battleships were needed in home waters in the event of a breakout by the German battleship *Tirpitz*. He hoped, however, to build up a balanced Far Eastern fleet by March 1942. Pound informed Churchill of the Admiralty's plans on 28 August. Between mid-September 1941 and early January 1942, four of the navy's unmodernized 'R'-class battleships would be sent to the Indian Ocean, where they would initially serve as troop convoy escorts; and between November 1941 and mid-January 1942, the battleships *Nelson* and *Rodney* and the battle cruiser *Renown* would move to either Trincomalee or Singapore. With the addition of an aircraft carrier, cruisers, and destroyers, these vessels would ultimately form a balanced fleet that could be stationed at Singapore.[102]

There was much to be said for this scheme, but Churchill swept it aside. 'It is surely a faulty disposition', he complained on 29 August, 'to create in the Indian Ocean a fleet considerable in numbers, costly in maintenance and man-power, but consisting entirely of slow, obsolescent, or unmodernised ships which can neither fight a fleet action with the main Japanese force nor act as a deterrent upon his modern fast, heavy ships, if used singly or in pairs as raiders.'[103]

Political considerations were even more important. Japan, he argued, would be unwilling to contemplate war with the 'combination now forming against her of the United States, Great Britain, and Russia, while already occupied in China'. It was very likely, he claimed, that Japan 'will negotiate with the United States for at least three months without making any further aggressive move or joining the Axis actively. Nothing would increase her hesitation more than the appearance of the force I mentioned, and above all of a KGV [*King George V*-class battleship]. This might indeed be a decisive deterrent.'[104]

Speed was therefore an essential element of these proposals. If the critical decisions about peace and war would be made in Tokyo before 1942, capital ships were needed in the Far East immediately. Churchill did not reject the Admiralty's goal of a large eastern fleet in 1942, he simply ignored it. His attention was focused entirely on short-term objectives. Since Britain could only spare a small force in 1941, he insisted on the dispatch of a fast, new battleship, which would be more likely to impress observers than the squadron of old, slow 'R'-class battleships proposed by the Admiralty.

The Admiralty's firm opposition deflected Churchill on this occasion, but the idea was taken up in September by Anthony Eden, the Foreign Secretary. Eden and the Foreign Office were optimistic that Japan could be deterred from war by a firm display of strength. On 12 September, the Foreign Secretary advised Churchill that Japan's leaders were 'hesitating', but that their 'better mood has only been brought about by the contemplation of the forces that may confront them'.

> Russia, the United States, China and the British Empire, to say nothing of the Dutch, is more than this probably over-valued military power is prepared to challenge. Our right policy is, therefore, clearly to keep up the pressure . . . We want the Japanese to feel that we are in a position to play our hand from strength.[105]

The desirability of impressing Japan with some show of force was backed up by leading civilian and military figures in the Far East, who emphasized the 'propaganda value of even one or two battleships at Singapore'.[106]

The fall of the Konoye government in Japan put the dispatch of capital ships back on the agenda. Eden warned Churchill on 16 October that the new Japanese government would probably be under the influence of 'extreme elements', but that it should still be possible to deter them. 'There is nothing yet to show in which direction they will move, if any', he concluded. 'But it is no doubt true that the stronger the joint front the ABCD [America, Britain, China, Dutch] powers can show, the greater the deterrent to Japanese action.' The 'possibility of capital ship reinforcements to the Far East' was, he claimed, now 'more urgent, and I should be glad if it could be discussed at the Defence Committee tomorrow afternoon'.[107]

The question of naval reinforcements was taken up by the Defence Committee (Operations) at two meetings, on 17 and 20 October.[108] The Admiralty fought to prevent the despatch of a deterrent squadron including the *Prince of Wales* to Singapore. According to Admiral Sir Tom Philips, the Vice-Chief of the Naval Staff, Churchill was 'scathing in his comments on the Admiralty attitude to this matter'.[109] Once again, the Prime Minister objected to the immediate transfer of older ships in the Far East. His reasons remained unchanged: a large force of old, unmodernized battleships could not engage the full weight of the Japanese fleet, he maintained, nor run away from a superior force. It would also be too slow to catch Japanese raiders in the Indian Ocean. A fast, powerful capital ship, on the other hand, could hunt down and destroy such vessels, and, by its presence in the Far East, tie down a much larger number of Japanese battleships. If the *Tirpitz* did break out into the Atlantic, Churchill insisted that carrier-borne aircraft could 'slow her up to become a prey for the heavy metal of our Capital Ships'.

Churchill clearly overestimated the impact of a few fast capital ships on Japanese naval strategy, but he emphasized their potential value in wartime principally as a means to circumvent the Admiralty's opposition to their employment as a peacetime deterrent. That mission was now highlighted by Eden, who informed the Defence Committee that the dispatch of a 'modern ship, such as the *Prince of Wales*, to the Far East would have a far greater effect politically, than the presence in those waters of a number of the last war's battleships. If the *Prince of Wales* were to call at Cape Town on her way to the Far East, news of her movements would quickly reach Japan and the deterrent effect would begin from that date.' These arguments were well received by the non-naval members of the Defence Committee, who concluded that the political advantages of this movement were great enough to 'outweigh objections hitherto advanced by the Admiralty'.[110] The *Prince of Wales*, together with the First World War-era battle cruiser *Repulse*, reached Singapore on 2 December.

These same calculations also played a role in the decision to dispatch two battalions of reinforcements to Hong Kong in late 1941.[111] The COS had rejected earlier proposals from Brooke-Popham to reinforce this exposed outpost, 'because they considered that it would only have been to throw good money after bad'. In September 1941, they were pressed again for additional forces, this time by a former General Officer Commanding, Hong Kong, who indicated that the Canadian government would be willing to supply the troops 'if the point were put to them'.[112] The Chiefs supported this request. The 'position in the Far East has now changed', they told the Prime Minister.

> Our defenses in Malaya have been improved and Japan has latterly shown a certain weakness in her attitude towards Great Britain and the United States.
>
> A small reinforcement of one or two battalions would increase the strength of the garrison out of all proportion to the actual numbers involved, and it would provide a strong stimulus to the garrison and the Colony. Further it would have a very great moral effect in the whole of the Far East and it would show Chiang Kai Shek that we really intend to fight it out at Hong Kong.
>
> The United States have recently dispatched a small reinforcement to the Philippines and a similar move by Canada would be in line with the present United States Policy of greater interest in the Far East.[113]

Churchill replied that he had 'no objection to the approach being made as proposed'.[114] Like his service advisers, he was eager to act in unison with the United States. As he remarked a few weeks later, the 'Far Eastern situation had undoubtedly changed' in recent months, and 'the United States Government was nearer to a commitment than they had been in the past'. Britain, he insisted, must 'regard the United States as having taken charge in the Far East. It was for them to take the lead in this area, and we would support them.'[115] The Canadian government agreed to release two infantry battalions for garrison duty at Hong Kong, and these forces arrived in the Far East shortly before the outbreak of war.

Neither Churchill nor the Chiefs of Staff believed that two additional battalions would enable them to hold Hong Kong indefinitely, or that a small squadron of capital ships could halt a determined invasion of Malaya. Japanese decision makers agreed. At the Imperial Conference of 1 December 1941, Admiral Nagano, the Chief of the Japanese Naval Staff, noted Britain's last-minute maneuvering, but concluded that these measures did 'not call for changes in the deployment of our forces. It will have no effect on our operations.'[116]

The decisions to dispatch these token forces to the Far East are only explicable within the context of Churchill's long-standing policy of aligning British and US policies so closely that both the Americans and the Japanese would take Anglo-American co-belligerency for granted. Churchill sent these forces to the Far East in 1941 for political not military reasons. British capital ships and Canadian infantrymen were symbols of resolve and determination, warnings that the British Empire still possessed considerable latent strength despite its preoccupations in Europe and the Middle East, and, most important, gestures of solidarity with the United States.

Churchill hoped that British strength would be sufficient to restrain Japan, but he believed that the only sure deterrent was the combined power of Britain and the United States. It seemed inconceivable to Churchill that Japan's leaders, who were still regarded as inherently cautious individuals, would risk certain defeat by attacking Britain if it meant war with the United States as well. This was the only real flaw in Churchill's deterrence strategy, but it was a decisive one. In Tokyo, a different cost-benefit analysis took place: once Anglo-American pressure became intolerable, confrontation was preferred to compromise, even though the prospects of a Japanese victory were small. Churchill, who had kept Britain in the war despite seemingly insurmountable odds in the summer of 1940, should have known better than to assume that foreign statesmen would not gamble if backed into a corner.

On 3 December 1941, President Roosevelt rewarded Churchill's efforts to form a united front with a pledge to support Britain in the event of an Anglo-Japanese war. Anticipating this decision, Japan's leaders had prepared a pre-emptive strike against the United States. Their success in neutralizing the US Pacific Fleet at Pearl Harbor on the morning of 7 December removed the most important obstacle to Japanese expansion in South-East Asia. Churchill's deterrents now found themselves caught up in the conflict they were meant to avert. On the evening of 8 December, the *Prince of Wales* and *Repulse* set out with an escort of four destroyers to disrupt Japanese landings in Malaya and Thailand. Lacking air cover, Admiral Phillips, the squadron's commander, had to count on speed and surprise for protection. The gamble did not pay off. On the morning of 10 December, Phillip's ships were caught off the coast of Malaya by Japanese land-based aircraft operating from bases in Indo-China. Within hours, both capital ships were sunk. Just over two weeks later, the remnants of two Canadian battalions surrendered at Hong Kong. The greatest and most humiliating disaster, however, was yet to come. Britain's defenses in Malaya collapsed with astonishing speed. On 15 February 1942,

Singapore capitulated to a numerically smaller Japanese force. Its defense resulted in 139,000 British and Imperial troops either killed or marched into captivity.

Churchill's deterrent strategy needlessly sacrificed two Canadian battalions and placed British capital ships in harm's way at the worst possible moment. The decision to use the *Prince of Wales* and *Repulse* to disrupt the Japanese invasion was taken by the man on the spot, Admiral Phillips, but moving these ships to Singapore made their destruction at least possible, if not probable. Churchill may have had different ideas about their deployment after 7 December, but he did not make his intentions clear in time to avert a catastrophe.[117]

The fall of Singapore, on the other hand, was a result of Churchill's determination to concentrate Britain's limited resources against Germany and Italy. Churchill chose to run serious risks in the Far East in 1940–41, but after the fall of France he had little choice but to concentrate resources in the decisive theater. Britain's survival was now at stake: its resources were dangerously overstretched and risks were being run everywhere. Further defeats in Europe and the Middle East would have had serious and immediate repercussions. The Far East, by contrast, remained calm. 'In war one only has to compare one evil with another', Churchill wrote in early 1939, 'and the lesser evil ranks as a blessing.'[118] So it was in 1941. Japan had not yet attacked British interests, and there was no certainty that it would. The choice for Churchill was an easy one: forces sitting idle in Malaya and Singapore would do nothing to stave off disaster in Europe.

The imperatives of grand strategy tell only part of the story, however. The Chiefs of Staff shared Churchill's broad priorities, but did not want to see Britain's defenses in the Far East cut to the bone. Although prepared to gamble in this region because there was no other reasonable choice, they would have hedged their bets by diverting at least modest reinforcements to the region. Churchill's intervention was decisive here. The Prime Minister was accustomed to differences with his service advisers and was willing to change course when he encountered firm resistance, but throughout 1941 he was not prepared to tolerate opposition to his Far Eastern policies. Both Dill and Pound saw their arguments for caution in this theater either dismissed or belittled. In the end, they decided to save their strength for other battles.

This uncompromising position grew from Churchill's conviction that the risks Britain was running in the Far East were in fact small. His reasons went beyond a simple underestimation of Japanese strength and fighting capabilities, although these were also important factors. In the decades leading up to war, Churchill's approach to the problem of British security in the Far East was generally both realistic and pragmatic. Unlike Britain's service leaders, who had ambitious plans for waging a protracted total war in the Far East, Churchill rightly concluded that Britain alone did not possess sufficient strength to inflict a decisive defeat on Japan. He was also more willing to sacrifice secondary British interests if they were not worth the cost of defending. These considerations dictated a defensive strategy in the Far East. Britain would have to defend Singapore, but only as a means of protecting its only vital interests in the region, Australia and New Zealand. Anything more than this would depend on US support.

It was clear to Churchill at an early date that Britain's position in the Far East ultimately rested on the ability and willingness of the United States to contain Japanese expansion. As Prime Minister, he willingly assumed a supporting role for Britain in the region. The steady improvement of Anglo-American relations in 1940–41 raised his hopes that Japan could be deterred from war, and provided a safety net in case he was wrong. If Britain could expect US support, which seemed increasingly likely in 1941, Japan's ultimate defeat was assured. Britain could make good its losses when the fighting was over, and, more importantly, the security of Australia and New Zealand would be assured. US belligerency would transform Britain's strategic position and make even Singapore expendable. 'I do not see why', he wrote in February 1941, 'even if Singapore were captured, we could not protect Australia by basing a fleet on Australian ports. This would effectively prevent an invasion.'[119]

Churchill does not seem to have realized how vulnerable Singapore had become by December 1941, but his propensity to gamble with its security was encouraged by the prospect of US support. This gamble, at least, paid off. Churchill's miscalculations about Japan's strength and intentions were important causes of the disasters of 1941–42, but they were balanced by a sound assessment of what constituted Britain's vital interests and a clear appreciation of the limits of British power. His policies towards the Far East may reveal his weaknesses as a strategist, but they also highlight many of his strengths.

NOTES

I am grateful to John R. Ferris for his comments on an earlier draft of this article.

1 NP (Naval Programme Committee) (27) 6th Mtg, 2 Feb. 1928, CAB 27/355.
2 Speech of 27 Jan. 1942, quoted in Robert Rhodes James, ed., *Winston S. Churchill: His Complete Speeches* (New York: Chelsea House Publishers/R. R. Bowker Company, 1974), vol. VI, p. 6561.
3 Churchill to Clement Attlee, cited in Winston S. Churchill, *The Second World War* (Boston, MA: Houghton Mifflin, 1948–53), vol. IV, p. 9.

4 Speech of 27 Jan. 1942, cited in Rhodes James, *Complete Speeches*, vol. VI, p. 6561.
5 Cabinet memorandum, 4 July 1921, cited in Martin Gilbert, ed., *Winston S. Churchill* (London: Heinemann, 1971–88) (hereafter cited as Gilbert, *WSC*), vol. IV, companion book 3, pp. 1539–42; also his earlier memorandum, 'The Anglo-Japanese Alliance', 17 June 1921, in Gilbert, *WSC*, vol. IV, book 3, pp. 1512–13.
6 Churchill to the Prince of Wales, 2 Jan. 1922, cited in Gilbert, *WSC*, vol. IV, book 3, p. 1710.
7 CP (Cabinet Paper) 2957: memorandum by the First Lord, 'Anglo-Japanese Alliance', 21 May 1921, CAB 24/123.
8 Keyes to Churchill, 24 March 1925, cited in Paul Halpern, ed., *Keyes Papers* (London: Navy Records Society, 1980), vol. II, p. 112.
9 On the history of the Singapore Naval Base, see James Neidpath, *The Singapore Naval Base and the Defence of Britain's Eastern Empire, 1919–1941* (Oxford: Clarendon Press, 1981) and W. David McIntyre, *The Rise and Fall of the Singapore Naval Base, 1919–1942* (London: Macmillan, 1979). The oil question is examined in Orest Babij, 'The Royal Navy and Inter-war Plans for War against Japan: The Problem of Oil Supply', in Greg Kennedy, ed., *The Merchant Marine in International Affairs, 1850–1950* (London: Frank Cass, 2000).
10 CP-3692, CAB 24/133.
11 'The Case for Singapore', *Sunday Chronicle*, 30 March 1924, reprinted in Michael Wolf, ed., *The Collected Essays of Sir Winston Churchill* (London: Library of Imperial History, 1976), vol. I, pp. 256–9.
12 Other speakers included Leo Amery and Lord Curzon. Stanley Baldwin and Lord Milner sent letters of support, *The Navy*, May 1924, pp. 132–9.
13 Speech of 28 March 1924, cited in *The Navy*, May 1924, p. 138; Rhodes James, *Complete Speeches*, vol. IV, pp. 3450–1.
14 Churchill to Baldwin, 15 Dec. 1924, T 161/243/S25613/ANNEX/5; Gilbert, *WSC*, vol. V, book 1, p. 304.
15 On the struggle over the 1925 navy estimates, see in particular John Ferris, *Men, Money and Diplomacy* (Ithaca, NY: Cornell University Press, 1989), ch. 10; B. J. C. McKercher, 'A Sane and Sensible Diplomacy: Austen Chamberlain, Japan and the Naval Balance of Power in the Pacific Ocean, 1924–1929', *Canadian Journal of History*, vol. 21 (1986), pp. 193–200, Stephen Roskill, *Naval Policy between the Wars* (London: Collins, 1968), vol. I, pp. 445–53; Gilbert, *WSC*, vol. V, chs 4–5.
16 Churchill to Baldwin, 15 Dec. 1924, T 161/243/S25613/ANNEX/5; Gilbert, *WSC*, vol. V, book 1, p. 304. On 29 Dec. 1924, Churchill also circulated to the Cabinet a Treasury memorandum belittling Japan's economic power: CP 554 (24), 'The Economic Power of Japan', CAB 24/169.
17 Ibid.
18 CID 193rd Mtg, 5 Jan. 1925, CAB 2/4.
19 CP 139/25: Admiralty memorandum, 'Political Outlook in the Far East', 5 March 1925, CAB 24/172; also NP (25) 5, CAB 27/273.
20 CID 193rd Mtg, 5 January 1925, CAB 2/4.
21 On the Treasury's strategic views, see Christopher M. Bell, *The Royal Navy, Seapower and Strategy between the Wars* (Stanford, CA: Stanford University Press, 2000), pp. 13–24.
22 CID 193rd Mtg, 5 Jan. 1925, CAB 2/4.
23 NP (25) 2nd Mtg, 5 March 1925, CAB 27/273.
24 Ibid.

25 CID 199th Mtg, 2 April 1925, CAB 2/4.

26 Ibid.

27 The CID's definition of the one-power standard was approved by the Cabinet in May. Cabinet 24 (25), CAB 23/50.

28 Keith Middlemas and John Barnes, *Baldwin: A Biography* (London: Weidenfeld & Nicolson, 1969), pp. 336–9; Robert Rhodes James, *Memoirs of a Conservative: J. C. C. Davidson's Memoirs and Papers, 1910–37* (London: Macmillan, 1969), pp. 213–16.

29 CID 209th Mtg, 18 Feb. 1926, CAB 2/4.

30 Churchill to Bridgeman, 18 Aug. 1927, T 161/281/S32700/1; Gilbert, *WSC*, vol. V, book 1, pp. 1044–5; Cabinet 48(27), 4 Aug. 1927; Cabinet 49 (27), 25 Aug. 1927, CAB 23/55.

31 NP (27) 1st Mtg, 10 Nov. 1927, CAB 27/355. Other members included Churchill, William Bridgeman (First Lord of the Admiralty), Arthur Balfour (Lord President of the Council), Lord Peel (First Commissioner of Works), Lord Salisbury (Lord Privy Seal), Neville Chamberlain (Minister of Health), and Douglas Hogg (Attorney-General).

32 NP (27) 1st Mtg, 10 Nov. 1927, CAB 27/355.

33 NP (27) 4th Mtg, 1 Dec. 1927, CAB 27/355.

34 CP 305 (27): 'Naval Programme Committee: Report on Cruisers', 14 Dec. 1927, CAB 24/190.

35 Churchill to Bridgeman, 16 Jan. 1928, T 161/285/S33101/2; Gilbert, *WSC*, vol. V, book 1, pp. 1182–5.

36 Undated Admiralty memorandum, 'Answers to Questions Asked by Colwyn Committee', ADM 116/2282.

37 Minute by Fraser (Treasury), 8 Feb. 1928, T 161/285/S33101/2.

38 Austen Chamberlain had informed the Naval Programme Committee as recently as 18 Nov. 1927 that it was 'common ground to those who have studied Japanese policy that never was Japan in recent times more pacifist – I will even say so pacifist – as she is at the present time'. NP (27) 2nd Mtg, CAB 27/355.

39 Ibid.

40 CP 47 (28): 'Naval Programme Committee: Report on Naval Oil Fuel Reserve', 20 Feb. 1928, CAB 24/192.

41 Churchill to Bridgeman, 20 Feb. 1928, T 161/285/S33101/4; Gilbert, *WSC*, vol. V, book 1, p. 1211.

42 Churchill to Bridgeman, 15 June 1928, ADM 116/3388.

43 CID 236th Mtg, 5 July 1928, CAB 2/5.

44 Ibid. Cabinet 39/28, 18 July 1928, CAB 23/58.

45 Minute by Sir Oswyn Murray, 18 Nov. 1928, ADM 116/3629.

46 Churchill to Bridgeman, 31 July 1928, ADM 116/3388.

47 Bridgeman to Churchill, 29 November 1928, ADM 167/78.

48 Churchill to Bridgeman, 14 Feb. 1929, ADM 116/3388; Gilbert, *WSC*, vol. V, book 1, p. 1424.

49 Quoted in Rhodes James, *Memoirs of a Conservative*, pp. 209–10.

50 For example, Middlemas and Barnes, *Baldwin*, p. 326; Stephen Roskill, *Churchill and the Admirals* (London: Collins, 1977), pp. 77–8; Vice-Admiral Sir Peter Gretton, *Former Naval Person* (London: Cassell, 1968), pp. 244–5; Robert Rhodes James, *Churchill: A Study in Failure* (London: Weidenfeld & Nicolson, 1970), p. 164.

51 Jon Sumida, 'Churchill and British Sea Power, 1908–1929', in R. A. C. Parker, ed.,

Studies in Statesmanship (London: Brassey's, 1995); John Ferris, *Men, Money and Diplomacy* (Ithaca, NY: Cornell University Press, 1989).

52 Bridgeman to Baldwin, 19 March 1928, ADM 116/3388.

53 For example, David MacGregor, 'Former Naval Cheapskate: Chancellor of the Exchequer Winston Churchill and the Royal Navy, 1924–29', *Armed Forces and Society* (Spring 1993), pp. 319–33.

54 John R. Ferris, 'The Last Decade of British Maritime Supremacy', in Keith Neilson and Greg Kennedy, eds, *Far Flung Lines* (London: Frank Cass, 1996).

55 Speech of 17 Feb 1933, Anti-Socialist and Anti-Communist Union Meeting, Queen's Hall, London, in Rhodes James, *Complete Speeches*, vol. V, pp. 5219–20.

56 Speech of 27 Feb. 1933, in Rhodes James, *Complete Speeches*, vol. V, pp. 5226–7; also speech of 7 Nov. 1933, in ibid., p. 5298: 'What could you expect of the League in far-off Asia?', he asked. 'China and Japan – what do they care for the League of Nations? Russia and the United States – neither of them members of the League. Those four countries comprise half the population of the globe. They form another world, a world in itself, and you should not judge of the success or power of a great international institution like this by the fact that it has not been able to make its will effective on the other side of the world.'

57 'Germany and Japan', 27 Nov. 1936, reprinted in Winston S. Churchill, *Step by Step 1936–1939* (London: Odhams, 1948), pp. 71–4. The articles in this volume were originally published in the *Evening Standard* between 13 March 1936 and 5 April 1938, and the *Daily Telegraph and Morning Post* from 14 April 1938 to 18 May 1939.

58 'The Mission of Japan', *Collier's*, 20 Feb. 1937, in Wolff, *Collected Essays*, vol. I, pp. 365–72.

59 Churchill, 'What Japan Thinks of Us', 21 Jan. 1938, in Churchill, *Step by Step*, p. 194.

60 For the navy's response to the problems posed by a two-hemisphere war, see Bell, *Royal Navy*, pp. 26–44, 99–111.

61 DRC (Defence Requirements Committee) 37: 'Third Report of Defence Requirements Sub-Committee', 21 Nov. 1935, CAB 16/112.

62 Bell, *Royal Navy*, p. 42.

63 Churchill to *Collier's* magazine, 30 Aug. 1937, in Gilbert, *WSC*, vol. V, book 3, p. 756.

64 Churchill, 'Germany and Japan', 27 Nov. 1936, in Churchill, *Step by Step*, p. 72.

65 Churchill, 'Future Safeguards of National Defence', *News of the World*, 1 May 1938, in Wolff, *Collected Essays*, vol. I, p. 398.

66 Ibid., pp. 400–1. 'Broadly speaking', he wrote, 'I do not believe that the air has deprived British sea power of its efficacy, or that it sets our Navy any task beyond its power, if properly maintained, to master.'

67 On British naval planning against Japan, see Bell, *Royal Navy*, ch. 3.

68 Remarks at a meeting of the 1922 Committee of the House of Commons, 7 Dec. 1936: report to the Cabinet, in Gilbert, *WSC*, vol. V, book 3, p. 467. See also 'Japan Guesses Wrong', *Collier's*, 30 July 1938, in Wolff, *Collected Essays*, vol. I, pp. 410–11: 'to invade the home waters of Japan and seek decisive action at close quarters would probably be beyond the present strength of either Britain or the United States alone'.

69 Churchill, 'Memorandum on Sea-Power, 1939', 27 March 1939, PREM 1/345; in Gilbert, *WSC*, vol. V, book 3, pp. 1414–17.

70 Ibid., p. 1416.

71 Ibid., p. 1415. 'One can take it as quite certain', Churchill wrote, 'that Japan would not run such a risk [of an attack on Australia]. They are an extremely sensible people.'

72 Churchill, 'Japan Entangled', 26 May 1938, in Churchill, *Step by Step*, pp. 233–6. Churchill returned to this theme in 'A Word to Japan!', *Daily Mirror*, 11 Aug. 1939, in Wolff, *Collected Essays*, vol. I, p. 468, and his speech of 28 June 1939 at the City Carlton Club, London, in Rhodes James, *Complete Speeches*, vol. VI, p. 6144: 'I do not believe', he told his audience, 'that Japan, deeply entangled in China – nay, bleeding at every pore in China – her strength ebbing away in a wrongful and impossible task, and with the whole weight of Russia upon her in the north of China, will wish to make war upon the British Empire until she sees how matters go in Europe.'

73 Churchill, 'Japan Entangled', in Churchill, *Step by Step*, pp. 233–6.

74 Churchill, 'The Mission of Japan', in Wolff, *Collected Essays*, vol. I, p. 365.

75 Churchill, 'Memorandum on Sea-Power, 1939', 27 March 1939, in Gilbert, *WSC*, vol. V, book 3, pp. 1414–17.

76 For Australia's position, see David Day, *The Great Betrayal* (New York: Norton, 1989), ch. 2.

77 DMV (Visits of Ministers from Dominions) (39) 8th Mtg, 20 Nov. 1939, ADM 1/11062.

78 Chamberlain to J. A. Lyons, Prime Minister of Australia, 20 March 1939, in R. G. Neale *et al.*, eds, *Documents on Australian Foreign Policy 1937–49* (Canberra: Australian Government Publishing Service, 1976–82), vol. II, p. 75.

79 DMV (39) 8th Mtg, 20 Nov. 1939, ADM 1/11062.

80 Ibid.

81 Ibid; WP (War Cabinet memorandum) (39) 135, 'Australian and New Zealand Naval Defence', 21 Nov. 1939, CAB 66/3; in Gilbert, *Churchill War Papers* (New York: Norton, 1993), vol. I, pp. 401–3.

82 Ibid.

83 WM 68(39) (War Cabinet conclusions), 2 Nov. 1939, CAB 65/2; Day, *Great Betrayal*, p. 24.

84 War Cabinet minutes, 5 July 1940, CAB 65/8; in Gilbert, *Churchill War Papers* (New York: Norton, 1995), vol. II, pp. 478–9.

85 War Cabinet minutes, 5 July 1940, CAB 65/8; in Gilbert, *Churchill War Papers*, vol. II, pp. 478–9.

86 COS (Chiefs of Staff Committee) minutes, 19 Sept. 1940, CAB 79/6; in Gilbert, *Churchill War Papers*, vol. II, p. 836. Also Churchill to General Hastings Ismay, 10 Sept. 1940, in ibid., p. 796: 'The presence of the United States Fleet in the Pacific must always be a main pre-occupation to Japan. They are not at all likely to gamble. They are usually most cautious, and now have real need to be, since they are involved in China so deeply.'

87 War Cabinet minutes, 8 Aug. 1940, CAB 65/14; in Gilbert, *Churchill War Papers*, vol. II, p. 634. Two weeks earlier, Churchill thought that Britain would have to rely 'mainly on submarines and a few fast cruisers at the outset'. Churchill to Ismay, 25 July 1940, in ibid., vol. II, p. 570.

88 War Cabinet minutes, 8 Aug. 1940, CAB 65/14; in Gilbert, *Churchill War Papers*, vol. II, p. 634.

89 See Gilbert, *Churchill War Papers*, vol. II, pp. 645–7.

90 COS (41) 80 (O), 'Despatch of a Fleet to the Far East', 18 May 1941; Menzies to Churchill, 11 Aug. 1941, PREM 3/156/1; *Neale et al., Documents on Australian Foreign Policy 1937–49*, vol. V, pp. 65–6.

91 FE (Far East Committee) (40) 65, 'Far Eastern Situation', 23 Nov. 1940, CAB 96/1. On Whitehall's views on the employment of capital ships as a deterrent, see Christopher M. Bell, 'The "Singapore Strategy" and the Deterrence of Japan: Winston Churchill, the Admiralty, and the Dispatch of Force Z', *English Historical Review*, vol. 116, no. 467 (June 2001), pp. 617–19.

92 Churchill to Menzies, 8 Dec. 1940, in Gilbert, *Churchill War Papers*, vol. II, pp. 1187–8; also Neale *et al.*, *Documents on Australian Foreign Policy 1937–49*, vol. IV, p. 315, where it is dated 23 Dec. 1940.

93 COS (40) 1053: 'Tactical Appreciation of Defence Situation in Malaya', report by Far Eastern Commanders-in-Chief, 16 Oct. 1940, CAB 80/24; S. Woodburn Kirby, *The War Against Japan* (London: HMSO, 1957), vol. I, pp. 48–9.

94 Churchill to COS, 13 Jan. 1941, COS (41) 33, CAB 80/24; J. R. M. Butler, *Grand Strategy* (London: HMSO, 1957), vol. II, p. 495; see also Churchill to Lord Cranborne, 15 Dec. 1940, in Gilbert, *Churchill War Papers*, vol. II, pp. 1237–8.

95 On British deficiencies in Malaya see John R. Ferris, 'The Singapore Grip: Preparing Defeat in Malaya, 1939–1941', in Ian Gow and Yoshi Hirama, eds, *The History of Anglo-Japanese Relations*, vol. III, *Military Dimensions* (London: Palgrave, 2003); Malcolm H. Murfett *et al.*, *Between Two Oceans* (Oxford: Oxford University Press, 2000), ch. 7.

96 Churchill to Ismay, 7 Jan. 1941, PREM 3/157/1; Winston S. Churchill, *Second World War*, vol. III, p. 177; Christopher M. Bell, '"Our Most Exposed Outpost": Hong Kong and British Far Eastern Strategy', *Journal of Military History*, vol. 60, no. 1 (January 1996), pp. 76–81.

97 Churchill to COS, 28 April 1941, PREM 3/156/6; DO (Defence Committee (Operations)) (41) 20th Mtg, 29 April 1941, CAB 69/2; COS (41)139(O), 16 July 1941, CAB 80/58.

98 Dill memorandum, 'The Relation of the Middle East to the Security of the United Kingdom', 6 May 1941, quoted in Churchill, *Second World War*, vol. III, pp. 421–2; Dill to Churchill, 15 May 1941, quoted in Butler, *Grand Strategy*, vol. II, p. 581; Ong Chit Chung, *Operation Matador: Britain's War Plans Against the Japanese 1918–1941* (Singapore: Times Academic Press, 1997), pp. 164–6.

99 Churchill to Dill, 13 May 1941, quoted in Churchill, *Second World War*, vol. III, pp. 422–3.

100 Ibid., p. 423. 'I have already given you the political data upon which the military arrangements for the defence of Singapore should be based', he informed Dill, 'namely that should Japan enter the war the United States will in all probability come in on our side . . .'.

101 Churchill to Pound and A. V. Alexander (First Lord of the Admiralty), 25 Aug. 1941, ADM 205/10; quoted in Churchill, *Second World War*, vol. III, pp. 854–5.

102 Pound to Churchill, 28 August 1941, ADM 205/10; in Churchill, *Second World War*, vol. III, p. 855–8.

103 Churchill to Pound, 29 Aug. 1941, ADM 205/10; in Churchill, *Second World War*, vol. III, pp. 858–9.

104 Ibid.

105 Eden to Churchill, 12 September 1941, FO 371/27981; Eden Diary, 12 September 1941, Papers of the first Earl of Avon, Special Collections Department, University of Birmingham; quoted in Antony Best, *Britain, Japan, and Pearl Harbor* (London: Routledge, 1995), p. 172.

106 JP (Joint Planning Committee) (41) 816, 'Japan: Our Future Policy', 7 Oct. 1941, annex I, CAB 84/35.

107 Eden to Churchill, 16 Oct. 1941, DO(41)21, CAB 69/3.
108 DO(41)65th Mtg, 17 Oct. 1941, CAB 69/2; DO(41)66th Mtg, 20 Oct. 1941, CAB 69/8.
109 Phillips to Pound, 17 Oct. 1941, ADM 178/322.
110 DO(41)66th Mtg, 20 Oct. 1941, CAB 69/8.
111 The reasons for this decision are explored in Bell, 'Our Most Exposed Outpost', pp. 75–88.
112 COS minutes, 3 Sep. 1941, CAB 79/14.
113 General L. C. Hollis to Churchill, 10 Sep. 1941, PREM 3/157/1; also War Office to Brooke-Popham, 6 Nov. 1941, WO 106/2409.
114 WO 106/2409.
115 WM (41) 103rd Conclusions, 16 Oct. 1941, Confidential Annex, CAB 65/23.
116 Nobutaka Ike, ed., *Japan's Decision for War* (Stanford, CA: Stanford University Press, 1967), pp. 280–1.
117 Churchill, *Second World War*, vol. III, pp. 547–8; Churchill to Commodore G. R. G. Allen, 11 Aug. 1953, CAB 103/327; Bell, 'Singapore Strategy', pp. 633–4.
118 'Memorandum on Sea-Power, 1939', 27 March 1939, in Gilbert, *WSC*, vol. V, book 3, pp. 1414–17.
119 Churchill to Pound and Alexander, 17 Feb. 1941, ADM 199/1932.

3

The Limitations of the Politician-Strategist: Winston Churchill and the German Threat, 1933–39

B. J. C. McKercher

'I find unendurable the sense of our country falling into the power, into the orbit and influence of Nazi Germany, and of our existence becoming dependent upon their goodwill or pleasure. It is to prevent that that I have tried my best to urge the maintenance of every bulwark of defense . . .'

Churchill, October 1938[1]

In the latter half of the 1930s, Winston Churchill emerged as the chief critic of British foreign and defense policy; the essence of his critique arose from his assertion that the strategic bases of government policy – indeed, that of successive British governments – was wrong. The contemporary disagreement about British strategy was emotive politically; to a large degree, the subsequent controversy about the accuracy of Churchill's strategic vision is subsumed within the so-called 'appeasement' debate, a dialectic within British historiography that revolves as much around the aims and abilities of Stanley Baldwin and Neville Chamberlain, the two leaders of the Conservative Party and, after June 1935, successive Prime Ministers.[2] Little doubt exists that on a range of foreign and defense issues after early 1938, Churchill, a government Member of Parliament, emerged as the focus of Conservative opposition to Chamberlain and his cabinet. But essential to understanding this fact is to appreciate that Churchill's dissenting opinions within his party on these and other policy matters surfaced in the early 1930s. And while his views of how to meet the growing German threat to British national and imperial security might well have had merit – those views changed between the early and later 1930s – one cannot lose sight of Churchill's naked political self-interest in arguing that his strategic vision was superior to that of his own party's leadership. Quite simply, he sought the premiership above all else; thus, his criticisms of British foreign and defense policy were less selfless than either he or his disciples later claimed. They were as much the reproaches of a politician on the make as those founded on a rational strategic basis and fostered out of a genuine conviction to meet an emerging threat to Britain.

When Chamberlain rose to the premiership in May 1937, he decided on a new basis for British foreign policy to meet the threat posed by the totalitarian powers in Europe and the Far East. For most of the period after the Great War, that policy had been based on the traditional strategy of maintaining balances of power on the European continent and in the wider world.[3] Chamberlain distrusted the balance because of the danger it posed if it broke down. Moreover, he also eschewed other available strategic options: constructing alliances (which, in his opinion, meant working with the unreliable French); conference diplomacy (which had failed again and again since 1932 over international arms limitation and financial cooperation); and League of Nations collective security (which had fizzled during the Abyssinian crisis in 1935–36). Instead, he believed that international stability – or, at least, stability for Britain – could be achieved through bilateral arrangements with each of Nazi Germany, Fascist Italy, and militaristic Japan to remove issues of contention. Here lay the essence of appeasement. But, importantly, Chamberlain, his senior ministers, and their advisers had no intention of relying solely on diplomatic means to remove tensions between Britain and the three totalitarian powers. Integral to keeping German, Italian, and Japanese demands reasonable stood the deterrent strength of effective British armed forces. From November 1931 to May 1937, Chamberlain had been Chancellor of the Exchequer in two successive coalition governments – the National governments of Conservative, National Labour, and National Liberals. These ministries had embarked on a program of strengthening the armed forces beginning in 1934.[4] Thus, three years later, as Chamberlain observed when he succeeded Baldwin as Prime Minister and Conservative Party leader: 'I believe the double policy of rearmament and better relations with Germany and Italy will carry us safely through the danger period, if only the Foreign Office will play up.'[5]

But difficulty for Chamberlain not only resided with the Foreign Office that, led by its formidable permanent under-secretary, Sir Robert Vansittart, advocated the balance of power.[6] On the left, the opposition Labour Party, supported by pacifist organizations like the Women's International League of Peace and Freedom, argued against rearmament. 'Under modern conditions neither aeroplanes nor armies, neither battleships nor fortresses can give security', the Labour *Daily Herald*, observed in a leading article in December 1933. 'There is no security except in peace.'[7] These comments appeared just after Adolf Hitler had taken Germany out of the League of Nations and, equally important, out of the

League-sponsored World Disarmament Conference. For these people, the League existed as the lynch-pin of the new international order that arose after 1918; and, even without Germany and Japan, which earlier in 1933 had also announced its withdrawal from the organization, they continued to believe in the collective action of its members as the best safeguard of peace and stability.[8] On the right, Churchill did not have a monopoly either about criticising the National government or in expressing worry about the strategic bases of British foreign policy.[9] Powerful newspaper proprietors, like Lord Rothermere, the owner of the *Daily Mirror*, and a small group of Conservative MPs and others were equally critical of both Baldwin and Chamberlain.[10] Yet, because his disagreement was unrelenting and articulate, and because he knew how to publicize his ideas,[11] Churchill became the focus of opposition to the National government's foreign and defense policies; ultimately, he proved the major difficulty confronting Chamberlain and his foreign and defense policy.

After the end of the Second World War, Churchill's view of the apparent inadequacies of Baldwin–Chamberlain foreign policy dominated the historiography of the British strategic response to the crises of the late 1930s. Admittedly, the anti-appeasement, anti-Chamberlain historico-polemic, *Guilty Men*, published in 1940, set the tone.[12] But Churchill went further in the first volume of his massive history of the Second World War, published in 1948, when he argued that it was 'an unnecessary war'; indeed, the 'theme' of the volume was: 'How the English-speaking peoples through their unwisdom, carelessness, and good nature allowed the wicked to rearm.'[13] This interpretation dominated all else for almost a generation for the simplest reason: since war with Germany broke out in September 1939, Chamberlain's strategy of appeasement failed.[14] A major British reinterpretation of Chamberlain's culpability finally emerged in 1961 with A. J. P. Taylor's iconoclastic study, *The Origins of the Second World War*.[15] Arguing among other things that appeasement did not go far enough – if Britain and its French partner had stood back in 1939, not only would Hitler's Germany have gone to war with Bolshevik Russia, but Britain would have avoided the enfeeblement that befell it after 1945 – Taylor saw Hitler as a diplomatic opportunist whose policies endangered peace. Taylor's work was a watershed. Coupled with the opening of British official archives in the late 1960s, it saw Churchill's assertion about an avoidable war crumble as younger historians produced more thoughtful assessments of the 1930s.[16] While not hiding that appeasement as the basis of national strategy was flawed, these less emotional analyses demonstrated that the problems in the 1930s were not so much the failure of Britain's response to the German threat as they were the result of Hitler's determination to overthrow the Treaty of Versailles and establish German hegemony on the continent. Put succinctly, the Second World War was Hitler's war, not Neville Chamberlain's. Although the appeasement debate still rages, no doubt exists that Churchill's censure of Chamberlain – and of Baldwin – was callow and vengeful against his political enemies.[17]

This situation has not stopped Churchill's admirers from conducting dogged rear-guard actions to deify 'the greatest Englishman of his time' and acclaim all his actions in war and peace. His official biographer has lately written: 'In the appeasement debate after Hitler's rise to power, Churchill's arguments centred around how to avert war.'[18] Of course, Chamberlain had the same goal, as did those before him like Baldwin and James Ramsay MacDonald, the Prime Minister of the National government from September 1931 to June 1935. And the same holds true for the Foreign Office, the Chiefs of Staff Committee (COS), the Treasury, and the bulk of the British public. The nub of the debate centers on whose method of doing so was correct. Churchill sat on the backbenches of the Commons in the 1930s. He might have been disconcerted about the international situation, but he had no responsibilities of state. Baldwin, Chamberlain, and the others on the front benches did. Along with their foreign and defense policy advisers, they had to balance Britain's financial resources with its domestic political reality and external commitments. There was more to policy-making than these systemic limitations on politicians in office; the connexion between personality and policy-making cannot be ignored.[19] The ambition to succeed marked both Churchill's and Chamberlain's characters – as it did for Baldwin and other members of the British foreign-policy-making élite; and so, too, did the desire to steal a march one against the other. To a large degree, therefore, Churchill's criticism of British foreign and defense policy in the six years after 1933 was as much a personal attack on those holding political power as it was to maintain what he called 'every bulwark of defense'. Still, the answers to two questions remain: what were Churchill's precise perceptions of the German threat, and, in contradistinction to Chamberlain's strategy built on the 'double policy of rearmament and better relations' with the totalitarian powers, what were Churchill's strategic alternatives to restrain Hitler's Germany?

In retrospect, Hitler's advent to the German chancellorship in January 1933 proved a divide in European great-power politics. It took, however, the tightening of Nazi control over the German government in March and early April before Churchill joined with other Conservative MPs, like Sir Austen Chamberlain, the former Foreign Secretary, to evoke a response. 'New discord has arisen in Europe of late years from the fact that Germany is not satisfied with the result of the late war', Churchill told the House of Commons on 13 April. 'I have indicated several times that Germany got off lightly after the Great War. I know that it is not always a fashionable opinion, but the facts repudiate the idea that a Carthaginian peace was in fact imposed on Germany.'[20] Regardless of Churchill's view about Germany getting off lightly, the Germans disagreed. So, too, as Churchill admitted about what was fashionable, did British public opinion.[21] While a range of British, French, and other statesmen might earlier have thought that the Treaty of Versailles was fair, they shared a belief by 1932–33 about loosening the bonds imposed in 1919. More specifically, the German question in the early 1930s touched two fundamentally important and intertwined international questions deriving from the peace settlement: reparations and disarmament. At Lausanne in June–July 1932, Neville Chamberlain, then Chancellor of the Exchequer, and his European counterparts ended the system of German reparations.[22] This decision occurred concurrently with a crisis in the World Disarmament conference: Berlin's discomfort about the course of the negotiations that produced the announcement in August of a German boycott of the Conference until Germany received *Gleichberichtigung*, 'equality of rights', in armaments. This German action produced a concerted effort by the National government, then led by MacDonald, to break the deadlock – a situation compounded by impending German elections in which the Nazis were making gains by chastising Versailles for keeping Germany militarily weak while its neighbors possessed substantial armed forces. In mid-November, Sir John Simon, the Foreign Secretary, outlined a plan that brought back the Germans: replacing Versailles' disarmament provisions with a new convention that would bind all signatories to the new disarmament treaty; as that convention would apply to Germany without the Versailles strictures, Germany would acquire equality of treatment.[23]

The World Disarmament Conference was to resume on 31 January 1933; the day before it convened, Hitler rose to the German chancellorship. Yet, in the two-and-a-half months before the Commons' condemnation of the Nazi regime, Churchill had other preoccupations. First, when the government announced reductions in the Royal Air Force (RAF) budget in March, he argued strongly for increased spending.[24] These reductions were tied to a new British disarmament plan, fostered by MacDonald in response to the Nazi seizure of power in Germany: a five-year period to allow Germany to attain equality with the other land powers and, with French concerns in mind, then having the continental European powers conclude an additional agreement to ensure their security.[25] Significantly, Churchill did not suggest that Hitler's Germany posed an air threat to British security, a difficult proposition given that Germany still had no air force. He argued, instead, for the possession of an RAF strong enough to deter an attack from any power. A more important preoccupation than air defense touched his opposition to the National government's determination to give India 'home rule'.[26] As an ardent imperialist, Churchill saw 'home rule' as weakening Britain's position as a global power; more prosaically, in purely racist terms, he distrusted Indian nationalist politicians.[27] 'I imagine HMG [His Majesty's Government] intend to do only provincial government now, minus the police', he wrote to Lord Salisbury, a senior Conservative peer on 13 February, '. . . but that they will incorporate into their Bill the whole Federal structure . . . The Indian political classes will be kept in continual agitation.'[28]

While Churchill obviously held sincere views about capable armed forces and the need to maintain the imperial status quo in 1933, his criticisms of government policy were just as much directed at discrediting the senior members of the coalition cabinet, especially Baldwin. After the May 1929 General Election, in which the Baldwin-led Conservatives lost power, Churchill, who had been Chancellor of the Exchequer, took a leading role in seeking to replace Baldwin as party leader. He failed.[29] The result when the Conservatives joined the National government in late 1931 was Baldwin's determination to keep Churchill out of office, a policy favored by the majority of Conservatives at Westminster who saw Churchill as slippery and self-serving. In the same way, his views about Hitler's Germany articulated in April 1933 were not directed simply at seeking to convince MPs and the voting public at large that Nazi Germany was a threat to Britain; rather, they were also a means to embarrass the National government at a time when it was seeking ways to keep alive the disarmament discussions at Geneva via the MacDonald Plan. As a junior Conservative minister wrote to Churchill on 13 April about the Indian question: 'By your words, and by your actions, you have shown that you intend to make it hot for all Conservative members who dare to stand by Mr Baldwin in regard to this problem.'[30]

Churchill's musings on the state of the armed forces, imperial unity, and the advent of the Nazi regime in Germany say much about his strategic beliefs in 1933. As the Conservative Chancellor of the Exchequer from November 1924 to June 1929, he had led the charge within the government to reduce public spending on the armed forces.[31] In fact, in July 1928, he succeeded in getting the so-called 'Ten-Year Rule' adopted by the senior cabinet body that coordinated foreign and defense policy, the Committee of Imperial Defence (CID).[32] This 'rule' held that 'it should be assumed, for the purpose of framing the Estimates of the Fighting Services, that at any given date there will be no major war for ten years'. Budget-cutting and a dearth of first-class strategic threats allowed the Baldwin government and its Labour and first National successors to follow this policy thereafter, with the stipulation that 'this should rule unless or until, on the

initiative of the Foreign Office or one of the Fighting Services or otherwise, it was decided to alter it'. The onset of the Great Depression in late
1929 permitted further retrenchment of arms spending – a situation compounded by the advent of the World Disarmament Conference.[33]
Although it would gall Churchill to be told so, he had major responsibility for the reductions in defense spending. The strength of the Treasury in
enforcing economies in government spending, especially in the first years
of the Depression, strengthened the application of the 'rule'. Thus, in
arguing for increased RAF spending in April 1933, Churchill was running
against a policy that he had helped put in place. This does not suggest that
he supported international arms limitation, he did not. He had been
dubious of the Preparatory Commission that paved the way for the
Disarmament Conference and of the Conference itself. In 1928, he used a
public platform to utter a famous condemnation that took the form of a
fable in which horned and toothed animals in a zoo could not agree on
how to disarm.[34] The horned animals sought the abolition of teeth;
toothed animals saw little purpose in horns. His argument, instead, was
that Britain should arm itself to meet its own requirements regardless of
what other powers decided. Moreover, Britain could best protect itself by
forbearing involvement in continental affairs.[35] 'I would far rather have
larger Estimates', he commented during the March 1933 Air Estimates
debate, 'and be absolutely free and independent to choose our own course
than become involved in this Continental scene by a well-meant desire to
persuade them to give up arms.' His problem was that the government and
the British public wanted a measure of arms limitation.

Churchill's notion of British unilateralism in armament policy tied
directly into his conception of the Empire. After the Great War and before,
Churchill stood as a proponent of 'Imperial isolationism'.[36] As the corner-
stone of Britain's global pre-eminence, the imperial edifice had to be pre-
served at all costs and, if possible, its economic and political strength
enhanced; to ensure strength and cohesion, Britain had to avoid a continental commitment. In this light, in 1925, Churchill had been an early
opponent within the Baldwin government of what became the Locarno
Treaty, a British guarantee of the Franco-German and German–Belgian
borders that finally brought stability to Europe after the Great War. 'If in
addition to sea superiority we had air supremacy, we might maintain ourselves as we did in the days of Napoleon for indefinite periods, even when
all the Channel ports and all the Low Countries were in the hands of a vast
hostile military power', he told Austen Chamberlain, the Foreign
Secretary. 'It should never be admitted in this argument that England [sic]
cannot, if the worst comes to the worst, stand alone.'[37] Although later supporting Locarno, Churchill's desire to strengthen the Empire at all costs

did not abate. Thus, in 1927, when Baldwin's government entered into naval arms-limitation talks with the Americans and Japanese, Churchill opposed an agreement by arguing that it would restrict Britain's ability to defend maritime lines of communication essential for imperial defense.[38] This attitude explains his adamant opposition to Indian home rule after 1933 – Britain's great-power status, fundamental to its wealth and ability to meet crises as they arose, would be eroded. In Churchill's estimation, the British armed forces existed not only to protect the home islands and the Empire, but to deter other powers from adventurism at British expense.

Although Nazi Germany had the potential to imperil British security in 1933, it did not yet have the ability to do so. For Churchill, the deterrent value of the RAF and the other fighting services offered means by which Germany or any other power would think twice about endangering that security. A strong indication that Churchill was undisturbed about the possibility of a German threat after his April 1933 speech can be seen in his reaction six months later to Hitler's diplomatic 'bombshell' of taking Germany out of both the League and the World Disarmament Conference. There was no reaction.[39] In October–November 1933, the publication of his book about his ancestor, the Duke of Marlborough, obsessed him. In terms of domestic politics, Indian home rule occupied his time and energy. The German question did not absorb Churchill much in 1933–34, because the material to criticize Baldwin, Chamberlain, and other Conservative leaders like Sir Samuel Hoare, the Indian Secretary, lay in other places.

However, Churchill's fertile mind did not ignore wider strategic questions. At the end of June 1934, Hitler strengthened his dictatorship by a blood-purge of Nazi radicals, an action supported by the German army, which now saw its future tied to the Nazi regime.[40] The balance of power on the continent seemed to shift in Berlin's favor, even though Hitler had not yet publicly confirmed German rearmament. Believing that Germany was rearming, Churchill now seemingly reversed himself about committing to the continent. In a newspaper article in the *Daily Mail*, owned by another of Baldwin's enemies, Lord Northcliffe, he argued for 'a definite defensive alliance with France, our nearest neighbour, almost the only other parliamentary country in Europe, a peace-loving country, and, luckily, with the best army in the world'.[41] These words constituted an apparent major shift in strategic thinking for a man who had opposed Locarno and, as late as March 1933, had been emphatic that Britain should be 'absolutely free and independent' to choose its course and avoid being involved on the continent. Yet, apart from the comment 'that we cannot get away' from Europe, he did not really pursue the idea.[42] He concentrated again on India and the RAF. While part of the reason for doing so was probably that he felt more fruitful political gains could be made by attacking the government on these issues, a more telling consideration was that high-placed friends, probably Vansittart, allowed him to see confidential Foreign Office assessments about German intentions.[43] In the latter part of 1934, Orme Sargent, the head of the Foreign Office Central Department, provided Churchill with material that suggested that while Hitler would rearm Germany, he was not bent on aggressive war: 'If Hitler were frankly aggressive the situation would be simpler, and peace – paradoxical though it may sound – more secure, for a frankly aggressive Germany would still unite all Europe against it.'[44]

Moreover, by late 1933, the National government had turned from pursuing an international arms-limitation agreement to embarking on limited rearmament – or, as it was referred to at the time, meeting defense deficiencies. By May 1933, the Foreign Office, Treasury, and three Chiefs of Staff (COS) had concluded that the 'Ten-Year Rule' had to be abandoned.[45] Animated chiefly by the changing situation in the Far East, their arguments convinced the CID in mid-October 1933 to establish a Defence Requirements Sub-Committee (DRC). Chaired by Sir Maurice Hankey, the secretary to both the cabinet and the CID, its other members were Vansittart, Sir Norman Warren Fisher, the Treasury permanent undersecretary, and the three Chiefs of Staff – Admiral Sir Ernle Chatfield, General Sir Archibald Montgomery-Massingberd, and Air Chief-Marshal Sir Edward Ellington. Its mandate centered on determining the forces needed for 'the Defence of our possessions and interests in the Far East; European commitments; the Defence of India'. To this end, the DRC was to 'prepare a programme for meeting our worst deficiencies for transmission to the Cabinet'.[46] Reporting in February, the DRC recommended additional spending of £71.3 million by 1939. Although at the cabinet level Neville Chamberlain succeeded in reducing spending to just over £50 million, the DRC determined the national strategy that guided British foreign and defense policy until late 1937: maintaining the balance of power in Europe by committing ground troops, the Field Force, to the continent; enhancing the deterrent strength of the RAF; and strengthening the Royal Navy in the Far East to keep Japan in check. This centerpiece of this strategy – a continental commitment – derived from Vansittart, who promoted the Field Force as a means to keep the Germans in check.[47] Additionally, over Chamberlain's objections, Vansittart won DRC and cabinet support for the notion that Germany constituted Britain's 'ultimate potential enemy'.[48]

Vansittart's strategy to contain German energy involved maintaining the continental balance of power via strengthened armed forces and cooperation with the French.[49] But he did not wish to antagonize Berlin unduly.

It seems that after the DRC, he worried that Churchill's rhetoric might unnecessarily inflame the situation.[50] Thus, giving Churchill confidential information about the European situation was a good political move for the Foreign Office position, as his general ideas about rearmament might be helpful in the future – Vansittart had told the cabinet that British foreign policy needed to be backed by armed strength.[51] Although Churchill's support for increased air strength did not abate throughout 1934 and into 1935, his perception of a looming German threat diminished. He told the House of Commons in late November 1934:

> To urge the preparation of defense is not to assert the imminence of war. On the contrary, if war were imminent preparations for defense would be too late. I do not believe that war is imminent or that war is inevitable, but it seems very difficult to resist the conclusion that, if we do not begin forthwith to put ourselves in a position of security, it will soon be beyond our power to do so.[52]

While his apprehension about German rearmament had not disappeared, he took the public position that Hitler might not be as threatening as he and others earlier thought. In 1935, he published a sketch of the German Chancellor that argued 'the world lives on hopes that the worst is over, and that we may yet live to see Hitler a gentler figure in a happier age'. Of Hitler, he observed: 'Those who have met Herr Hitler face to face in public business or on social terms have found a highly competent, cool, well-informed functionary with an agreeable manner, a disarming smile, and few have been unaffected by a subtle personal magnetism.'[53]

In this way, as 1935 dawned, Churchill's strategic prescription for British foreign and defense policy found basis on the deterrent strength of the RAF. While he was anxious about a potential German threat – conditioned by his belief in the justice of the Treaty of Versailles and the advent of the brutish Nazi regime – that threat remained more potential than real. Despite toying briefly with the idea of an Anglo-French 'defensive alliance' in the summer of 1934, Churchill's strategic focus concentrated on Britain's ability to stand alone in defending its interests. No doubt Vansittart's intervention in allowing Churchill to see confidential assessments of the German question were important in this regard, though Vansittart's efforts were certainly designed to safeguard the efforts of the DRC to begin meeting defense deficiencies. As Churchill's rather optimistic pen-portrait of Hitler showed, the potential German threat seemed to be diminishing as Hitler entered his third year in office. The Nazi regime pursued authoritarian internal policies but, as the Foreign Office showed, it had done little in foreign policy that could be considered aggressive. Just as important, in early 1935, given Churchill's later charge about the National government's 'unwisdom, carelessness, and good nature' in allowing 'the wicked to rearm' – notwithstanding the efforts of the DRC – he had done little other than to demand increased spending on the RAF. His chief preoccupation was to embarrass the Conservative Party leaders, Baldwin and Chamberlain primarily; and in this regard, India took as much or more of his energies than foreign and defense policy.

This situation changed in March 1935. On 4 March, the National government issued a White Paper that outlined increased spending to meet British defense deficiencies – an election would have to held later in the year and these expenses had to be justified to a British electorate still buffeted by the ill winds of the Great Depression. Using this British action as a pretext, the more so as the White Paper referred to Germany's illegal rearmament, Hitler announced 11 days later that Germany would no longer be bound by the disarmament strictures of Versailles.[54] Churchill wrote immediately to his wife: 'The Russians, like the French and ourselves, want to be left alone and the nations who want to be left alone to live in peace must join together for mutual security. There is safety in numbers.'[55] No one doubts that Churchill held legitimate concerns about the German threat at this moment but, then and later, his critique of British foreign and defense policy remained excessively overstated. On 17 March, for instance, he wrote to Baldwin: 'I believe that the Germans are already as strong as we are and possibly stronger, and that if we carry out our new programme as prescribed [in the White Paper], Germany will be 50 per cent stronger than we by the end of 1935 or the beginning of 1936.'[56] Though equally concerned, especially after Simon returned from Berlin in late March when Hitler told him the new *Luftwaffe* equalled the RAF,[57] the government investigated the situation carefully. At Simon's request, a CID Sub-Committee on Air Parity looked carefully at the situation, reporting to the cabinet in mid-May that Hitler's claim was wide of the mark.[58] Nine days later, Baldwin told the House of Commons that earlier government statements about German air strength were wrong, although based on the best available information at the time.[59] Indicating that there was little reason 'for panic', he indicated that the National government as a whole would take the blame for those earlier statements, that the German air threat remained more potential than real, and that the government would increase RAF first-line strength to 1,500 airplanes.

To Churchill's dismay, Baldwin's performance let the government escape a crisis; he wrote later that 'I felt a sense of despair'.[60] In fact, Churchill's later criticisms of the British reaction to the changing international situation held that: 'After the loss of air parity [untrue in 1935–36], we were liable to be blackmailed by Hitler.'[61] In this context, it is important to understand the National government's response to Hitler's actions. Almost immediately, Baldwin, Chamberlain, and their cabinet colleagues moved bolster the British position in Europe. In late April, MacDonald met with Étienne Flandin, the French premier, and Benito Mussolini, the Italian dictator, at Stresa and successfully created a front to contain German power.[62] In addition, by June, to obviate an Anglo-German naval race *à la* that of pre-1914 vintage, the National government concluded a naval agreement with Germany that was to keep the *Reichsmarine* surface fleet at 35 per cent of Royal Navy strength. In the same month, these efforts were tied to a re-shuffling of the cabinet that saw Baldwin become Prime Minister, MacDonald move to the Lord Chancellorship, and Hoare replace Simon at the Foreign Office. Then, in July, the DRC was revived to assess the new situation.[63] By November, it reported twice to a special cabinet sub-committee on Defence Policy and Requirements (DPR). An 'Interim Report' of 24 July discussed when British forces should be ready for war.[64] There was no unity of opinion. Attempting to see the world from the vantage-point of their German opposites, the COS believed that 1942 seemed likely; Vansittart and Warren Fisher opted for 1939, their argument being that Germany might provoke war 'by miscalculation or political error of judgement'. With Hoare's patronage, the DPR endorsed the Vansittart–Warren Fisher assessment.[65] Given European developments and the need to maintain the Far Eastern naval and political balance, the DPR's action meant that the cabinet had to go beyond meeting defense deficiencies and expand the armed forces.[66] Circulated on 21 November, the 'Third Report' addressed the nature of this expansion.[67]

The 'Third Report' had two parts: a narrow one pertaining to the technical side of armed forces expansion; and a broader one about how those forces should be deployed for home and imperial defense.[68] The DRC reaffirmed the need for balanced armed strength. The March 1935 White Paper had modified spending programs set by the ministerial committee in 1934, weighting them in favor of the RAF. Hence, the 'Third Report' called for a two-power naval standard against Japan and Germany; it recommended army expansion to provide adequate imperial garrisons, ensure home defense, and 'enable us to honour our international obligations . . . [including] the occupation for ourselves and the denial to the enemy of an advanced air base in the Low Countries'; it sought additional air strength to permit operations against Japan, strengthen the Fleet Air Arm, and ensure cover for the 'Field Force'.[69] The projected cost by 1 January 1939 was estimated at £239 million; additional spending for upgrading and replacement, another £178.5 million (totalling £417.5 million), was required by the end of 1940.

As to the strategic basis of foreign and defense policy, the Foreign

Office and Treasury – the axis of Vansittart and Warren Fisher – won the argument that Germany and Japan, in that order of priority, persisted as the principal dangers to international stability and, hence, British security.[70] A dangerous wrinkle emerged after October 1935, when Mussolini's forces invaded Abyssinia. This action broke Stresa, which had already been weakened via the Anglo-German naval agreement and the conclusion of a Franco-Soviet security pact in May 1935. Still, disparaging imminent Italo-German rapprochement, Vansittart forecast that Mussolini might later assist Hitler in realizing his aspirations in central and eastern Europe, especially in Austria. Anglo-German cooperation remained possible on particular issues – unmentioned, the naval agreement certainly stood at the fore in his thinking – but Hitler had now to be forestalled. Strengthened British armed forces tied to an 'Entente' rather than an alliance with France could meet this end. Yet, European and Mediterranean questions were connected to the Far East. For Vansittart, 'a policy of friendliness towards Japan' backed by a regional naval presence to hinder Japanese covetousness toward British markets, colonies, and Australia and New Zealand was essential. Britain should only support League collective security if sanctions gave legal cover to the protection of British strategic or economic interests.

By the end of 1935, the National government had decided to increase extra defense spending eight times above the level determined by the DCM in 1934; and it looked to maintain the linked balances of power on the continent, in the Mediterranean, and in the Far East. Churchill might well have despaired about British foreign and defense policy in May 1935, but his focus on air power and the German threat thereafter followed the pattern of over-statement and exaggeration set immediately after Hitler's announcement of rearmament. Suffusing it all was his continual effort to discredit the Conservative Party leadership. Even before the March 1935 White Paper, Churchill and Austen Chamberlain had jointly lobbied MacDonald to set up a CID committee to examine issues of air defense.[71] A new CID sub-committee on Air Defence Research (ADR) was accordingly formed and, though a backbencher and because of his public pushing, Churchill contributed to its deliberations.[72] After Hitler announced German rearmament, however, Churchill continued his campaign for expanded air power by using *Daily Telegraph* reports that the *Luftwaffe* possessed twice 'the first-line military aircraft' of the RAF.[73] Baldwin's steady performance in the Commons on 22 May took some of the steam out of Churchill's attack.

Although probably aware of the reconstituted DRC, Churchill did not relent. He used his considerable political abilities to take the government to task to improve air defenses: 'our safety requires air parity with

Germany'. In private and in public, he promoted a national strategy based on the deterrent strength of the RAF. As he told Baldwin when he was appointed to the ADR, 'I must be perfectly free to criticise air policy and air strength.'[74] For political reasons – Baldwin eventually called a general election for 14 November 1935 – the Prime Minister allowed Churchill to comment on some CID memoranda concerning national defense. Concerning air power, Churchill became unyielding in arguing for expanded funding, better efforts by the Air Staff, the training of 'high-class military pilots', and the planning and construction of new aerodromes.[75] Churchill did not ignore the state of the army or the Royal Navy in his efforts to foster expanded and strengthened armed forces.[76] However, the RAF had pride of place in his thinking. The advent of the Abyssinian crisis crystallized his views. As pointed out above, until early in the 1930s, he had never been an advocate of active involvement on the continent to maintain the balance of power – for him, the Empire stood as the *raison d'être* of British great-power status.[77] But if he began to muse sporadically about the efficacy of the balance in 1934, he embraced it by the late summer of 1935. 'Mussolini's Italy may be quite different to that of the Great War', he told Hoare in August. 'The only safe ruling is to provide superior material forces easily concentratable and if our sailors are better that is a make-weight.'[78] His goal involved keeping Anglo-Italian relations on an even keel to maintain the balance against possible German pretensions – beyond rearming, Hitler had thus far conducted a relatively quiescent foreign policy. In this respect, the League might provide a forum for resolving the crisis. As he remarked to Vansittart: 'It seems to me the only chance of avoiding the destruction of Italy as a powerful and friendly factor in Europe.'[79]

As 1936 began, and as Baldwin's political position became impregnable because of the National government's victory in the November 1935 General Election, Churchill's conception of British strategy and that of the National government were essentially at one: increase the strength of the armed forces and rely on the balance of power to preserve stability on the continent. The difference between Churchill and the government lay with the speed of British rearmament. At the base of this difference resided Churchill's personal political ambitions. Even before the election, he and his supporters looked to pressure Baldwin and Chamberlain, who had emerged as Baldwin's successor as Conservative leader and Prime Minister, to create a Ministry of Defence with a single minister. 'On 2 June', he learnt in September 1935 from the influential editor of the *Observer*, J. L. Garvin, 'I gave Baldwin the terse memorandum urging him to make you the creator of Air Parity which by a grand effort – with our financial resources and unemployed – could be done in a year, giving us time to make the rest secure and to *re*make the Navy.'[80] In late 1935 and early 1936, private lobbying became public in part when the former Chief of the Air Staff, Lord Trenchard, criticized the COS in the *The Times* for being unable to make decisions on essential issues of defense.[81] Added to increasing public concern over the need to improve British defense, in which Sir Basil Liddell Hart, *The Times'* military correspondent, supported Trenchard, the matter entered Parliament. On Valentine's Day 1936, the Commons debated a private member's bill on reorganizing defense.[82] The bill never came to a vote, but it proved to be a catalyst within the government to resolve this pressing matter. For more than a month, Baldwin, Chamberlain, and a clutch of senior civil service advisers had considered the matter. Taking the point for those who opposed the creation of a Minister of Defence – the service ministries did not want their influence diminished – Hankey argued for 'defense co-ordination' rather than a new department of state. He won the day with a proposal that a Deputy Chairman of the CID be appointed and be responsible to the Prime Minister; that he chair the CID and DPR in the Prime Minister's absence; and that he have other duties like chairing the COS.[83] This formed the basis of the 24 February decision to create the new post of Minister of Defence Co-ordination: his essential function would involve managing British rearmament, especially arms production, supply, and improving armed forces manpower.[84] Although one critic has characterized this new position as a 'modest' reform,[85] it was more. It gave British rearmament central direction within the government.

Baldwin had no difficulty in keeping Churchill out of this new office. That the Prime Minister saw the importance of the position came with him trying to get Chamberlain to take it, Chamberlain refused. Baldwin then found his man: Sir Thomas Inskip, the Attorney-General. A former cabinet secretary told a friend when it was clear that Churchill would be passed over: 'Those who desired Winston will be disappointed . . . '.[86] But Baldwin would never have Churchill in his cabinet; thus Churchill could only content himself with sniping at what he saw as both the continuing slow pace of rearmament and apparent strategic weaknesses. He put his thoughts in this regard before Hankey in April 1936.[87] Churchill felt that Inskip's mandate as determined by the cabinet seemed misdirected. Inskip would be bogged down in the minutiae of supply – 'Mr Churchill's main criticism was on [Inskip's] assumption of the Chair of the Principal Supply Officers Sub-Committee.' When Hankey enquired about Churchill's vision of the new minister's role, he learnt that it 'should be confined to questions of general policy, such as bombs versus battleships, the value of Russia as an ally, and so forth'. Churchill's prescription for improving British forces now involved the formation of a Ministry of Supply or Ministry of Munitions. He disavowed the post for himself, probably because it lay outside his grasp. Hankey's response to this idea constituted an irritating surprise for Churchill; Hankey pointed out that when Churchill had been concurrently the Air and War Secretaries immediately after 1918, he had successfully engineered the abolition of the wartime Ministry of Munitions.

Equally important for examining Churchill's strategic thinking at this juncture comes from the rest of this conversation in which he rambled over a range of policy considerations. As the Abyssinian crisis had still not ended, Churchill proposed that unless the Italians conformed to League proposals to return to peace, Britain should close the Suez Canal to Italian shipping and: 'Shortly before the presentation of the ultimatum we should notify the French of our intention, demand their co-operation, and intimate that failing that co-operation we should ourselves come to terms with Germany.' 'He talked in this connection', Hankey remarked incredulously, 'of our delivering heavy bombing attacks on Italy which showed he had not thought out how it was to be done, from what bases or with what aircraft.' In almost the same breath, Churchill then expounded on the German threat – which Hankey characterized as 'positive'. Churchill wanted:

> to hammer away at the League for a complete encirclement of Germany (I do not think he used the word 'encirclement'). The various countries of the Baltic, Holland, Belgium, France, Italy, Switzerland, Austria, the Balkan States, Russia and Poland must all as Members of the League be induced to make such an effort as to deter and, if necessary, stop an aggression by Germany.

But these positive thoughts were under-cut by another flight of strategic whimsy when Churchill proposed keeping a permanent Royal Navy force in the Baltic that would always be larger than the *Reichsmarine* and 'based in a Russian port of which we should obtain the use as a part of the Plan'. As far as Russia was concerned – Churchill had long been the implacable enemy of Bolshevism – Hankey noted: 'In view of the danger from Germany he has buried his violent anti-Russian complex of former days and is apparently a bosom friend of M. Maisky [the Russian ambassador at London].' Yet, Churchill also admitted to Hankey that he had been reading a book about domestic Russian conditions and seemed now to have 'the impression that Russia may perhaps present only a facade with nothing behind'.

One cannot help concluding that by early 1936, Churchill's strategic thinking stood at a distance from reality. He saw two threats to stability in Europe: Italy and Germany. He advocated the hardest of hard lines against Mussolini's regime; in taking such a line, he reckoned an Anglo-

German entente of some kind could be arranged if the French – heretofore his chief choice of ally – refused to fight against the Italians. Yet, Churchill pushed for the containment of German ambitions via all of Europe united through the medium of the League. This policy was to be tied to a naval arrangement with Bolshevik Russia, a state Churchill admitted might be a hollow shell. Admittedly, the National government suffered a number of diplomatic setbacks over the winter of 1935–36. An ill-starred and cynical Anglo-French initiative to resolve the Abyssinian crisis in Italy's favor had led to severe domestic criticism of the government, the fall of Hoare in December, and his replacement by Anthony Eden, who had a decided personal animus to Mussolini.[88] Then, in March 1936, with the British, French, and Italians enmeshed in that crisis, Hitler had remilitarized the Rhineland in another violation of the Treaty of Versailles.[89] Churchill had condemned this action in the House of Commons – and Neville Chamberlain believed that 'Winston made a constructive and helpful speech.'[90] Yet, despite these reverses, British policy remained coldly realistic. Military operations against Italy lay pregnant with danger, especially as a European crisis might embolden the Japanese in the Far East. A fight over the Rhineland did not have the backing of British public opinion, especially since Hitler made a convincing public case that the Rhineland was German territory and subject to the sovereign will of Berlin. London would have to re-examine its strategic options on the continent now that Italy was estranged – which Vansittart and the Foreign Office attempted to do.[91] Nonetheless, it would do so within the existing balance of power and within the realm of possibility. Basing a permanent Royal Navy Baltic fleet at a Russian port lay firmly outside that realm in April 1936. Perhaps most important given Churchill's constant theme in defense policy since at least 1933, the British armed forces needed to be built up and expanded further on sea, land, and air before London could even think of pursuing the kind of strategy envisaged in this conversation with Hankey.

As it happened, Churchill ceased to be an effective force in British politics for two years after mid-1936. In December 1935, King George V died, and the new king, Edward VIII, almost immediately indicated that he would not end his personal relationship with his mistress, a married American, Wallis Warfield Simpson. Baldwin, the rest of the Royal Family, the leadership of the Church of England, and the British 'Establishment' in general became increasingly discomforted at Edward's determination to keep Mrs Simpson at his side. When she divorced her husband in October and the King indicated his desire to marry her – a violation of Church of England teachings about marriage and divorce – the matter created a constitutional predicament.[92] Churchill chose to support the King.[93] Like his earlier differences with the Conservative Party leadership over the RAF and Indian 'home rule', this decision severely undermined his position in Parliament, made weaker his standing in the Conservative Party, and isolated him further from Baldwin and senior ministers like Neville Chamberlain. His career went into eclipse – in the interim, Edward VIII abdicated the throne in favor of his younger brother; more important, in May 1937, Baldwin retired and Chamberlain became leader of the Conservative Party and Prime Minister.

During the first year of his premiership, Chamberlain set his mark on British foreign and defense policy by overturning the reliance on the balance; he looked instead to 'the double policy of rearmament and better relations with Germany and Italy'. In terms of the former, Chamberlain's new government, through Inskip, undertook a major defense review. Examining the changing international situation, Inskip won cabinet approval in February 1938 that defense spending by 1941 would now have to total £1,650 million.[94] He underscored the need to weigh economic well-being with effective armed force. The cabinet agreed, deciding that defense programs already approved would not be touched, while those accepted in principle were open to Treasury scrutiny. The army was the big loser: its continental role would be abandoned. Imperial defense had a greater priority and, besides, the French supposedly no longer envisioned a British continental commitment.[95] When considering that the modified first DRC spending proposals contemplated extra spending of £50 million by 1939, the Chamberlain government's defense review produced a total 3,300 per cent higher. This sum represented the maximum amount the armed forces could spend while the government looked to turn to pressing domestic issues.

The other half of Chamberlain's 'double policy'– better relations with the dictator powers – embraced 'appeasement'. By early 1938, the changing international situation that underpinned the Inskip Report revolved, first, around the emergence of an Italo-German 'axis' on the continent with implications for the Mediterranean and, second, Japan's attack beginning in July 1937 on China south of the Great Wall that portended much for the Far East. In these calculations, COS appreciations played an important role.[96] Britain could fight and win in a war with any one of the three dictator powers; however, it could not do so when confronting two or more. Therefore, Chamberlain's concept of appeasement involved removing points of friction with Germany, Italy, and Japan that did not endanger British interests. However, there were limits to which Britain could or should go. Improved and expanded armed forces were designed to deter Berlin, Rome, and Tokyo from going too far, demanding too much. The 'danger period' that Chamberlain earlier mentioned was the length of time it was going to take Britain to rearm to the levels ultimately determined by Inskip. To ensure his new diplomatic course – which also meant that Downing Street rather than the Foreign Office dominated in policy-making – Chamberlain successfully removed Vansittart as Foreign Office permanent under-secretary and, with Eden, replaced him with the pliable Sir Alexander Cadogan.[97]

The course of Chamberlain's foreign policy in Europe from the summer of 1937 and March 1939 allowed Churchill to rehabilitate himself politically. In each of the major crises that mark this period – the German absorption of Austria in March 1938; the September 1938 crisis resolved at the Munich conference when Britain and France allowed Germany to take the Sudetenland from Czechoslovakia; and the German occupation of the rump of Czechoslovakia in March 1939[98] – the appeasement of Hitler seemed only to whet Nazi Germany's territorial appetite. Over Austria and the Sudetenland, Hitler argued that he had only brought ethnic Germans into the Reich; however, with the occupation of the Czech rump, non-Germans found themselves brutally made German subjects. Hitler had violated the Munich agreement. Within his own government, Chamberlain had difficulties. After Munich, his new Foreign Secretary, Lord Halifax, became increasingly uncomfortable with appeasement.[99] He also faced some high-profile defections. In February 1938, Eden resigned as Foreign Secretary because of the Prime Minister's meddling; then, because of what he saw as the sell-out of Czechoslovakia at Munich, Alfred Duff Cooper quit as First Lord of the Admiralty.[100] Because Churchill continued to criticise the government's foreign policy, these dissidents gravitated toward him, as did other Conservative backbench critics. It followed that when the Germans occupied Prague and appeasement's failure to maintain order became clear, Churchill emerged as the increasingly prominent chief critic of Chamberlain and his policies.

The point to consider is that initially – beginning with Germany's annexation of Austria – Churchill's criticism of government policy seemed designed more to embarrass Chamberlain than to offer an effective strategic alternative:

> Our affairs have come to such a pass that there is no escape without running risks. On every ground of prudence as well as of duty I urge His Majesty's Government to proclaim a renewed, revivified, unflinching adherence to the Covenant of the League of Nations. What is there ridiculous about collective security.[101]

There was nothing ridiculous about League collective security; but it had been shown to be hollow over the Abyssinian crisis. Economic sanctions, the first phase of any collective action, would not work without the willingness of powerful non-League members, especially the United States, to support Geneva. A lack of US willingness in 1935 to join a League oil embargo had played a crucial role in the failure to restrain Italy.[102] Furthermore, should economic sanctions fail, 'collective security' in early 1938 meant that other powers, especially great ones, had to be willing to join with Britain in imposing military sanctions on Germany. France faced a major ministerial emergency at that moment; Churchill himself had been in Paris at the end of March 1938 when he recorded: 'How can they expect us to open these serious matters [respecting military cooperation] to Ministers who expect to quit at any moment.'[103] It follows that the League of Nations lacked the willingness and ability of important member powers and influential non-members to enforce peace. Lacking an effectual strategic base, therefore, Churchill's critique seemed designed more to belittle the Chamberlain government in the eyes of British public opinion.

After the Munich conference, apart from condemning the sellout of Czechoslovakia, Churchill's public stance respecting national strategy involved building up the armed forces:

> I have been casting about to see how measures can be taken to protect us from the advance of the Nazi Power, and to secure those forms of life which are so dear to us. What is the sole method that is open? The sole method that is open is for us to regain our old island independence by acquiring that supremacy in the air which we were promised, that security in our air defenses which we were assured we had, and thus to make ourselves an island once again.[104]

As just indicated, these sentiments constituted his public stance: returning to his old view of Britain as an island fortress and allowing the continental powers to fend for themselves. Out of the public glare, he flew to Paris on an unsuccessful private mission to galvanize French opponents of 'the policy of peace'.[105] The two responses to Munich were linked. His discussions with French opponents of Munich, tied to the constitutional instability of the Third Republic he witnessed in March, showed the impossibility of a firm Anglo-French stance against Germany. But here, too, Churchill was at little distance from Chamberlain and his supporters. France seemed an unreliable reed on which to tie a firm British response to Germany. The National government had committed itself to further – and massive – rearmament by adopting the Inskip Report. The difficulty lay in the fact that that rearmament had only just begun.[106] Chamberlain's 'danger period' had not yet passed; thus, Munich offered the chance for long-term peace. Hitler, after all, had promised that he had no more territorial ambitions. Despite Churchill's opposition, Duff Cooper's resignation, and even

Halifax's suspicion that appeasement had flaws, British public opinion seemed supportive of the Prime Minister's efforts.[107] Churchill gained some strength in his opposition to Chamberlain, but he still seemed a voice in the wilderness in October 1938.

German occupation on the rump of Czechoslovakia proved a watershed. For all those who had subscribed to appeasement, Hitler's move meant the sudden death of Chamberlain's diplomatic strategy. Perhaps the best assessment came from Cadogan's pen: 'I must say it is turning out – at present – as Van[sittart] predicted and as I never believed it would.'[108] Although the Prime Minister seems to have held a residual belief that appeasement might be resurrected, his cabinet, the Conservative backbenches, and most of British public opinion demanded a different strategy. In practice, a single policy – deterrence – replaced the double one. Relying on rearmament more than ever, the Chamberlain government looked to organize the continental powers to contain German and Italian zeal. At the end of March, Chamberlain's government combined with Paris to guarantee the sovereignty of Poland, to which Hitler's interest now turned; and, when Mussolini annexed Albania on 7 April, they followed this with guarantees for Romania and Greece.[109] In May, conscription was introduced for the first time in peacetime Britain.[110] This decision derived from the need to commit ground forces to the continent to show that Britain would support France in the event of a German attack. The further pursuit of allies to facilitate Anglo-French containment of Germany came to rest on Bolshevik Russia.

> On the public platform after the German occupation of Prague, Churchill took the tack: Nothing with which Napoleon threatened England is half as intimate or direct as the destruction and ordeal which would fall upon this country should we be involved in a modern war. I think it very remarkable that this House of Commons . . . is ready quite calmly and resolutely, and not in any mood of excitement – far from it – to accept the perils with which we may be confronted, with a feeling that, God helping, we can do no other.[111]

Politically, his remarks were astute. He supported government efforts to meet the German threat, he sought to calm fears, and he believed – as Chamberlain and his advisers did – that war might be avoided. The Polish, Romanian, and Greek guarantees indicated the limits beyond which the Germans and their Italian ally could not go with impunity. Likewise, the search for allies to contain the Axis powers in Europe showed a British resolve to meet the threat to European stability. At the base of this new British strategy resided rearmament. The challenge in this regard derived from the fact that the timetable posited by Inskip had yet to be met and, indeed, there were problems in meeting those initial deadlines for 1939.[112]

On 27 March 1939, two weeks after the occupation of Prague and just as the British and French guaranteed Polish sovereignty, Churchill committed his grand-strategic ideas to paper and circulated them to a small circle of influential men, including Chamberlain.[113] It embodied a cold calculation of gain and loss. Given the limited size of the British army – conscription had not yet come – and the need for imperial garrisoning, the Royal Navy would play a major role should war break out with Germany and Italy. The North and Baltic Seas, plus the Mediterranean, should be the principal theater of operations. The Royal Navy could keep Atlantic sea lanes open and keep the *Reichsmarine* in the Baltic Sea; concurrent air attacks on the Kiel Canal would make 'that side door useless'. Working with the French, Royal Navy command of the Mediterranean would isolate Italian ground forces in Libya and Abyssinia. With simultaneous military operations against Germany to maintain the balance, 'a series of swift and striking victories in this theatre, which might be obtainable in the early weeks of the war, would have a most healthy and helpful bearing upon the main struggle with Germany. Nothing should stand between us and these results, both naval and military'.

Churchill saw the Far East offering especial difficulties. With the Royal Navy concentrated west of Suez, he thought that the 'farthest point we can hold in the conditions imagined is Singapore'. Nonetheless, other factors reenforced imperial security in the region. Engaged in a border war in northern Manchuria with Bolshevik Russia at that moment, Japan could not exploit a European crisis to its advantage. Even when peace returned, Tokyo would wait until it knew the outcome of a European conflict. Yet, should the Japanese decide to take advantage of Britain's commitment to Europe, they could only 'take Hong Kong and Shanghai; and clean us out of all our interests there'. Singapore, Churchill surmised, could resist a Japanese onslaught: 'Over these two thousand miles of salt water, Japan would have to send the bulk of her fleet, escort at least sixty thousand men in transports in order to effect a landing, and begin a siege which would end only in disaster if the Japanese sea-communications were cut at any stage.' Finally, Britain could probably count on US intervention should Japan seek to reorganize the Far Eastern balance of power to its advantage. In Churchill's estimation, Britain's global position was not desperate; protecting it required the resolute implementation of national-security policies that tied together the European balance of power with the defense of the Empire. In this calculation, the Americans remained critical. They would be fundamental to secure British trade routes across the Atlantic to guarantee access to the material resources of the United States; as an extra, should Washington decide to thwart Tokyo's ambitions south of the equator in the Pacific, a rough balance of power could be maintained until Britain could direct its energies eastward.

In the complicated diplomacy of the summer of 1939, of course, Hitler proved a formidable adversary. The competition to win Bolshevik Russian support – for Anglo-French containment of Germany, on one side, and non-aggression, on the other – saw Berlin triumph. With a high order of *realpolitik*, the German Chancellor buried his virulent anti-communism and purchased a Nazi–Soviet non-aggression pact on 23 August with the currency of eastern European territory coveted by Moscow.[114] Britain and its French ally could not pay, a function of the Polish guarantee. Eight days after signing the Russo-German agreement, Nazi Germany invaded Poland and the Second World War began. Always the politician on the make, Churchill spoke in the House of Commons on 3 September not about the need to go to war to defend Britain's narrow national interests. Instead, he waxed eloquently that: 'This is no war of domination or imperial aggrandizement or material gain; no war to shut any country out of its sunlight and means of progress. It is a war, viewed in its inherent quality, to establish, on impregnable rocks, the rights of the individual, and it is a war to establish and revive the stature of man.'[115] That same day, Chamberlain restructured his cabinet and offered Churchill the post of First Lord of the Admiralty. Churchill was back at the highest levels of government. He had arrived there as a result of carving for himself the position as chief critic of a range of his own party's policies for almost a decade, especially foreign and defense policy.

Churchill's ten years on the backbenches following the Conservative government's defeat in June 1929 – what his official biographer laments as Churchill's 'wilderness years'[116] – resulted from his own follies, primarily his antipathy to Baldwin and Neville Chamberlain. They were men who blocked his rise to the premiership, and he used every device at his finger tips to undermine both their authority and credibility in the country at large and in the Conservative Party in particular. Whether the issue at hand was Indian 'home rule', support for the peculiar marital ambitions of the King, or the nature and purpose of foreign and defense policy, Churchill looked always for political arguments that would enhance his chances for high office. Given the deleterious impact of the Second World War on Britain's position as a world power – indeed, in 1939, the only world power – the subsequent historical debate about the strategic basis of British foreign policy in the 1930s had special significance. After the war, Churchill used his memoirs to castigate mercilessly Baldwin, Chamberlain, and other of his political opponents; as 'the greatest Englishman of his time', his words had weight for a generation. Although his interpretation of the foreign and defense policy debates of the 1930s have been seriously questioned, his opinions still have influence.

Yet, it remains that careful examination of the *ex post facto* justification of Churchill's actions in meeting the German threat, and his disparaging of those who held power in the 1930s, shows that his is a flawed history – a self-serving, self-promoting dialectic – obscuring more than it illuminates. No one would dispute that Churchill held honest views about the weaknesses of the British armed forces after 1933; nor is there a question about his desire to ensure that the country and Empire had a foreign policy that, through its strategic objectives, best protected British interests. However, Baldwin and Chamberlain and the others responsible for British foreign and defense policy shared these same views and desires. In the period before Chamberlain became Prime Minister and instituted his defense review, the main difference between Churchill and the National government concerned the pace of rearmament. The DRC in its various incarnations showed the government's desire to meet, first, defense deficiencies and, later, the need to rearm significantly. It did so within the strictures placed upon it by the financial constraints of the Great Depression. It also did so with a sound and effective diplomatic strategy – the balance of power – that gave the cabinet and the Foreign Office flexibility in dealing with Germany. After the Inskip report, differences revolved around how to respond to an increasingly ambitious Germany.

In all of this, Churchill consistently exaggerated threats. More than this hyperbole, his strategic prescriptions bore little connexion with reality. In the first years of Hitler's regime, Churchill propounded isolation from the continent, with an armed Britain cocooned within the Empire. As a League of Nations member, a signatory of the Locarno pact, and a supporter of the World Disarmament Conference, the National government could adhere to such solitude to its peril. Then when the situation began to change, because German policy had changed, Churchill gradually came to support involvement on the continent in alliance with France – and, later, the League. When Hitler exploited the situation presented to him in Austria and Czechoslovakia after early 1938 – and perhaps as early as his remilitarization of the Rhineland – Churchill's strategic prescription shifted again: a return to an armed island. When looking beyond grand strategy to its component parts, Churchill lacked perspective. He was consistent in wanting a strong and capable RAF, but in almost the same breath to threaten aggressive Italy with bombing and seek French support by threatening to align with Germany and, then, advocate containing Germany with every European power, including Italy and Bolshevik Russia, was to invite a serious questioning of his prescription. In 1938, when he demanded the government embark on a policy of collective security, he knew full well that internal problems in France precluded such an eventuality. Even his March 1939 prescription had major flaws: over-estimating British military capabilities and assuming that the United States would support Britain in the Far East. Hence, while Churchill's desire to improve the British armed forces and construct a foreign-policy strategy to protect adequately British interests can be lauded, the means by which he worked to achieve these ends lacked a grasp of reality. His strategy was that of a politician-strategist; it was bent and twisted – and was sometimes contradictory – by his desire to use it as a political weapon to attack his leaders. There is certainly much to criticize in the foreign and defense policy record of the various British governments of the 1930s. However, there is more to criticize in Winston Churchill's contemporary and historical assertions about the flawed strategic base of government policy.

NOTES

Unless otherwise stated the place of publication is London.

1 House of Commons Speech, 5 October 1938, in R. Rhodes James, ed., *Churchill Speaks, 1897–1963: Collected Speeches in War and Peace* (New York: Garland, 1998), p. 661.

2 Two of the best studies are R. A. C. Parker, *Chamberlain and Appeasement: British Policy and the Coming of the Second World War* (Basingstoke: Macmillan, 1993); and his *Churchill and Appeasement* (Basingstoke: Macmillan 2000). Cf. R. J. Caputi, *Neville Chamberlain and Appeasement* (Selinsgrove, PA: Susquehanna University Press, 2000); M. Gilbert and R. Gott, *The Appeasers* (Weidenfeld & Nicolson, 1963); K. Robbins, *Appeasement*, 2nd edn (Oxford: Blackwell, 1997); W. R. Rock, *British Appeasement in the 1930s* (Arnold, 1977); P. Shen, *The Age of Appeasement: The Evolution of British Foreign Policy in the 1930s* (Phoenix Mill, UK: Sutton, 1999); G. Stewart, *Burying Caesar: Churchill, Chamberlain and the Battle for the Tory Party* (Weidenfeld & Nicolson, 1999).

3 For example, see B. J. C. McKercher, 'Old Diplomacy and New: The Foreign Office and Foreign Policy, 1919–1939', in M. Dockrill and B. McKercher, eds, *Diplomacy and World Power: Studies in British Foreign Policy, 1890–1950* (Cambridge: Cambridge University Press, 1996), pp. 79–114; and M. L. Roi, *Alternative to Appeasement: Sir Robert Vansittart and Alliance Diplomacy, 1934–1937* (Westport, CT: Praeger, 1997). Cf. M. L. Roi and B. J. C. McKercher, '"Ideal" and "Punch-Bag": Conflicting Views of the Balance of Power and Their Influence on Interwar British Foreign Policy', *Diplomacy and Statecraft*, vol. 12 (2001), pp. 47–78.

4 See N. Gibbs, *Grand Strategy*, vol. I: *Rearmament Policy* (HMSO, 1976); B. J. C. McKercher, 'From Disarmament to Rearmament: British Civil–Military Relations and the Policy-Making Process', *Defence Studies*, vol. 1 (2001), pp. 21–48.

5 Quoted in I. Colvin, *The Chamberlain Cabinet: How Meetings in 10 Downing*

Street, 1937–1939, Led to the Second World War – Told for the First Time from the Cabinet Papers (New York: Taplinger, 1971), p. 46.

6 See Simon Bourette-Knowles, 'The Global Micawber: Sir Robert Vansittart, the Treasury, and the Global Balance of Power, 1933–1935', pp. 91–121; B. J. C. McKercher, 'The Last Old Diplomat: Sir Robert Vansittart and the Verities of British Foreign Policy', pp. 1–38; M. L. Roi, 'From the Stresa Front to the Triple Entente: Sir Robert Vansittart, the Abyssinian Crisis, and the Containment of Germany', all in *Diplomacy and Statecraft*, vol. 6 (1995), pp. 61–90.

7 'Re-Arming', 27 November 1933, *Daily Herald*, 10. Cf. Anon., 'Policy and Armaments', *New Statesman*, 9 (16 March 1935), pp. 372–3; C. R. Buxton, *The Alternative to War: A Programme for Statesmen* (1936); A. Henderson (Labour Party Pamphlet No. 15), *Arbitration, Security and Disarmament* (1934); H. M. Swanwick, *New Wars for Old* (1934);

8 H. R. G. Greaves (New Fabian Research Bureau), *The Prevention of War, or Labour and the League of Nations* (1934); P. J. Noel-Baker, 'The Future of the Collective System', in Geneva Institute of International Relations, *Problems of Peace*, 10th Series (1934), pp. 178–98; A. Zimmern, 'Organize the Peace World', *Political Quarterly*, vol. 5 (1934), pp. 153–66.

9 See N. J. Crowson, 'Conservative Parliamentary Dissent Over Foreign Policy during the Premiership of Neville Chamberlain: Myth or Reality?', *Parliamentary History*, vol. 14 (1995), pp. 315–36; N. Thompson, *The Anti-Appeasers: Conservative Opposition to Appeasement in the 30s* (Oxford: Oxford University Press, 1971); A. Turner, 'Austen Chamberlain, *The Times*, and the Question of Revision of the Treaty of Versailles in 1933', *European History Quarterly*, vol. 18 (1988), pp. 51–70. Cf. P. Beck, 'Politicians versus Historians: Lord Avon's 'Appeasement Battle' Against 'Lamentably, Appeasement-minded' Historians', *Twentieth Century British History*, vol. 9 (1998), pp. 396–419.

10 For instance, Austen Chamberlain to Hilda, his sister, 4 July 1936, AC (Austen Chamberlain MSS, University Library, Birmingham University, Birmingham) 5/1/739; Rothermere to Churchill, 23 Feb. 1936, CHAR (Winston Churchill (Chartwell) MSS, Churchill College, Cambridge) 2/266A.

11 See W. S. Churchill, *India* (Butterworth, 1931); idem., *Great Contemporaries* (Butterworth, 1937); idem., *Arms and the Covenant: Speeches* (Harrap, 1938); idem., *Step by Step, 1936–1939* (Butterworth, 1939); and 'Debate on Defence. We have to abandon our Foreign Affairs Committee as Winston is to make a great speech. He does.': in Nicholson (Labour MP) diary, 12 November 1936, cited in H. Nicholson, *Diaries and Letters 1930–1939* (Collins, 1966), p. 278.

12 'Cato' [Michael Foot, Frank Owen, and Peter Howard] *Guilty Men* (Gollancz, 1940).

13 W. S. Churchill, *The Second World War*, vol. I: *The Gathering Storm* (Cassell, 1948). The 'theme' is stated on the frontispiece.

14 For example, A. Duff Cooper, *Old Men Forget* (Ruper Hart-Davis, 1953); M. George, *The Warped Vision: British Foreign Policy, 1933–1939* (Pittsburgh, PA: University of Pittsburgh Press, 1965).; L. B. Namier, *Diplomatic Prelude, 1938–1939* (Macmillan, 1948).

15 A. J. P. Taylor, *The Origins of the Second World War* (Hamish Hamilton, 1961). See G. Martel, ed., *The Origins of the Second World War Reconsidered: The A. J. P. Taylor Debate after Twenty-five Years* (Boston, MA: Unwin Hyman, 1986).

16 See S. Aster, *1939: The Making of the Second World War* (New York: Simon & Schuster, 1973); D. Dilks, 'Appeasement Revisited', *University of Leeds Review*, 15

(1972); D. Cameron Watt, 'The Breakdown of the European Security System 1930–1939', in Comité Internationale des Sciences Historiques/American Historical Association, *Papers Presented to the XIVth International Congress of Historical Sciences* (San Francisco, CA, 1975); G. L. Weinberg, *The Foreign Policy of Hitler's Germany*, vol. I: *Diplomatic Revolution in Europe, 1933–36* (Chicago, IL: University of Chicago Press, 1970).

17 In this respect, see J. Charmley, *Chamberlain and the Lost Peace* (Hodder & Stoughton, 1989); and idem., *Churchill, The End of Glory: A Political Biography* (Hodder & Stoughton, 1993). While some of Charmley's conclusions are weak – for instance, that Churchill's Britain should have aligned with Nazi Germany after 1940 to fight Bolshevik Russia to avoid not only its ultimate loss of global power but subservience to the United States – he is insightful about Churchill. For a corrective of Charmley, see D. Reynolds, 'Churchill the Appeaser? Between Hitler, Roosevelt and Stalin in World War Two', in Dockrill and McKercher, eds, *Diplomacy and World Power*, pp. 197–220. Then cf. L. W. Fuchser, 1st edn (New York 1982); F. McDonough, *Neville Chamberlain and Appeasement: A Study in the Politics of History Neville Chamberlain, Appeasement and the British Road to War* (Manchester: Manchester University Press, 1998); Stewart, *Burying Caesar*; D. Cameron Watt, *How War Came: The Immediate Origins of the Second World War, 1938–1939* (New York: Viking, 1989).

18 M. Gilbert, 'Churchill and the European Idea', in R. A. C. Parker, ed., *Winston Churchill: Studies in Statesmanship* (Brassey's, 1996), p. 208. Cf. M. Gilbert, *Winston S. Churchill*, vol. V: *The Prophet of Truth* (Heinemann, 1977); I. S. Wood, *Churchill* (New York: Palgrave, 2000), pp. 73–93.

19 D. Cameron Watt, 'The Nature of the Foreign-Policy-Making Élite in Britain', in idem., *Personalities and Policies: Studies in the formulation of British Foreign Policy in the Twentieth Century* (Longman, 1965), pp. 1–15.

20 House of Commons Speech, 13 April 1933, in Rhodes James, *Churchill Speaks*, p. 563.

21 C. D. Krull and B. J. C. McKercher, 'The Press, Public Opinion, Arms Limitation, and Government Policy in Britain, 1932–1934: Some Preliminary Observations' (forthcoming).

22 See. H. G. Bickert, 'Die Vermittlerolle Grossbritanniens während der Reaparationskonferenz von Lausanne 1932', *Aus Politik und Zeitgeschichte*, supplement to *Das Parliament*, vol. 23 (1973), pp. 12–22; J. W. Wheeler-Bennett, *The Wreck of Reparations, Being the Political Background of the Lausanne Agreement, 1932* (Allen & Unwin, 1933).

23 See C. J. Kitching, *Britain and the Problem of International Disarmament, 1919–34* (London, New York: Routledge, 1999), 151–3; B. J. C. McKercher, *Transition of Power: Britain's Loss of Global Preeminence to the United States, 1930–1945* (Cambridge: Cambridge University Press, 1998), pp. 148–50.

24 House of Commons Speech, 14 March 1933, in Rhodes James, *Churchill Speaks*, pp. 557–62.

25 *Draft Convention Submitted by the United Kingdom Delegation* (16 Mar. 1933), LND (League of Nations Document, League of Nations Archives, Palais des Nations, Geneva) Conf.D.157.

26 S. Gopal, *The Viceroyalty of Lord Irwin, 1926–1931* (Oxford: Oxford University Press, 1957). Cf. *Report of the Indian Statutory Commission/Presented by the Secretary of State for the Home Department to Parliament by Command of His Majesty. May, 1930*, 2 vols (1930).

27 Gilbert, *Churchill*, vol. V, 464-84.
28 Churchill to Salisbury, 13 February 1933, in M. Gilbert, ed., *Winston S. Churchill*, vol. V, Companion Part 2, Documents: *The Wilderness Years* (Heinemann, 1981), p. 527.
29 S. R. Ball, *Baldwin and the Conservative Party: The Crisis of 1929-1931* (New Haven, CT: Yale University Press, 1988).
30 Ormsby-Gore (1st Commissioner of Works) to Churchill, 13 April 1933, in Gilbert, *Churchill*, vol. V, Companion Part 2, pp. 572-3.
31 For instance, 'Memorandum of a Meeting' (between Churchill and William Bridgeman, First Lord of the Admiralty, undated, but 18 Oct. 1927); Churchill to Bridgeman, 20 and 28 October 1927, all CHAR 18/44. Cf. J. R. Ferris, *Men, Money, and Diplomacy: The Evolution of British Strategic Policy, 1919-26* (Ithaca, NY: Cornell University Press, 1989), pp. 158-78.
32 Gibbs, *Grand Strategy*, pp. 55-9. Cf. Ferris, *Men, Money, and Diplomacy*, pp. 158-78; R. Rhodes James, *Churchill, A Study in Failure* (Weidenfeld, 1970), pp. 212-17. See also P. Silverman, 'The Ten Year Rule', *Journal of the Royal United Services Institute*, vol. 116 (1971), pp. 42-5; and responses from K. Booth, 'The Ten Year Rule: An Unfinished Debate', ibid., pp. 58-73; S. W. Roskill, 'The Ten Year Rule: The Historical Facts', *Journal of the Royal United Services Institute*, vol. 117 (1972), pp. 69-71.
33 For the National Government's own assessments, see 'Appendix II: Defence Services. Net Effective Expenditure, Years 1913-1934 (in £ millions)' in CID 'Material for Memorandum', undated (but early 1935), CAB (Cabinet Archives, Public Record Office, Kew) 21/392.

	Navy (£)	Army (£)	Air (excluding Civil Aviation) (£)	Total (£)
1926	48.9	35.4	14.8	99.1
1927	49.7	35.5	14.5	99.7
1928	48.7	32.5	15.5	96.7
1929	47.4	32.4	16.3	96.1
1930	43.6	31.4	16.9	91.9
1931	42.2	29.9	17.2	89.3
1932	41.2	27.8	16.3	85.3
1933 (estimated)	44.4	29.7	16.5	90.6

34 Gilbert, ed. *Churchill*, vol. V, p. 305.
35 House of Commons speech, 14 March 1933, in Rhodes James, *Churchill Speaks*, p. 559.
36 Watt, 'Élite'.
37 Churchill to Chamberlain, 23/25 February 1925, with enclosure, Chamberlain FO (Foreign Office Archives, Public Record Office, Kew) 800/257.
38 See Churchill memorandum (CP 189(27)), 29 June 1927, CAB 24/187; Cabinet Conclusion 43(27)1, plus Appendices, CAB 23/55; Beatty (former 1st Sea Lord) to Churchill, 14 July 1927, CHAR 2/152.
39 Apart from a private characterization of Hitler as a 'gangster' on 10 July 1933 (p. 627) and a public comment on the possibility of a plebiscite in the Saar on 23 February 1934 (p. 717, n.1), the companion volume of documents amassed by Churchill's official biographer for this period shows no consideration by his

subject of contemporary Germany from mid-April 1933 to July 1934. See Gilbert, *Churchill*, vol. V, companion 2, pp. 570–825. Gilbert has been exhaustive in collecting and publishing these documents.

40 See I. Kershaw, *Hitler*, vol. I: *1889–1936: Hubris* (Penguin, 1998), pp. 505–24.

41 Churchill, 'How I Would Procure Peace', *Daily Mail* (9 July 1934), quoted in Gilbert, *Churchill*, vol. V, companion 2, pp. 825–6, n.3. Cf. Gilbert, *Churchill*, vol. V, p. 550.

42 Churchill speech, 'The Causes of War', 16 November 1934, in Rhodes James, *Churchill Speaks*, pp. 586–9.

43 On the Churchill–Vansittart friendship: 'I am hurrying to answer the question that Tania's friend was asking about Daddy's closest friends. Except for Anthony Eden and of course Churchill[,] there were no really intimate friends . . . Winston was always about picking his brains and literally using all possible information.' In Lady Vansittart to her daughter, 11 March 1964, Vansittart MSS (Hoover Institution, Stanford University, Palo Alto, CA).

44 Sargent to Churchill, 13 November 1934, with enclosure, CHAR 2/229; Foreign Office to Churchill, 22 November 1934, enclosing 'Memorandum on German Rearmament', 22 November 1934, CAB 21/417.

45 COS papers on 'Imperial Defence Policy' (COS 306), 24 April 1933, enclosing memoranda from the Colonial Office, India Office, Home Office, CID, and Joint Oversea and Home Defence Committee; and COS papers on 'Imperial Defence Policy' (COS 307), 20 May 1933, enclosing Foreign Office 'Memorandum on the Foreign Policy of His Majesty's Government in the United Kingdom', 19 May 1933, both CAB 53/23. Cf. COS, 'Annual Review for 1932 by the Chiefs of Staff Sub-Committee' (COS 295), 23 February 1932, CAB 53/22.

46 'Terms of Reference' (DRC 1), 10 November 1933, CAB 16/109. Because of Hitler's actions at Geneva, the DRC received additional instructions to consider 'the point of view of their effect on German armaments' and 'stipulations . . . necessary from the point of view of the United Kingdom'; Hankey memorandum (DRC 4), 23 November 1933, with enclosures, in ibid.

47 For example, 'Minute by Sir R. Vansittart' (DC(M)(32) 117), 2 June 1934, CAB 27/510.

48 The rest of this paragraph is based on McKercher, 'Disarmament to Rearmament'. Cf. Gibbs, *Grand Strategy*, pp. 91–9; G. Post, Jr, *Dilemmas of Appeasement: British Deterrence and Defense, 1934–1937* (Ithaca, NY: Cornell University Press, 1993), pp. 32–8, 43–8; S.W. Roskill, *Naval Policy between the Wars*, vol. II: *The Period of Reluctant Rearmament, 1930–1939* (Collins, 1976), pp. 169–73; W. K. Wark, *The Ultimate Enemy: British Intelligence and Nazi Germany, 1933–1939* (Ithaca, NY: Cornell University Press, 1985), pp. 28–34.

49 See Vansittart minute, 22 February 1934, FO 371/18518/1830/1; Vansittart memorandum, 'The Future of Germany' (CP104(34)), 9 April 1934, CAB 16/111; Vansittart minute, 2 May 1934, FO 3371/18524/4153/1.

50 Vansittart to MacDonald, 21 February 1934, CAB 21/471.

51 'The Foreign Office has long endeavoured to make bricks without straw . . . In the present temper and material preparations not only of Europe, but of the world – Russia, the United States and Japan as well – British shrinkage will become the more apparent if it continues.' In 'Minute by Sir R. Vansittart' (DC(M)(32) 117), 2 June 1934, CAB 27/510.

52 House of Commons Speech, 28 November 1934, in Rhodes James, *Churchill Speaks*, pp. 589.

53 Later re-published in Churchill, *Great Contemporaries*, p. 268.
54 Cmd. 4827: *Statement Relating to Defence: Issued in Connexion with the House of Commons Debate on March 11, 1935*. Cf. Weinberg, *Hitler's Germany*, pp. 204–6.
55 Churchill to his wife, 8 March 1935, in Gilbert, *Churchill*, vol. V, companion Part 2, pp. 1107–8.
56 Churchill to Baldwin, 17 March 1935, in ibid., p. 1119.
57 'Notes of Anglo-German Conversations, held at the Chancellor's Palace, Berlin, on March 25 and 26, 1935', in Foreign Office, *British Documents on Foreign Policy*, Second Series, vol. XII (hereafter *DBFP*, Ser. 2, 12) (1972), pp. 703–46.
58 See Simon to MacDonald, 10 April 1935, Baldwin MSS (University Library, Cambridge University, Cambridge) 1; and Air Parity Sub-Committee 1st Report (CP 100(35)), 13 May 1935, CAB 24/255. Cf. COS 139th–144th Meetings, 9–29 Apr. 1935, CAB 53/5; Air Ministry memorandum, 'German Air Programme and Its Bearing on British Air Strength' (COS 373), 17 Apr. 1935, all CAB 53/24; Sub-Committee on Industrial Intelligence in Foreign Countries memorandum, 'German Aircraft Industry' (CID 1170B), 11 Apr. 1935, Air Staff memorandum, 'German Air Rearmament' (CID 1180B), 14 June 1935, all CAB 4/23.
59 The speech is quoted in Churchill, *Second World War*, vol. I, p. 121. Cf. Hankey minute to MacDonald, 2 May 1935, CAB 21/404, which discusses Parliament's view that Britain is 'in something of approximating to a state of emergency in Defence matters'.
60 Churchill telegram to his son, Randolph, 23 May 1935, in Gilbert, *Churchill*, vol. V, companion Part 2, p. 1180; Churchill, *Second World War*, vol. I, p. 121.
61 Gilbert, *Churchill*, vol. V, p. 147.
62 'Notes of Anglo-French-Italian Conversations held at the Palazzo Borromeo, Isola Bella, Stresa, from April 11 to 14, 1935', *DBFP*, Ser. 2, 12, pp. 862–912. See also Roi, *Vansittart*, pp. 77–82.
63 Pownall (CID) memorandum, 9 July 1935, CAB 16/112.
64 DRC meetings 13–14, 'Interim Report' (DRC 25), 24 Jul 1935, in ibid.
65 CC 40(35), 24 Jul 1935, CAB 23/82, DPR meeting 4, 29 July 1935, CAB 16/136.
66 Vansittart to Hoare, 9, 19 Aug. 1935, Hoare to Eden, 15 Sep. 1935, all Hoare FO 800/295.
67 DRC meetings 15–26 (3 Oct.–14 Nov. 1935), DRC 'Third Report' (DRC 37), 21 Nov. 1935, CAB 16/112.
68 'The soldiers, sailors and airmen are gradually beginning to show signs of no longer being the worst pacifists and defeatists in the country': Hoare to Eden, 17 Sep. 1935, Hoare FO 800/295.
69 'Summary of Conclusions and Recommendations', 'Third Report', pp. 38–44, CAB 16/112. Cf. War Office memorandum, 'Army Requirements' (DRC 28), 2 Oct. 1935, Air Ministry memorandum, 'Royal Air Force Requirements additional to the Expansion of First Line Strength for Home Defence' (DRC 30), 2 Oct. 1935, Admiralty memorandum, 'Naval Requirements' (DRC 33), 9 Oct. 1935, all in ibid. For balanced analysis of the report, see Gibbs, *Grand Strategy*, pp. 254–68; Post, *Dilemmas*, pp. 107–15.
70 DRC Meetings 14–18, 20, 22–24, CAB 16/112.
71 See Chamberlain to Churchill, 9 January 1935; Chamberlain and Churchill to MacDonald, 9 January 1935; Churchill minute, 28 January 1935, on Chamberlain minute, undated, to Churchill and Lindemann (Churchill adviser), all CHAR 2/243.
72 See ADR Meeting 1, CAB 16/132.

73 Churchill telegram, 26 April 1935, to Austen Chamberlain and other parliamentarians (Robert Horne, Lord Winterton, Lord Wolmer, Henry Page-Croft, General Seely Mottistone, Captain Guest, Lloyd George, Archibald Sinclair), CHAR 2/243. Cf. Churchill to Hankey, 29 April 1935, enclosing Churchill memorandum, 28 April 1935, CAB 21/419. Admittedly, he ignored Rothermere's wild claim that Germany had 20,000 planes by late April 1935; Rothermere to Churchill, 29 April 1935, CHAR 2/243.

74 Churchill to Winterton, 29 September 1935, in Gilbert, *Churchill*, vol. V, companion Part 2, p. 1272.

75 See House of Commons Speech, 31 May 1935, in Rhodes James, *Churchill Speaks*, 598–600; Churchill memorandum, 'Air Defence' (ADR 21), 23 July 1935, CAB 16/133; Churchill to Cunliffe-Lister (Air Secretary), 16 August 1935, with enclosure, in Gilbert, *Churchill*, vol. V, companion Part 2, 1233–8; Churchill notes (2) on CID Paper 1205B, both 9 Dec. 1935, CHAR 2/244.

76 For example, Churchill to Hoare, 25 August 1935, Hoare FO 800/295; Churchill to Chatfield, 21 September 1935, in Gilbert, *Churchill*, vol. V, companion 2, pp. 1264–5.

77 For insight, see B. J. C. McKercher, 'Churchill, the European Balance of Power and the USA', in R. A. C. Parker, ed., *Winston Churchill: Studies in Statesmanship* (1995), pp. 42–64.

78 Churchill to Hoare, 29 August 1935, CHAR 2/244.

79 Churchill to Vansittart, 28 September 1935, in Gilbert, *Churchill*, vol. V, companion Part 2, pp. 1271–2.

80 Garvin to Churchill, 3 September 1935, in Gilbert, *Churchill*, vol. V, companion Part 2, pp. 1255–6. Emphasis in original.

81 Trenchard to Hankey, 19 December 1935, 21 and 27 February 1936, and the responses, 21 December 1935, 18 and 26 February 1936, all CAB 21/424.

82 The debate showed there must be 'some concession for a Minister of Defence': Hankey to Warren Fisher, 14 February 1936, CAB 21/424. The best account is Post, Jr, *Dilemmas of Appeasement*, pp. 175–82.

83 Warren Fisher minute, 'Minister of Defence', to Baldwin, 13 January 1936, CAB 24/424; Hankey Memorandum on 'Defence Co-ordination' (CP30(36)), 7 February 1936, CAB 24/259. Hankey minute, 'Defence Co-ordination: A Suggested Compromise', to Baldwin, 14 February 1936, CAB 21/424.

84 CC 9(36)1, CAB 23/82; 'Report of the Ministerial Committee' (CP51(36)), 20 February 1936; 'Revised Report of the Cabinet Committee' (CP51(36) (Revise)), n.d., both CAB 24/260.

85 Post, *Dilemmas*, p. 182.

86 Jones to a friend, 21 February 1936, in Gilbert, *Churchill*, vol. V, companion Part 3, p. 55.

87 The rest of this paragraph and the next are based on Hankey 'Note of a Conversation with Mr Winston Churchill on Sunday, 19th April, 1936', CAB 21/435. He sent copies to Inskip and Sir Alfred Duff Cooper, the War Secretary, among others.

88 See S. U. Chukumba, *The Big Powers against Ethiopia: Anglo-French-American Maneuvers during the Italo-Ethiopian Dispute, 1934–1938* (Washington, DC, 1977); M. Roi, '"A Completely Immoral and Cowardly Attitude": The British Foreign Office, American Neutrality, and the Hoare–Laval Plan', *Canadian Journal of History*, vol. 29 (1994), pp. 331–51.

89 See Emmerson, *The Rhineland Crisis, 7 March 1936: A Study in Multilateral*

Diplomacy (Ames, IA: University of Iowa Press, 1977); D. C. Watt, 'German Plans for the Reoccupation of the Rhineland: A Note', *Journal of Contemporary History*, vol. 1 (1966), pp. 193–9.

90 Chamberlain diary, 10 March 1936, in Gilbert, *Churchill*, vol. V, companion Part 3, p. 66.

91 See Roi, 'Stresa Front to the Triple Entente'.

92 See Lord Beaverbrook, *The Abdication of King Edward VIII* (Hamish Hamilton, 1966); P. Brendon, *The Dark Valley: A Panorama of the 1930s* (Jonathan Cape, 2000); B. Inglis, *Abdication* (1966); K. Middlemas and J. Barnes, *Baldwin: A Biography* (Weidenfeld & Nicolson, 1969), pp. 1018–51.

93 Gilbert, *Churchill*, vol. V, pp. 809–31; Rhodes James, *Churchill Speaks*, pp. 344–55.

94 See Inskip 'Interim Report on Defence Expenditure in Future Years' (CP 316(37)), 15 December 1937, CAB 24/273; Inskip 'Report on Defence Expenditure in Future Years' (CP 24(38)), 8 February 1938, CAB 24/274; CC 5(38)9, 16 February 1938, CAB 23/92. Cf. Warren Fisher memorandum, 'Defence: Sir T. Inskip's New Report', 18 Dec 1937; Warren Fisher minute, 15 February 1938, both Warren Fisher (British Library of Economic and Political Science, London), p. 1.

95 See the discerning M. L. Dockrill, *British Establishment Perspectives on France, 1936–40* (Macmillan, 1999), pp. 77–107.

96 For instance, COS 'Comparison of the Strength of Great Britain with that of Other Nations as at January, 1938' (CP 296(37)), 12 November 1937, CAB 24/273; COS memorandum, 'Planning for War with Germany' (COS 644JP), 13 November 1937, CAB 53/34; COS memorandum, 'Mediterranean, Middle East and North-East Africa Appreciation' (COS 691), 21 February 1938, sections 32, 162, CAB 53/37. Cf. COS meetings 216, 221, both CAB 53/8.

97 McKercher, *Transition*, p. 249. Cf. McKercher, 'Last Old Diplomat'.

98 See Aster, *1939*; Dilks, 'Appeasement Revisited'; P. M. Kennedy, 'The Tradition of Appeasement in British Foreign Policy, 1865–1939', *British Journal of International Studies*, vol. 2 (1976), pp. 195–215; McDonough, *Chamberlain*, pp. 45–91; Watt, *How War Came*, pp. 76–161; G. L. Weinberg, *A World at Arms: A Global History of World War II* (Cambridge: Cambridge University Press, 1994), pp. 6–47.

99 A. Roberts, *'The Holy Fox': A Biography of Lord Halifax* (Macmillan, 1991), pp. 131–48.

100 D. Carlton, *Anthony Eden: A Biography* (Allen Lane, 1981), pp. 124–33; Duff Cooper, *Old Men Forget*.

101 House of Commons Speech, 14 March 1938, in Rhodes James, *Churchill Speaks*, p. 644.

102 See Ashton-Gwatkin (FO Economic Section) memorandum, 'Raw Materials', 7 Sep. 1935, Hoare FO 800/295; Hoare telegram to Lindsay (British ambassador, Washington), 4 Dec. 1935, Lindsay telegram to Hoare, 6 Dec. 1935, both *DBFP II*, vol. XV, pp. 377–8, 383–4; Hoare memorandum, 8 Dec. 1935, Templewood (University Library, Cambridge University, Cambridge) VIII/I. Cf. G. W. Baer, *Test Case: Italy, Ethiopia, and the League of Nations* (Stanford, CA: Stanford University Press, 1976); R. A. C. Parker, 'Great Britain, France and the Ethiopian Crisis', *English Historical Review*, 89 (1974), pp. 293–332.

103 Churchill to Phipps (British ambassador, Paris), 1 April 1938, in Gilbert, *Churchill*, vol. V, companion 3, pp. 969.

104 House of Commons Speech, 5 October 1938, in Rhodes James, *Churchill Speaks*, p. 662.

105 Hankey diary, 2 October 1938, in Gilbert, *Churchill*, vol. V, companion 3, p. 1196.
106 See S. Cox, 'British Military Planning and the Origins of the Second World War', in B. J. C. McKercher and R. Legault, eds, *Military Planning and the Origins of the Second World War in Europe* (Westport, CT: Praeger, 2001), pp. 103–19; G. A. H. Gordon, *British Seapower and Procurement Between the Wars: A Reappraisal of Rearmament* (Basingstoke: Macmillan, 1988); S. Ritchie, *Industry and Air Power: The Expansion of British Aircraft Production, 1935–41* (Frank Cass, 1997).
107 See A. Adamthwaite, 'The British Government and the Media, 1937–1938', *Journal of Contemporary History*, vol. 18 (1983), pp. 281–97; R. Crockett, *Twilight of Truth: Chamberlain, Appeasement and the Manipulation of the Press* (New York: St Martin's, 1989); A. Foster, 'The 'Times' and Appeasement: The Second Phase', *Journal of Contemporary History*, vol. 16 (1981), pp. 441–65.
108 Cadogan diary, 26 March 1939, D. Dilks, ed., *The Diaries of Sir Alexander Cadogan, OM* (New York: Putnam, 1972), p. 163.
109 See S. Conkov, 'The British Policy of Guarantees and Greece (March–April 1939)', *Studia Balcanica*, vol. 4 (1971), pp. 187–202; D. Lungau, 'The European Crisis of March–April 1939: The Romanian Dimension', *International History Review*, vol. 7 (1985), pp. 390–414; S. Newman, *The British Guarantee to Poland: A Study in the Continuity of British Foreign Policy* (Oxford University Press, 1976).
110 P. Dennis, *Decision by Default: Peacetime Conscription and British Defence Policy 1919–1939* (Routledge, 1972).
111 House of Commons Speech, 3 April 1939, in Rhodes James, *Churchill Speaks*, p. 680.
112 Ritchie, *Air Power*, is helpful in this regard.
113 Churchill, 'Memorandum on Sea-Power, 1939', 27 Mar. 1939, in Gilbert, *Churchill*, vol. V, companion Part 3, pp. 1414–17. All quotes in this paragraph and the next are from this source.
114 See R. Manne, 'The British Decision for Alliance with Russia, May 1939', *Journal of Contemporary History*, vol. 9 (1974), pp. 3–26; A. Prazmowska, *Britain, Poland, and the Eastern Front, 1939* (Cambridge: Cambridge University Press, 1987); Watt, *How War Came*, pp. 447–61. Cf. M. J. Carley, *1939: The Alliance That Never Was and the Coming of World War II* (Chicago, IL: Ivan R. Dee, 1999), p. 114. House of Commons Speech, 5 October 1938, in Rhodes James, ed., *Churchill Speaks*, p. 661.
115 Quoted in Gilbert, *Winston S. Churchill*, vol. V, p. 112.
116 Gilbert, *The Wilderness Years*.

4

CHURCHILL AND TECHNOLOGY

David Jablonsky

Winston Spencer Churchill was born in 1874, the Indian summer of the Victorian era. As a result, he was imbued early on with the Victorian's optimistic secular faith that progress was mankind's destiny and that technology was instrumental in achieving that destiny. It was a faith that despite its obeisance to continuity and tradition in other fields would brook no resistance to technological change. Thus at mid-century, Charles Dickens could scornfully dismiss as driveling idiots those who were concerned about railroad construction across the lagoon into Venice. Instead, he pointed out, they should be grateful for living in an era when iron was used for something positive like railroads instead of for driving screws into the skulls of innocent men. And in Rome, the famed author rejoiced at telegraph wires passing 'like a sunbeam through the cruel old heart of the Coliseum'.[1] Churchill was equally dismissive of any challenges to the progressive primacy of technology. In his background description of the 1898 River War in the Sudan, he noted that the height of the reservoirs of the British-built Aswan Dam had been limited because of protests by archeologists ('profitless chippers of stone, rummagers in the dust heaps of the past') that the release of any higher level would submerge the ptolemaic Temple of Philae. 'The State must struggle and the people starve', the young Victorian concluded, 'in order that professors may exult and tourists find some space on which to scratch their names.'[2]

For the late Victorians, then, technology and progress continued to be linked as products of a rational, harmonious, and teleological world. In 1891, oxygen was liquefied and the zipper was invented. By 1895, there were the discoveries of x-rays and diptheria antitoxin and the invention of the safety razor. Everything seemed to be on the verge of being completely understood to the young Churchill. Years later, he recalled his wonderment of the period in 'the palmy days of Queen Victoria. . . '.

The Victorian Age was the age of . . . growth and gathering in every land of all those elements and factors which go to make up the power of States . . . Door after door had been unlocked. One dim mysterious gallery after another had been lighted up, explored, made free for all: and every gallery entered gave access to at least two more. Every morning when the world woke up, some new machinery had started running. Every night while the world had supper, it was running still. It ran on while all men slept.[3]

The purpose of this chapter is to illustrate how this Victorian attitude to technology affected Churchill's outlook on the nature of war, on the use of technological surprise in war, and on policy direction for the development and use of technology in war. It is not always a clear-cut relationship; and in many cases as the British statesman responded to the cataclysmic events in the first half of the twentieth century, his Victorian outlook appeared to falter. In times of crisis, however, that outlook reasserted itself and allowed Churchill to outstrip a narrow utilitarian view of science, providing him with both an optimism that led him to see many possible, and some impossible, applications of technology, and to have an unlimited confidence in the ability to solve any technical problem. 'Churchill's appreciation of the actual and potential contribution of science and technology to modern warfare', Michael Handel pointed out in this regard, 'combined with his fertile imagination are unique among modern leaders and certainly ahead of most military professionals of his time.'[4]

Technology and the Nature of War

In 1895, Churchill graduated from Sandhurst and for the next five years passed through four different regiments and fought in three different conflicts in the twilight of the Victorian era. The first of these so-called 'small wars' was against the Pathan tribesmen on India's north-west frontier in 1897, where the young officer served in Sir Bindon Blood's Malakand Field Force.[5] The following year, he participated in Lord Herbert Kitchener's campaign against the Dervish tribesmen in the Sudan – a campaign that ended with the British victory at Omdurman. Finally, the Boer War ushered in the new century – straining but not breaking for Churchill the late Victorian linkage of technology and progress.

In the first two of these conflicts, Churchill was somewhat ambivalent concerning the technological advantage over the Pathan and the Dervish tribesmen. On the one hand, the 'paramount and sacred law of self-preservation' justified the employment of any advanced technology in small wars against an enemy so fanatical that at one point in the Malakand campaigns the tribesmen attacked using only stones as weapons.[6] In another instance, the 'tidal wave of fanaticism' was so great that one cavalry officer recommended a *pennon* should be knotted about 18 inches below the point of a spear to prevent the enemy, once struck with the lance, from wriggling any further on to the spear in order to attack the lancer.[7] In the Sudan, 'any means' were also justified against 'a mighty avalanche' of fanatical Dervish warriors, 'stern, unflinching, utterly irresistible'.[8] From this perspective, Churchill had only praise for the expansive character of the new Dum-Dum bullet, 'a wonderful and from the technical point of view a beautiful machine', since it 'tears and splinters everything before it, causing wounds which in the body must be generally mortal and in any limb necessitate amputation.'[9] In any event he concluded, 'bullets are primarily intended to kill, and these bullets do their duty most effectively without causing any more pain to those struck by them than the ordinary lead variety'.[10]

Churchill was equally pragmatic about the advantages afforded by other weapons, to include the 10-shot Mauser model 1896 pistol that he used against the Dervish in the cavalry charge of the 21st Lancers at Omdurman. Forced to replace his sword with this pistol as a result of a recurring dislocated shoulder, Churchill later considered it 'the best thing in the world', providing him an immense advantage over the Dervish who, as he wrote to his mother, 'fell AOT [arse over tip]. . . '.[11] Any preference for cold steel over such a weapon, he concluded, was 'purely sentimental!'[12] How far the technological pragmatist had come was illustrated as Churchill worked on *The River War* back in India in Bangalore, a city in which 6,500 people had recently died in four months of plague, 'an unnoticed slaughter' that he estimated was nearly as great as at Omdurman. 'The machinery of modern war is still defective', he wrote. 'Some day science may call the mighty *bacillus* into the disputes of nations.'[13]

On the other hand, after riding with another officer over the killing grounds several days after the Battle of Omdurman, Churchill was aghast at the effect of modern technology on small wars. Both men ministered to the wounded, struck by how in the 'horrors of the field' a 'nameless man with a revolver and a big bag of cartridges would have seemed merciful'.[14] Soon, Churchill as a war correspondent was informing the British public of his disillusionment at what modern technology had done to the romance of war, rendering the Sudan campaign 'a tale which from beginning to end has been a record of slaughter' and, more specifically concerning Omdurman, 'the mechanized scattering of death by well-armed men on the defensive upon badly armed men in the open'.[15] For a 'civilized' soldier, there was a nobility in death, an 'honourable exit', that could still excite admiration in the comrades left behind. But there was nothing '*dulce et decorum*' when it came to the effects that 'the terrible machinery of scientific war' had on the Dervish foe, Churchill informed his newspaper readers in his first visceral reaction to the field at Omdurman after the battle. 'All was filthy corruption.'[16] Ultimately, he concluded in *The River War*, as he looked back on the effect of technology in the conduct of a small wars,

> The mind turns with disgust from the spectacle of unequal slaughter. The name of the battle, blazoned on the colours preserved for future generations the memory of a successful expedition. Regiments may exult in the part they played. Military experts may draw instruction from the surprising demonstration of the power of modern weapons. But the individual soldier will carry from the field only a very transient satisfaction, and the 'glory of Omdurman' will seem to any who may, five years hence, read this book a very absurd expression.[17]

Nevertheless, Churchill could not have it both ways. In October 1899, the editor of *Concord*, a pacifist magazine, wrote to the *Westminster Gazette* deploring 'massacres' of the Dervish forces during and after the Battle of Omdurman as 'deliberately planned and executed in cold blood'. The letter cited 'Lieutenant Churchill's account of how the enemy was 'destroyed, not conquered by machinery'.[18] In reply, Churchill pointed out that the 'ethics of human destruction must necessarily be somewhat obscure', if there were to be a reasonable chance of success in the conduct of small wars. 'Had "The Editor of *Concord*" . . . seen 40,000 savages advancing with hostile intent', he wrote, 'he would not have protested against the soldiers opening fire . . . I submit, that it is unfair, as well as irrational to attribute cruelty and blood thirstiness to soldiers who, placed in a position where they have to defend their lives, use the weapons with which they are armed with skill, judgment, and effect.'[19]

In the end, however, this lack of proportionality on the part of the Kitchener expedition in the conduct of the River War was rationalized by Churchill in the broader positive context of empire and 'scientific civilization'. In this approach, technology was a means by which civilized powers could 'chastise' their enemies with a 'strong and implacable arm', unlike earlier times when it was not possible for civilizations to devise instruments of war superior to those of the uncivilized.[20] As demonstrated in the Sudan, Churchill concluded, if Britain's imperial force had not been 'sheltered in the strong arms' of science and technology, the Dervish hordes might have swept civilization from the Middle East and, combined with the 'militant and proselytizing faith' of Mohammedanism, even from Europe.[21]

The Boer War was different. In South Africa, the British were not dealing with the Pathan and Dervish tribesmen. This time it was the Boers with a panoply of modern war technology ranging from machine-guns, which shredded the dense ranks of the Queen's army, to distant artillery known as Long Toms, which were emplaced far beyond the reach of the British cavalry, rapidly firing 40-pound, 4.7-inch shrapnel shells that dismembered men in the attack or in static positions. Added to this were the sandbagged entrenchments and the barbed wire. As British casualties mounted at such battles as Spion Kop and Vaal Krantz, regimental histories began to record phrases that would become set-pieces for the total wars of the twentieth century. Battles became 'enshrined forever' in history; engagements were 'imperishable' and 'immortal'.[22]

The impact of the new technology was not lost on Churchill, who along with Ghandi served at the battlefields along the Tugela River. 'Colenso, Spion Kop, Vaal Krantz, and the third day at Pieters were not inspiring memories', he wrote. At the Battle of Pieters, he watched as British units were repeatedly cut down by the 'hideous whispering death' from Mauser bullets. And Spion Kop left an indelible impression concerning the effects of artillery shrapnel on a 2,000-man British brigade crowded into a space 'about as large as Trafalgar' on the bare top of the kop – 'scenes . . . among the strongest and most terrible I have ever witnessed'.[23]

Nevertheless, the effect of the new technology on Churchill's Victorian perception of war should not be overstated. Two generations later, on a particularly grueling day in September 1940 that included a visit to one of the worst-bombed areas of London, the Prime Minister could still reminisce late at night about the Boer conflict, 'the last enjoyable war'.[24] During that same war, Churchill's physician noted that 'the PM always goes back to the Boer War when he is in good humour. That was before war degenerated. It was great fun galloping about.'[25] Certainly, there was a tendency at the time of the South African conflict for Churchill to gloss over the evolving impact of technology on the nature of warfare. At Diamond Hill on 14 June 1900, there was an almost palpable sense of relief when the British reverted to a cavalry charge, 'a fine gallant manoeuvre, executed with a spring and an elasticity wonderful and admirable. . . '.[26] As for the new technologies, Churchill also had a warning firmly grounded in the small wars of the late nineteenth century. 'Battles now a-days are fought mainly with firearms', he wrote, 'but no troops . . . can enjoy the full advantage of their successes if they exclude the possibilities of cold steel and are not prepared to maintain what they have won, if necessary with their fists.'[27]

There was, of course, no denying the immense effect of new technology in terms of the squalid, indecisive attritiveness of the First World War. The frustration at this turn of events was captured by Dick Divers in F. Scott

Fitzgeralds's novel *Tender is the Night* when he visited the Somme Valley after that war. 'See that little stream', he said, 'we could walk to it – a whole empire walking very slowly, dying in front and pushing forward behind. And another empire walked very slowly backwards a few inches a day leaving the dead like a million bloody rugs.' Churchill was no less frustrated. 'Something must be discovered', he wrote in 1915, 'which would . . . make it unnecessary for soldiers to bare their breasts to the machine gun hail.'[28] A year later, that frustration was mixed with anguish for Churchill, recently returned from battalion command on the Western Front, as he reminded his listeners in the Commons that every 24 hours nearly a thousand men, 'Englishmen, Britishers, men of our own race, are knocked into bundles of bloody rags . . . '.[29]

The basic problem, Churchill came to realize, was that technology had changed the scale of warfare. Now it was possible to mobilize not only armies, but entire populations and national economies for total war, in which all elements of national power could be continuously applied. It was a 'frightful bondage' to all that modern technology could accomplish, particularly since advances in technology had not been accompanied by similar progress in restraint: 'When all was over, Torture and Cannibalism were the only two expedients that the civilized, scientific, Christian states had been able to deny themselves; and these were of doubtful utility.'[30] With new technologies, then, came enormous new responsibilities not easily understood. 'Death stands at attention . . . ready, if called on, to pulverize . . . what is left of civilization', Churchill concluded. 'He awaits only the word of command . . . from a frail, bewildered being . . . '.[31]

In the interwar years, Churchill returned repeatedly in his speeches and writings to the 'melancholy and degraded epoch' of the Great War, in which the 'slaughter of men by machinery' had reduced combat 'to a business like the stockyards of Chicago'.[32] If war should come again, he reflected bitterly, 'it may well be that chemists will carry off what credit can be found', in a competition 'to kill women and children and the civil population generally, and victory will give herself in sorry nuptials to the diligent hero who organizes it on the largest scale'.[33] By enlarging the scale and destruction of modern warfare, technology had produced mass, impersonal death, which meant the end of the very basis for Victorian wars. Looking back on the Battle of Omdurman, Churchill commented in sorrow on the passing of that 'sporting game' under the onslaught of technical innovation.

> This kind of war was full of fascinating thrills. It was not like the Great War. Nobody expected to be killed. Here and there in every regiment or battalion, half a dozen, a score, at the worst thirty or forty,

would pay the forfeit; but to the great mass of those who took part in the little wars of Britain in those vanished light-hearted days, this was only a sporting element in a splendid game. Most of us were fated to see a war where the hazards were reversed, where death was the general expectation and severe wounds were counted as lucky escapes, where whole brigades were shorn away under the steel flail of artillery and machine guns, where the survivors of one tornado knew that they would certainly be consumed in the next or the next after that.[34]

It was not, however, in Churchill's nature to remain immersed too long in such melancholy reflections. He still retained his lifelong fascination with technology, despite its major role in the unprecedented cataclysm of the First World War. Moreover, as he realized from his experiences in that conflict, if technology could transform warfare into immobile attritiveness, it also had the potential to reverse that process. Equally important, technology might fall into the wrong hands in which a type of reverse social Darwinism might obviate the heroic traits of Victorian England forever. In previous times, he pointed out in a 1924 article entitled 'Shall We All Commit Suicide?', war meant that 'in the hard evolution of mankind the best and fittest stocks came to the fore'. But a technological breakthrough could allow 'a base degenerate, immoral race' to conquer 'an enemy far above them in quality . . .'. Such a breakthrough, he conjectured with his ever-active imagination, could come from a panoply of weapons that might include:

electric rays which could paralyse the engines of a motor-car, could claw down aeroplanes from the sky, and conceivably be made destructive of human life or human vision. Then there are Explosives. Have we reached the end? Has Science turned its last page on them? May there not be methods of using explosive energy incomparably more intense than anything heretofore discovered? Might not a bomb no bigger than an orange be found to possess a secret power to destroy a whole block of buildings – nay, to . . . blast a township at a stroke? Could not explosives . . . be guided automatically in flying machines by wireless or other rays, without a human pilot, in ceaseless procession upon a hostile city, arsenal, camp, or dockyard?[35]

Churchill was aided in the article by a noted scientist, Professor F. A. Lindemann, later Viscount Cherwell, and known simply to Churchill as 'The Prof.' The two men had met in 1921. Churchill, who valued eating, drinking and smoking, took to the non-smoking, abstemious vegetarian primarily because of the value he put on what he described as Lindemann's 'beautiful brain', and on the ability of the Prof. to explain even the most complicated and arcane scientific issues in clear, concise, understandable terms. Sarah Churchill recounted, in this regard, how one day at lunch her father asked the Prof. to explain in five minutes, in words of one syllable, the quantum theory. That was, she recalled, 'quite a tall order: however, without any hesitation, like quicksilver, he explained the principle and held us all spell-bound. When he had finished we all spontaneously burst into applause.'[36] That type of close, unofficial tutelage was to continue throughout their long relationship, even under the most adverse conditions, such as the time in December 1931 when Churchill was struck by a car on Fifth Avenue while visiting New York City. Upon learning the details of the accident from Churchill, who was convalescing in a New York hospital, Lindemann immediately wired his friend from England: 'Collision equivalent falling thirty feet on to pavement . . . Equivalent stopping ten pound brick dropped six hundred feet or two charges buckshot point-blank range.'[37]

Lindemann continued that tutelage in the 1930s as Churchill increasingly became involved in the British government's development of war technology ranging from the design of bombsights to air defense research. In 1931, aided by the Prof., Churchill produced a wide-ranging, upbeat article entitled 'Fifty Years Hence' that bridged the gap produced by the Great War in his Victorian outlook on technology. While acknowledging that science and technology had altered war for the worst, he focused on what they could do for man in the future, whether in the form of television, peaceful nuclear energy or the use of hormones to control growth ('We shall escape the absurdity of growing a whole chicken in order to eat the breast or wing, by growing these parts separately under a suitable medium.') Both elements had been instrumental in the progress of the previous century, he pointed out; it was thus important to regain a faith in science, which in turn would find Britain realistically ready to deal with friendly or enemy technological innovations in warfare. It was a faith that returned Churchill to Tennyson and the poems of his youth as an optimistic link to the future from an uncertain present. That future was described in 'all the wonder that would be' of 'Locksley Hall', a couplet of which he could even see in his rejuvenated faith as presaging the League of Nations.

> Till the way-drum throbb'd no longer, and the
>   battle flags were furl'd
> In the Parliament of man, the Federation of the world.[38]

This type of optimism enabled Churchill to use technology to great effect in the Second World War – a development recorded in detail by 1949 in his memoirs of that conflict. Without the new technology and 'unless its strange sinister resources had been effectively brought to bear on the struggle for survival', he wrote, 'we might well have been defeated, and, being defeated, destroyed'.[39] The reference to 'strange sinister resources' was typical of the British statesman's continued ambivalence toward modern science and technology. Already in his 18 June 1940 'Finest Hour' speech after Dunkirk, he would warn that if Britain should fail, then the entire world would 'sink into the abyss of a new dark age made more sinister . . . by the lights of perverted science'.[40] By 1945, he was admonishing Parliament to avoid any tendencies to turn government over to scientists: 'It is the duty of scientists, like all other people, to serve the State and not to rule it because they are scientists', he stated. 'If they want to rule the State they must get elected to Parliament . . . '.[41] In his 'Iron Curtain' speech at Fulton, Missouri, the next year, Churchill cautioned that the 'dark ages may return – the Stone Age may return on the gleaming wings of science, and what may shower immeasurable material blessing upon mankind, may even bring about its total destruction'.[42]

The British leader, of course, was referring to nuclear power and the advent of the atomic bomb. But it was the hydrogen bomb that most disturbed him, particularly after the second American explosion at Bikini in 1954. In his final speech on defense as Prime Minister on 1 March 1955, his last great oration in Commons, Churchill expressed his concerns. 'The atomic bomb with all its terrors', he emphasized, 'did not carry us outside the scope of human control or manageable events in thought or action, in peace or war.' But with the H-bomb, he continued, 'the entire function of human affairs was revolutionized, and mankind placed in a situation both measureless and laden with doom.' Nevertheless, the outgoing Prime Minister would not completely yield his Victorian optimism, choosing instead to quote from his 1931 article 'Fifty Years Hence' on the benefits of technology while finding some solace in the future efficacy of nuclear deterrence. 'Then it may be well', he concluded, 'that we shall by a process of sublime irony have reached a stage in this story where safety will be the sturdy child of terror, and survival the twin brother of annihilation.'[43]

Ironic or not, and despite a continued acknowledgement of how far in weapons technology 'scientific knowledge has outstripped human virtue', the end of Churchill's active career marked a return once again to the Victorian linkage of technology and progress.[44] After retirement in April 1955, the former Prime Minister expressed regret that he had not done more to expand higher education in technology – 'an all-important subject in which Great Britain has allowed herself to fall behind'.[45] One result was the establishment of Churchill College at Cambridge with a primarily technical focus in its curriculum. On 17 October 1959, in a tree-planting ceremony to mark the foundation of the college, Churchill paid tribute to 'Lord Cherwell – the Professor – who strove so earnestly and so well to awaken our country to the shortages we faced in the sphere of technology.'[46] It was a speech that captured the mix of optimistic faith, awe, and wonderment concerning technology from the elder statesman's youth. 'Let no one believe', Churchill concluded in words that any Victorian would have understood,

> that the lunar rockets, of which we read in the Press, are merely ingenious bits of prestige. They are manifestations of a formidable advance in technology. As with many vehicles of pure research, their immediate uses may not be apparent. But I do not doubt that they will ultimately reap a rich harvest for those who have the imagination and power to develop them and to probe ever more deeply into the mysteries of the universe in which we live.[47]

Technology and Surprise

Churchill's natural interest in technology deepened as the First World War progressed. Increasingly, he saw the unilateral introduction of a new weapon or the use of a known weapon in an innovative way as a means to break the military deadlock, much as the scythed chariot or the longbow had enabled armies to achieve surprise and win unexpected victories in the past. Unless such devices were developed and introduced in such a way as to achieve 'the priceless element of surprise', Churchill asserted to Commons in 1917, 'I do not see how we are to avoid being thrown back on those dismal processes of waste and slaughter which are called attrition.'[48] This focus on technological surprise by the future British leader would pay even greater dividends in the next war.

Innovation

The tank was the quintessential British invention for technological surprise in the First World War. As early as December 1915, Churchill analyzed the importance of that element in any armor attack, emphasizing the primacy of 'novelty and suddenness'.[49] But that novelty, he soon realized, could be dissipated quickly. Less than a year later at the Somme, 35 tanks were dispersed in small, ineffective groups along the entire front of the Fourth Army as it attacked. Just prior to the assault, Lloyd George informed Churchill, who was 'shocked at the proposal to expose this tremendous secret to the enemy upon such a petty scale . . . '.[50] The attack was a limited success which, in Churchill's opinion, 'recklessly revealed to the enemy a secret that might have produced allied victory in 1917'.

> The immense advantage of novelty and surprise was thus squandered while the number of the tanks was small, while their condition was experimental and their crews almost untrained. This priceless conception . . . was revealed to the Germans for the mere petty purpose of taking a few ruined villages . . . The enemy was familiarized with them by their piecemeal use . . .[51]

On 9 November 1916, less than a month after the ineffective British armor attack at the Somme, Churchill summed up in a memorandum to the government what was by then an axiom for him concerning technological surprise. 'Don't familiarize the enemy by degrees with these methods of attack. Apply them when all is ready on the largest possible scale, and with the priceless advantage of surprise.'[52] Later, as he looked back on the war, his thinking on the subject was reinforced by his study of the Eastern Front, where, in at least one incident, technological surprise had been sacrificed to reinforce a deception operation. In April 1915, German forces were withdrawn from the Western Front to participate in the Gorlice–Tarnow offensive that was to begin on 2 May. To cover the withdrawal, 'lively activity' was prescribed for the Western Front, the most formidable being the gas attack at Ypres that began on 22 April. Although gas had been used in a minor role with artillery shells, the attack at Ypres involved for the first time the continuous discharge of gas from cylinders. 'The precipitate exposure of this deadly device at a time when no German reserves were at hand to exploit its surprising effects', Churchill observed, 'was one of the debts which the Western allies owed to the Eastern Front.'[53]

Churchill's objections were finally answered at the Battle of Cambrai on 20 November 1917, when the British combined massed armor with tactical and operational surprise to achieve a decisive breakthrough in the German lines. 'All the requisite conditions were at last accorded', he wrote. 'The tanks were to operate on ground not yet ploughed up by artillery, against a front not yet prepared to meet an offensive. Above all, Surprise! The tanks were themselves to open the attack.'[54] In fact, surprise was also achieved because of the synergistic effects of technological progress in other areas such as the science of gunnery. By the autumn of 1917, as a consequence, artillery did not require preliminary registration to be on target, and the British were able to open accurate, pre-planned fire at H-Hour.[55]

The following August, General Rawlinson's great armored attack met with equal success. There were nearly 600 tanks involved, assisted not only by a thick morning mist, but by special noise barrages and artificial fog as well. In addition, there were 120 brigades of British artillery of all types ready to fire, but only after the assault commenced. 'Everything was subordinated to the surprise of the tank attack', Churchill noted, owing to Rawlinson's imaginative combination of new technology and doctrine. 'He had put aside old fashioned ideas, he had used new weapons as they should be used, he had reaped swift and rich reward.'[56] Unlike Rawlinson, however, the majority of the Anglo-French commanders, in Churchill's judgment, had been captured by technology instead of harnessing it to restore maneuver to warfare. Ultimately, he concluded, technological innovations had to be pressed from above upon Marshals Haig and Foch in the summer of 1918 before victory could be achieved: 'Both were now provided with offensive weapons which the military science of neither would have conceived . . . The Goddess of surprise had at last returned to the Western Front.'[57]

The linkage of such experiences from the First World War to Churchill's involvement with technological surprise in the Second World War is best illustrated in his 1917 proposal to Lloyd George for amphibious landings on the Frisian Islands north of mainland Germany. To facilitate the landing, he also proposed to create an artificial island constructed from concrete flat-bottom barges. Almost 23 years later, on 6 June 1940, the new Prime Minister revived the details of this proposal and pressed for further development. By May 1942, he was able to provide the Chief of Combined Operations further guidance remarkable in its detail and faith in the ability to solve any technological problem.

> They must float up and down with the tide. The anchor problem must be mastered. The ships must have a side-flap cut in them and a drawbridge long enough to overreach the moorings of the piers. Let me have the best solution worked out. Don't argue the matter. The difficulties will argue for themselves.[58]

The result was a concept that became the basic assumption for the 1944 cross-Channel invasion of Europe: 'Mulberry' harbors used throughout the Normandy invasion to the great surprise of the Germans and decisive for the success of the Allied landings. Strategically, as Michael Handel pointed out, Mulberry provided the planners with the freedom to select landing zones well away from the heavily fortified harbors on the continent; psychologically, it gave the Allied leaders a degree of confidence, without which they might never have attempted what they perceived as an extremely hazardous operation.[59] In the end, that 'single brilliant technical device', in Albert Speer's description, allowed the Allies to bypass the Atlantic Wall, thus rendering the German coastal defense system irrelevant.[60]

Counter-measures

'One of the most serious dangers that we are exposed to', Churchill wrote to the Prime Minister in 1915, 'is the possibility that the Germans are . . . preparing . . . surprises and that we may at any time find ourselves exposed to some entirely new form of attack'.[61] This concern with counter-measures against emerging enemy technology was spurred by his already effective campaign as First Lord against German U-boats – 'a close and fruitful union between the scientist, the inventor and the submarine officer' – using such new technology as nets with necklaces of explosives, depth charges, horned mines, and hydrophones for detecting the beat of a submarine propeller.[62] Moreover, the enemy reactions to British technological advances must also be considered. Shortly after the piecemeal armor commitment at the Somme, Churchill recommended in a memorandum marked by its rational, deductive approach, that an Anti-Tank Committee be established 'to study the methods by which tanks can be defeated'.

> This body should work in the closest harmony with those concerned in the production and design of tanks, each striving to defeat the other, exchanging information and perfecting their methods. It is not to be supposed that the Germans will not develop tanks in their turn. We have the enormous advantage of being able to experiment on ourselves with them, and to find out the best ways by which they may be defeated.[63]

In the Second World War, Churchill was aided in the development of technological counter-measures by German mistakes and the high quality of British intelligence, which revealed new enemy technologies and programs for weapons development. In some cases this meant that deception was necessary to disguise the effectiveness of British counter-measures against enemy technological surprise. There were, for example, the elaborate efforts Churchill directed as First Lord to convince the Germans that their magnetic mine, which had been initially so effective against British shipping, was still a powerful weapon, even though in fact effective counter-measures had been devised. By 24 December 1939, de-magnetization experiments had proved successful enough to prompt a triumphant telegram from Churchill to Roosevelt. That same day, he minuted the Admiralty that 'wherever ships are lost by mines in future it will be well to state that they are sunk by magnetic mines whenever this possibility exists'.[64]

In other cases, it was often a race to develop the appropriate counter-measures as the intelligence on enemy technology developed. On 23 May 1940, Dr R. V. Jones, a scientist in the Air Ministry, informed Lindemann of the possibility that the Germans had developed a system of intersecting radio beams for the purpose of guiding bombers accurately to their targets. The information on that possibility began to accumulate rapidly thereafter. A radio intercept of 5 June pinpointed an area in Britain under the code name 'Knickebein', literally translated as 'crooked legs'. The analysts examining the decrypt a few days later realized that two airfields had been bombed near the area on the evening after the dispatch of the coded message. On 11 June, there was further confirmation from a captured German flier. Jones continued to investigate other leads, becoming increasingly convinced that Knickebein was a device for dropping bombs automatically when an airplane reached the point where two radio beams intersected.[65]

On 21 June 1940, in a meeting with Churchill and his key military and scientific advisers, Jones briefed the situation and was directed to continue his research. 'If our good fortune holds', he wrote a week after the meeting, 'we may yet pull the crooked leg.'[66] This was accomplished before the end of the summer. Not only was the beam located, but shortly after it became operational, it was successfully 'bent'. For the two critical months of September and October 1940, as Churchill noted, 'the German bombers wandered around England bombing by guesswork, or else being actually led astray'.[67] At one point during this period, an officer on Churchill's staff sent his family to the country to escape the London raids. They were astonished to see on one occasion more than 100 bombs fall in fields over 10 miles from the nearest town. The officer, unaware of Knickebein, recounted this to his colleagues, some of whom were in the small inner circle privy to the sensitive 'beam' information. 'The very few who knew', Churchill summed up the episode, 'exchanged celestial grins.'[68]

Finally, despite or in some instances because of the plethora of intelligence on a specific German technology, there were cases in which the timing for introducing counter-measures remained a problem. The classic example was 'Window', the tin-foil chaff that could be dropped to confuse German radar during British bombing raids. In 1942, the Prime Minister supported experiments under Lindemann's direction which clearly indicated by June 1943 that Window was not only effective, but would save one-third of British bomber casualties. Nevertheless, Churchill hesitated, concerned that the Germans might use Window to renew heavy-bomber raids on Britain. The turning point came in an acrimonious staff meeting on 17 July when the British leader turned to the head of Fighter Command and asked him for advice, since he would have to 'carry the can' if Britain's defenses failed. The commander did not discount the fact that his defenses might be neutralized, but acknowledged that he would take responsibility, since the focus must now be on reducing losses in Bomber Command. 'Very well', Churchill concluded the meeting, 'let us open the Window.'[69]

Sigint

The advent of wireless communication opened up an entirely new means for technological surprise during the First World War in the form of signal intelligence (Sigint). Early British code-breaking success by the Royal Navy in that conflict began Churchill's lifelong enthusiasm for this field, in which, as Michael Handel has observed, he was always 'ready and eager to open other gentlemen's mail'.[70] The idea of plucking the enemy's most recent thoughts from the air was a source of excitement and enthusiasm for a man whose imagination could surround even ordinary events with romance and enchantment. As First Lord in November 1914, Churchill issued a memorandum for which he devised a new formula, 'Exclusively Secret', directing the study of all decoded intercepts 'in order to penetrate the German mind and movement'.[71] By the end of that year, a small staff of cryptographers was implementing that charter from Room 40 of the Admiralty Old Building, and as their numbers grew, from a series of adjoining rooms, but still known by the innocuous collective title as 'Room 40 O.B.'. Churchill's enthusiasm for this new organization was quickly justified. In January 1915, Admiral von Pohl submitted a memo to William II recommending German submarine attacks on merchant shipping and the dispatch of airships to attack Britain. 'So excellent was our Intelligence Service', Churchill wrote later of the signal intercepts, 'that reports of what was passing in the minds of the German Naval Staff reached us even before Admiral von Pohl's memorandum had been laid before the Emperor.'[72]

Churchill's trust in Room 40's ability was confirmed the following month in the Battle of the Dogger Bank. Based on that organization's analysis of German message decrypts and the calculations for the interception of the German fleet, Churchill dispatched the messages that began to move the British ships out to sea. That night at a French Embassy dinner, the First Lord's faith in Room 40's capacity for technological surprise allowed his romantic imagination free rein as he contemplated the next day's events. 'One felt separated from the distinguished company who gathered there', he later recalled, 'by a film of isolated knowledge and overwhelming inward preoccupation.' Now, there would be a battle between Dreadnoughts for the first time in history. Equally important for the young First Lord, 'there was added a thrilling sense of a Beast of Prey moving stealthily forward hour by hour towards the Trap'.[73]

In the next war, Churchill kissed hands as Prime Minister in the same month as the initial British breakthrough into the German 'Enigma' machine, the multi-purpose and infinitely variable cipher used by the German military for most of its radio communication. Once again, Churchill was fascinated with the technological possibilities of Sigint, this time in the form of the British decrypts of the Enigma ciphers that came to be known as Ultra. 'Where are my eggs', he would demand imperiously, referring to the box containing the latest Ultra intercepts.[74] From that box would emerge secrets with an irresistible appeal for the schoolboy who was never very far from the surface. These were also secrets that fundamentally changed the course of the war; for with Ultra, Churchill was able to move inside the German mind as events occurred or before they took place – to read operations orders, to monitor battlefield maneuvers, to follow the fortunes of German commanders and to learn about German weapons-technology development. It was thus not surprising that the British leader referred to the Ultra cryptologists as 'the geese who laid the golden eggs but never cackled'.[75]

Those code-breakers were members of the Government Code and Cipher School (GC & CS), established as a successor to Room 40 at Bletchley Park – an organization that came to owe its huge success in the Second World War to Churchill's personal protection and interest.[76] On some occasions it might be a direct call from the Prime Minister in search of the latest news, to a surprised officer in one of the Bletchley huts. At other times, it could be a translated Enigma decrypt returned to Bletchley with Churchill's handwritten query. Finally, there were the visits, by which Churchill could express his personal gratitude and maintain the morale of the cryptoanalysts. 'You all look', he began a speech on one such visit to the assembled staff, 'very . . . innocent.'[77]

How direct Churchill's top–down interest in the activities at Bletchley could be was illustrated in October 1941, when four cryptoanalysts wrote a letter directly to the Prime Minister complaining of the lack of sufficient staff as well as of administrative, bureaucratic problems. One of the four code-breakers was selected to deliver the letter in person. Years later, he recalled his sense of 'total incredulity' when, upon arriving by train in London, he hailed a taxi and told the driver to take him to 10 Downing Street. He became more amazed as he approached the Prime Minister's residence when one uniformed policeman waved the taxi through a wooden barrier. At the door of No. 10, he paid off the taxi, rang the bell and was ushered into the residence, where he was told he could not see the Prime Minister personally, but that his letter would be delivered. After reading the letter the next day, Churchill immediately minuted:

ACTION THIS DAY
Make sure they have all they want on extreme priority and report to me that this has been done.[78]

Policy and Technology

Churchill's thoughts concerning the connection between policy and technological development were initially formed as First Lord of the Admiralty between 1911 and 1915. From the beginning, this ex-lieutenant of Hussars enthusiastically set out to learn about all aspects of naval technology, spending 182 days at sea during his first 18 months at the Admiralty, visiting almost every dockyard, shipyard, naval installation, and important ship in the British Isles and Mediterranean. 'These were great days', he recalled. '. . . I got to know what everything looked like and where everything was, and how one thing fitted into another.'[79] Almost immediately, the new First Lord was involved in three interrelated technology decisions concerning the 1912 battleship program, in which 'each link forged the next'.[80] The first decision was to introduce 15-inch naval guns – a considerable gamble, since even though a prototype gun could be hurried into construction, there would still be more than a year of suspense before the outcome was known. Moreover, the new guns would require enlarging the ships and redesigning 'every detail in these vessels, extending to thousands of parts', thus increasing the cost and guaranteeing opposition in the cabinet. Nevertheless, Churchill moved forward, working closely with engineers and scientists on the Ordnance Board. 'Risks have to be run in peace as well as in war', he wrote at the time, 'and courage in design now may win a battle later on.'[81]

The second decision was to form a fast division out of the new Dreadnoughts. This innovation led Churchill to his most important decision of converting the fast division from coal to oil – a move that not only increased the speed of the ships, but enabled the fleet to refuel at sea without having to send a quarter of its strength into harbor for coal. Once the large ships had been converted in this manner, the decision to convert the smaller vessels followed naturally. 'The camel once swallowed', Churchill noted, 'the gnats went down easily enough.'[82] All this, as the First Lord well realized, posed considerable dangers, since the Royal Navy would become completely dependent on overseas oil, while abandoning the huge supply of the best steam coal in the world located in Britain. The result was the Anglo-Persian oil convention carried masterfully through the Commons against a 'confusing variety of oppositions' that ranged from economists opposed to naval expenditure increases and MPs from coal-mining constituencies to armchair strategists who believed that the Persian fields and oil tankers were vulnerable to wartime attacks by land and sea, respectively.[83]

Churchill had equally momentous policy involvement in other fields of technology. At the beginning of the war, as Michael Howard has pointed out, the First Lord 'was virtually inventing both air and armored warfare'.[84] The two areas were not unconnected. Prior to the war, Churchill had learned to fly and logged in almost 140 flights in the highly dangerous primitive aircraft of the time. One result was the impetus he provided to naval air, despite strong institutional resistance from the navy bureaucracy and in Parliament. In 1913, the first torpedo was launched from a British aircraft; and that same year the cruiser *Hermes*, with an air-craft launching platform installed on the forecastle, was highly successful in North Sea maneuvers. Once hostilities began, however, the critics of naval air reversed themselves and begin to clamor for greater activity – a situation succinctly summed up at the time by one naval air pioneer: 'They have pissed on Churchill's plant for three years – now they expect blooms in a month.'[85]

Another outcome of this activity was that in September 1914 Lord Kitchener requested that Churchill and the Admiralty take on responsibility for air defense of the British Isles. The First Lord approached the task with his usual enthusiasm, concluding that preemptive attacks would be the most effective form of air defense. As a consequence, he created air bases in France and Belgium as well as Britain with the goal of commanding the air within 100 miles of the English coast. A month later, Churchill began to use armored car squadrons to patrol inland from Dunkirk in order to protect advance British airfields and to prevent the Germans from establishing similar bases. At the same time, he initiated studies addressing ways and means of moving those vehicles over obstacles and trenches. There was something anomalous in the involvement by the head of the Admiralty in land operations and fighting methods. But, as the tank pioneer Ernest Swinton noted, 'in the circumstances and, in this connection a fortunate one for the nation'.[86]

Swinton's appraisal reflected the absolutely essential policy role that Churchill and the Admiralty played in the evolution of the tank even as the army armor pioneers proceed on a similar research and development track in the War Office. On 5 January 1915, Churchill dispatched a memorandum to the Prime Minister suggesting the development of steam tractors on an armored caterpillar system carrying men and machine-guns. Given the nature of trench warfare, he wrote, 'an obvious measure of prudence would have been to have started something like this two months ago. It should certainly be done now.'[87] The next month, Churchill established an 'Admiralty Landships Committee', which by April 1915 was well underway in the production of prototype tanks. Nevertheless, when he lost his office in May 1915 because of the faltering Galopoli campaign, the fortunes of the new weapon were still uncertain, with the Board of Admiralty much inclined to reject the project. Churchill appealed personally to the new First Lord, who allowed one experimental model to proceed. The following December, despite the lack of an official position, he submitted to the commander of the British Army a memorandum that outlined possible offensive roles for an armored caterpillar system. Sir Douglas Haig read the memorandum on Christmas Day and immediately began to exert command pressure to continue the project. By the following month, the surviving experimental machine, 'Mother', succeeded in trials, becoming the model for the tanks that fought on the Somme in August 1916. There were many parents for these new machines; but without Churchill's policy impulsion, as Basil Liddell Hart observed, 'the new idea might never have survived the chill of that first winter in official Army quarters'.[88]

The experience with the tank convinced Churchill of the need for overall, centralized political direction of technological development in modern war. In 1915, he had already tied the lack of progress in tank development directly to decentralized government indifference. 'The problem', he wrote, 'of crossing two or three hundred yards of open ground . . . ought not to be beyond the range of modern science if sufficient authority . . . backed the investigation. The absence of any satisfactory method cannot be supplied by the bare breasts of gallant men.'[89] And after the war, Churchill returned to the subject in his praise for the efforts of the armor pioneers, who lacked, however, 'the executive authority which alone could ensure progress . . . They were unfortunate in not being able to command the resources necessary for action, or to convince those who had the power to act.'[90]

With that authority, Churchill realized, must also come coordination, extending from the laboratory to the trenches. 'A hiatus exists between inventors who know what they could invent, if they only knew what was wanted', he noted in 1916, 'and the soldiers who know, or ought to know, what they want and would ask for it if they only knew how much science could do for them.'[91] This perspective was further enlarged the following year with his appointment as Minister of Munitions. In this capacity, Churchill reinforced his belief that the war was now one of *matériel* – particularly concerning the new weapons technology of aircraft and tanks, which he had done so much to develop. To his prescience concerning the effect of this new technology on warfare, the Minister of Munitions now was able to add implementation in the form of mass manufacture. 'Let me have on a single sheet of paper the following broad facts about the Tank programme', he minuted at the time in a typically detailed approach to the production of technology.

How many Tanks, and of what patterns, are to be ready month by month for the next 12 months? By whom, and to what extent, have these programmes been approved? How much steel do they require?

How much do they cost? How much labour skilled and unskilled do they require in those 12 months? What are the principal limiting factors in material and class of labour? Apart from the number of Tanks, what quantity of spares, and what maintenance plants are required?[92]

Most important, what became clear to Churchill by the end of the war was that the political-policy level, with its broad view of all elements of national power, must determine the use of technology in modern war. When that did not happen, when in fact military strategy dominated policy as it did in Germany during the closing years of the war under the Hindenburg–Ludendorff dictatorship, the results could be disastrous. Serving that dictatorship was the 'military priesthood' of the German General Staff, a 'small gathering', in Churchill's estimate, of 'competent experts in blinkers, their eyes riveted on . . . their own job, with supreme knowledge in their sphere and little inkling that other or larger spheres existed'.[93] One result was the German decision to renew unrestricted submarine warfare that brought the United States into the war – an example of how a narrow military framework could become focused on technology to the exclusion of all other considerations. 'They staked too much upon a purely mechanical device', he concluded after the war. 'They looked too little to the tremendous psychological reactions upon the Allies, upon the whole world, and above all their own people, which must follow the apparition of a fresh, mighty antagonist among the forces against Germany.'[94]

Churchill brought these policy lessons into the next war. Until that conflict, technological 'facts' were what the authorized experts articulated, to be challenged only at great peril. Within weeks of assuming office as Prime Minister, Churchill began to extend such challenges, forcing the experts to justify conclusions by observational evidence, removing their screen of unchallengeable authority and thereby making most of them who responded the stronger for it. 'I knew nothing about science', Churchill recalled in his memoirs, 'but I knew something of scientists, and had much practice as a Minister of handling things I did not understand. I had, at any rate, an acute military perception of what would help and what would hurt, of what would cure and what would kill.'[95] In fact, the new Prime Minister recognized more than any other political leader of the time that the most effective use of technology in modern war could result only from an overall political direction that brought scientists and technologists together with leaders of the armed forces.

To aid him in this political direction, Churchill relied on his old friend, 'the Prof.', whom he established at 11 Downing Street with a door leading directly to the Prime Minister's residence – an example of, as one analyst has described it, 'almost medieval or Renaissance propinquity' between ruler and adviser.[96] It was a propitious combination for the Prime Minister of intimacy and frequency of contact. In his seven varied ministerial positions since early in the century, Churchill had always absorbed an immense amount of detail, some of it, as in the case of the Admiralty, extremely technical. As Prime Minister, he maintained those habits, bringing everything he saw under intense scrutiny, then following up with comment and exhortation. Time was therefore limited; and it was precisely the value of this commodity to Churchill that made his intimate relations with Lindemann such an asset. For the Prof. had a special way of stripping a document to its base components and providing synthesized results that permitted rapid and easy understanding – particularly important in the case of statistics, which were always difficult for Churchill to understand.

> Lindemann could decipher the signals from the experts on the far horizons and explain to me in lucid homely terms what the issues were . . . Anyone in my position would have been ruined if he had attempted to dive into the depths which not even a lifetime of study could plumb. What I had to grasp were the practical results, and . . . so I made sure . . . that some at least of these terrible and incomprehensible truths emerged in executive decisions.[97]

This dependence on the Prof. was often criticized, particularly since, as C. P. Snow pointed out, 'he had more direct power than any scientist in history'.[98] This power compounded errors throughout the war which vanity or miscalculation often caused Lindemann to perpetuate. He was a passionate advocate of 'area bombing', for instance, but his damage estimates were later shown to be six times too high.[99] Equally serious, he consistently underestimated the German potential to develop rocket weapons. Nevertheless, as the 1943 War Cabinet arguments on this subject revealed, Lindemann often encouraged advisers with opinions counter to his to make presentations to Churchill.[100] In any event, as John Keegan has pointed out, in the fields of science and technology Churchill had 'a remarkably sure touch in choosing between good and bad advice . . . '.[101]

Much of this ability derived from the British leader's experiences in the previous war with the dangers of colored appreciations. 'The temptation to tell a Chief in a great position the things he most likes to hear', he wrote of the battle of the Somme, 'is one of the commonest explanations of mistaken policy.'[102] As a result he was generally able after 'his passing wrath' to recognize that unpleasant truths presented to him had to be faced while acknowledging the courage that had been required to bring them to his notice. In any case, as R. V. Jones observed, the decision concerning policy organization for the development and use of technology was Churchill's to make:

In 1940, the nation had been led into disaster by a Government that depended on conventional bureaucratic arrangements in, among other things, scientific advice. *In extremis*, it called in Churchill, and it was bound to accept, as part of his method of leadership, whatever arrangement he thought would enable him to take the best decisions. Having seen the dangers of bureaucracy . . . and of hierarchic attenuation of front-line experience, Churchill decided to have personal advisers who could range for him over whole fields at any level. For science and technology, he chose Lindemann as a man, not necessarily unique, but of whose foresight he had direct experience and on whose friendship he could rely. It has not been shown that any alternative arrangement is in principle better.[103]

The policy essence of the Churchill–Lindemann duo was a focus on the problem at hand. 'Assemble your ideas and facts', the Prime Minister directed the scientists in his efforts to develop a proximity fuse, 'so that I may give extreme priority and impulse to this business.'[104] During the Battle of Britain, he used this focus to impel innovations in air defense such as experimental searchlight radar. 'Some must be in action during the next moon phase', he minuted in September 1940. 'Report to me how this will be achieved. Use all necessary authority.'[105] The primary vehicle for these efforts was the committee. That same autumn, Churchill formed the Night Air Defence Committee with himself in the chair as Minister of Defence. And in order to reduce British shipping losses, he created and chaired the Cabinet Anti-U-boat Warfare Committee, which in addition to Service Chiefs and Ministers, also included a high-level group of scientists. The result of such dynamism and organization, as one member of the committee recalled concerning the Battle of the Atlantic, was an 'anti-submarine campaign waged . . . under closer scientific control than any other campaign in the history of the British Armed Forces . . . '.[106]

On a smaller scale of policy direction, Churchill had also come away from the First World War with the firm conviction that technology must also serve the front-line combatant directly. That conviction, coupled with his fascination for gadgets and his short-term need for special weapons in the summer of 1940, resulted in the creation of an unorthodox section called MD 1, so named because it was the first department established directly under the Minister of Defence. The organizational linkage was no accident. Both Churchill and Lindemann were convinced from Robert Watson-Watt's triumph with radar that one man or a small group of men cut off from the bureaucratic morass could achieve similar accomplishments. Hence, MD 1 was responsible through Lindemann directly to Churchill. This special connection to the Prime Minister ensured almost unlimited support for the organization, which eventually contained an experimental station and proving ground complete with fully equipped workshops, factories, and firing ranges. From this station came such invaluable inventions as the Limpet magnetic mine and its smaller version, the Clam, the 'L' delay-action fuse, and the Jefferis Shoulder Gun, which as the PIAT (Projector Infantry Anti-Tank) became standard equipment.[107]

Churchill's personal connection to MD 1 was indispensable throughout the war. As an organization outside the civil and military bureaucracy, it not surprisingly occasioned a great deal of resistance. When that occurred, the Prime Minister would not interfere until, as in the case of MD 1's anti-tank device, known as the Sticky Bomb, the impasse could not be resolved. At that point, he would bring his supportive powers to bear as he did very succinctly in a memorandum concerning that device. 'Sticky Bomb. Make one million. *WSC.*' At other times, his support could be even more immediate. 'As Prime Minister', he told the MD 1 personnel, after a successful firing demonstration of a weapon at Chequers in 1940, 'I instruct you to proceed with all speed with the development of this excellent weapon. As First Lord of the Treasury, I authorize expenditure of £5,000 on this work to tide you over until proper financial arrangements are made.'[108]

The guiding hand behind such demonstrations was Lindemann, whose love of technological gadgetry and surprise at least equaled the Prime Minister's. Their common delight in such matters, not to mention one aspect of the decision-making process, was illustrated at a dinner at Chequers one night in July 1940. After listening to reports from the military guests which displeased him, Churchill turned to Lindemann and demanded: 'Prof! What have *you* got to tell me today?' An uneasy look spread along the faces of the other dinner guests as Lindemann slowly and with great pride produced a Mills hand grenade from his pocket. 'This, Prime Minister, is the inefficient Mills bomb', he replied, 'issued to the British infantry . . . Now I have designed an improved grenade, which has fewer machined parts and contains a fifty per cent greater bursting charge.' Churchill was ecstatic. 'Splendid, Prof, splendid!', he shouted. 'That's what I like to hear.' And turning to the Chief of the Imperial General Staff: 'Have the Mills bomb scrapped at once and the Lindemann grenade introduced.' The general attempted to explain that contracts for millions of the Mills grenades had been signed in both the United States and England and that it would be impractical to alter the design. But the Prime Minister brushed the arguments aside.[109]

At the strategic level, this impulsiveness could have adverse results at times, particularly when combined with Churchill's deep-seated perception of technology as a panacea for deterring and surprising the enemy. In some cases, the Prime Minister's impulses were checked early on in the project. In July 1943, for example, Churchill asked the Chiefs to examine, under the code name 'Habbakuk', the possibility of turning icebergs into floating air bases that would be virtually unsinkable because of their massive size. The Habbakuk iceberg bases would include installations built from frozen wood pulp and could be used not only against Norway, but eventually Japan as well. In the end, the project never went beyond the memorandum stage because of a general skepticism, the nature of which could be gauged by one scientist's proposal to use the term 'mili-habbakuk' as a new unit for measuring impracticability.[110]

In other cases, such as the dispatch of the *Repulse* and the *Prince of Wales* to 'exert a paralyzing effect upon Japanese naval action', Churchill simply ignored the evidence from the Norwegian campaign and under-estimated the power of air technology against large surface ships.[111] And despite his abiding interest in the tank, he was surprised by the German *Blitzkrieg* and the 'incursion of a mass of fast-moving heavy armour'.[112] In June 1940, he initiated a crash project to create a new type of tank with 500–600 models due by March 1941 over and above the current armor programs. The result was the A22 model, the 'Churchill' tank, literally ordered off the drawing board and, as a consequence, requiring major reworking as the first models began to emerge from the production line. As late as November 1941, the War Office reported that without at least 16 modifications, those products of Churchill's impetuous and impulsive directive would be useless not only for the Middle East, but for sustained operations in Britain as well. By July 1942, these problems were well known as Churchill defended his ministry in the Commons on a vote of confidence. At one point, his speech was interrupted by queries concerning the new tank. 'This tank', the Prime Minister replied in a response that defused the attacks, 'had many defects and teething troubles, and when these became apparent the tank was appropriately re-christened the "Churchill".'[113]

Generally, however, Churchill's firm control over technology development and use had more positive results. The General Strike of 1926 had been a clear indication to him of the power of radio to affect the course of events; and during the next war, the British leader combined his matchless oratorical skills with the new medium to mobilize not only the British people, but the Grand Alliance as well.[114] His policy of severely restricting Ultra recipients and going to any lengths to deceive the Axis concerning British possession of Enigma decrypts ensured effective use of the technology until the German surrender.[115] Equally important, the Prime Minister approved a policy in 1940 of 'bringing American scientists into the war before their Government'.[116] In September of that year, Churchill dispatched a group of serving officers and scientists to the United States with a black leather suitcase containing reports, blueprints, even samples, of almost all important new British war technology – 'the most valuable cargo', one American recipient noted, 'ever brought to our shore'.[117] This 'imaginative act of trust' allowed for the first time the American counterparts to hear civilian scientists discuss authoritatively the new technology of warfare and service representatives describe the practical experience.[118]

Finally, since Churchill viewed the threat as one to national survival, he established an overarching policy that in principle there would be no technological limits in the war. This policy was set in sharp relief to the British leader's disillusioned realization after the First World War that science and technology 'may destroy all that makes human life majestic and tolerable'.[119] That disillusionment continued to contribute to his ambivalent feelings on the matter throughout the next war. 'There is no doubt', he wrote after learning the full extent of the mass extermination of the Jews, 'that this is probably the greatest and most horrible crime ever committed in the whole history of the world, and it has been done by scientific machinery . . .'.[120] Nevertheless, such misuse of technology only reinforced Churchill's perception of how high the stakes had become in total war. The result was a pragmatic acceptance of the extent to which technology had changed the nature of war; and the British leader would often vent his combative indignation against those who opposed this outlook. As early as December 1939, for instance, he was angered as First Lord to read a note prepared by the Air Staff that opposed, for legal reasons, his scheme for mining the Rhine river. In place of the note's formal title, he wrote: 'Some funkstick in the Air Ministry running for shelter . . .'.[121]

Nowhere was this fundamental policy more in evidence than in Churchill's approach to weapons of mass destruction. For him the atomic bomb was just a larger weapon that would make no difference in the principles of war; and as with other war devices, he was quick to share early British research on the technology with the United States even prior to Pearl Harbor. 'Although personally I am quite content with the existing explosives', he minuted the Chiefs of Staff when first informed of the bomb's potential, 'I feel we must not stand in the path of improvement.'[122] As for biological weapons, when the Prof. recommended in February 1944 that Britain stockpile N-bombs, a weapon containing anthrax spores, Churchill agreed, pointing out that if the Germans possessed that type of weapon, 'the only deterrent would be our power to retaliate'.[123] In terms of poison gas, however, the British leader's considerations went beyond just deterrence. In July 1944, during the height of the V-1 rocket assault, Churchill advised the Chiefs of Staff to consider using gas 'to drench' the cities of Germany. 'I want the matter studied in cold blood by sensible people', he concluded, 'and not by that particular set of psalm-singing uniformed defeatists which one runs across . . .'.[124] The Joint Planning Staff provided a comprehensive critique by the end of the month that argued against the use of poison gas. Churchill was not convinced by the negative report. 'But clearly', he responded, 'I cannot make head against the parsons and the warriors at the same time.'[125]

Conclusion

In Winston Churchill's lifetime, weapons and transportation technology advanced from the Lee-Metford rifle and the horse used by the Malakand Field Force to the H-bomb and supersonic aircraft of the Cold War. These developments indelibly changed warfare from the 'sporting game' of his youth – straining but never breaking the British statesman's fundamental faith in what technology could accomplish. In the First World War, that faith was channeled into a pragmatic acceptance of how new technology had immobilized warfare and why it would take technological innovation and counter-measures in areas such as signal intelligence and submarine warfare to remedy the situation. At the same time, Churchill's experiences at the highest political levels of government and as a tactical military commander taught him that policy must direct and organize the development and use of new devices for war, no matter how horrific the outcome, if technology was to be effective in modern conflict.

Britain's victory in the next conflict, then, was a triumph for the cross-currents set in motion for Churchill so many years before in the late Victorian era and honed in the crucible of the Great War. The belief in science and technology as progressive entities made the British leader alive to their possibilities in the struggle for national survival. Accompanying this was the small boy's perpetual delight in tricking and diverting the enemy. To this outlook, Churchill added policy machinery for centralized, pragmatic coordination that allowed him throughout the war to support instantly and unstintingly the many technological initiatives undertaken by Britain. The result was top–down, informed, imaginative, detailed involvement and encouragement in esoteric projects ranging from Ultra and Mulberry to Knickebein and Window. Only in such a milieu could a young scientist like R. V. Jones have made such an immediate contribution. Only in such a milieu could the full brunt of the power of a modern nation-state have been brought to bear so effectively by this late Victorian on the development and use of technology in the greatest cataclysm in human history.

NOTES

1 Edgar Johnson, 'Dickens and the Spirit of the Age', in Warren D. Anderson and Thomas D. Clareson, eds, *Victorian Essays* (Oberlin, OH: Kent State University Press, 1967), p. 30. For this overall progressive outlook on history, see H. Butterfield, *The Whig Interpretation of History* (New York: Charles Scribner's Sons, 1951); and for the particular application of this outlook to Churchill, see J. H. Plumb, 'The Historian', in A. J. P. Taylor, ed., *Churchill Revised: A Critical Assessment* (New York: The Dial Press, 1969) and Maurice Ashley, *Churchill as Historian* (New York: Charles Scribner's Sons, 1968). 'A sense of safety, a pride in the rapidly-opening avenues of progress', Churchill later wrote, 'was the accepted basis upon which the eminent Victorians lived and moved. Can we wonder? Every forward step was followed by swiftly-reaped advantages . . . '. Winston S. Churchill, *Great Contemporaries* (London: Thornton Butterworth, 1937), p. 96. In the first three volumes of his *History of the English-Speaking Peoples*, ending with the Battle of Waterloo, however, Churchill overlooked the massive technological changes underway. There is no mention, for example, of inventions such as the steam engine or inventors like James Watt. R. V. Jones, 'Churchill and Science', in Robert Blake and Wm Roger Louis, eds, *Churchill* (New York: W. W. Norton, 1993), p. 433.

2 Winston Spencer Churchill, *The River War: An Historical Account of the Reconquest of the Soudan*, 2 vols, (London: Longmans, Green, 1899), vol. II, p. 19. The massive dam was set stupendously in the desert around the first cataract of the Nile. It controlled the entire Egyptian irrigation system with a reserve of water that could be released downstream in dry periods to eight smaller barrages that distributed the water among the irrigation canals. James Morris, *Farewell the Trumpets: An Imperial Retreat* (New York: Harcourt Brace, 1978), pp. 351–42.

3 Winston S. Churchill, *The World Crisis, 1911–1914* (New York: Charles Scribner's Sons, 1928), pp. 1 and 4. Churchill considered the Victorian era to be 'the British Antonine Age'. Churchill, *Great Contemporaries*, p. 95. See also Janet and Peter Phillips, *Victorians at Home and Away* (London: Croom Helm, 1978), p. 181.

4 Michael I. Handel, *War, Strategy and Intelligence* (London: Frank Cass, 1989), p. 175. See also A. M. Low, 'Churchill and Science', in Charles Eade, ed., *Churchill by His Contemporaries* (New York: Simon & Schuster, 1954), p. 377.

5 This was the official classification of these conflicts by the British War Office. The type of fighting in small wars against 'savages and semi-civilised races', the official regulation pointed out, was 'distinct from the conditions of modern regular warfare', particularly in terms of treatment to be expected at the hands of 'barbarous' foes: 'A reversal means not defeat alone, it means destruction.' C. E. Callwell, *Small Wars: Their Principles and Practice* (London: Her Majesty's Stationery Office, 1896), pp. 19–20 and 71.

6 Churchill, *River War*, vol. II, p. 338 and Randolph Spencer Churchill, *Winston S. Churchill: Companion Volume I* (Parts I and II hereafter, Randolph Churchill, *WSC*, vol. I, *C*) (Boston, MA: Houghton Mifflin, 1967), p. 792.

7 Winston L. Spencer Churchill, *The Story of the Malakand Field Force: An Episode of Frontier War*, 2nd edn (London: Longmans, Green, 1901), pp. 128, 293.

8 Churchill, *River War*, vol. II, p. 338 and ibid., vol. I, p. 430.

9 Churchill, *Malakand Field Force*, p. 228. See also Churchill's defense of the Dum-Dum at Churchill, *River War*, vol. II, p. 338: 'After all no wounds are more

appalling than those caused by splinters of shell, a projectile whose legitimacy has never been challenged.' In a letter to his grandmother, however, Churchill referred to the 'appalling' effects of the Dum-Dum. Randolph Churchill, *WSC*, vol. I, *C*, p. 810.

10 Churchill, *Malakand Field Force*, p. 288. There was no such effectiveness in the Mark II, nickel-cased Lee-Metford bullets that accompanied the British brigade to the Sudan. As a result, the brigade commander ordered that a million rounds of this ammunition be converted into Dum-Dum bullets by filing off the tips and exposing the heavy core inside the outer case. 'These missiles', Churchill observed, 'were afterwards . . . found satisfactory as far as killing power was concerned.' Churchill, *River War*, vol. I, p. 367.

11 Quoted in Randolph Churchill, *Winston S. Churchill*, vol. I. *Youth: 1874–1900* (hereafter Randolph Churchill, *WSC*, vol. I) (Boston, MA: Houghton, Mifflin 1966), p. 403. Churchill had left his revolver behind. 'Now I have nothing but this new-complicated-and-untried-though apparently excellent Mauser Pistol', he wrote his mother from Luxor on 5 August 1898. Randolph Churchill, *WSC*, vol. I, *C*, p. 957.

12 Churchill, *River War*, vol. II, p. 349. 'I write as the only British officer who has used this weapon in actual war.' Ibid., p. 351. 'The pistol . . . is incomparably more terrible than any *arme blanche*.' Ibid., p. 347.

13 Churchill, *River War*, vol. I, p. 142. In February 1944, Churchill agreed to a recommendation that Britain should stockpile N-bombs, a weapon containing anthrax spores to which there was no 'known cure and no effective prophylax'. Quoted in Martin Gilbert, *Winston S. Churchill*, vol. VII: *Road to Victory* (hereafter Gilbert, *WSC*, vol. VII) (Boston, MA: Houghton, Mifflin, 1986), p. 776.

14 Churchill, *River War*, vol. II, pp. 223–4 and Frederick Woods, ed., *Winston S. Churchill: War Correspondent, 1895–1900* (London: Brassey's 1992), p. 146. But see Churchill's callous observations to his mother: 'I am just off with Lord Tullibardine to ride over the field', he wrote. 'It will smell I expect as there are 7,000 bodies lying there. I hope to get some spears, etc.' Randolph Churchill, *WSC*, vol. I, *C*, p. 974.

15 Churchill, *River War*, vol. II, pp. 322 and 375 and Frederick Woods, ed., *Artillery of Words: The Writings of Sir Winston Churchill* (London: Leo Cooper, 1992), p. 42.

16 Woods, *Churchill: War Correspondent*, p. 145; Churchill, *River War*, vol. II, p. 221; and Woods, *Artillery of Words*, pp. 41–2.

17 Churchill, *River War*, vol. II, p. 197. See also ibid., p. 143, in which Churchill noted that 'war, disguise it as you may, is but a dirty, shoddy business, which only a fool would undertake'.

18 Randolph Churchill, *WSC*, vol. I, p. 409.

19 Ibid. See also G. W. Stevens, *With Kitchener to Khartoum* (1898; reprint, London: Greenhill Books, 1990), p. 285: 'It was impossible not to kill the Dervishes: they refused to go back alive.'

20 Churchill, *River War*, vol. II, p. 38 and Kirk Emmert, *Winston S. Churchill on Empire* (Durham, NC: Carolina Academic Press, 1989), p. 30.

21 Churchill, *River War*, vol. II, p. 250.

22 Winston S. Churchill, *London to Ladysmith via Pretoria* (London: Longmans, Green, 1900), p. 429; William Manchester, *The Last Lion: Winston Spencer Churchill: Visions of Glory, 1874–1932* (Boston, MA: Little, Brown, 1983), p. 317; and Randolph Churchill, *WSC*, vol. I, *C*, p. 1147.

23 Churchill, *London to Ladysmith*, pp. 416 and 429 and Winston S. Churchill, *A Roving Commission* (New York: Charles Scribner's Sons, 1951), p. 309. Churchill noted that the artillery effect had been produced by far less than a battery of howitzers. 'Yet in a European war', he concluded presciently, 'there would have been . . . three or four batteries. I do not see how troops can be handled in masses in such conditions.' Churchill, *London to Ladysmith*, p. 420.

24 Martin Gilbert, *Winston Churchill*, vol. VI: *Finest Hour, 1939–1941* (hereafter Gilbert, *WSC*, vol. VI) (Boston, MA: Houghton Mifflin, 1983), p. 800.

25 Quoted in Lord Moran, *Churchill: Taken from the Diaries of Lord Moran: The Struggle for Survival, 1940–1965* (Boston, MA: Houghton, Mifflin, 1966), p. 254.

26 Winston S. Churchill, *Ian Hamilton's March* (London: Longmans, Green, 1900), p. 386.

27 Ibid., p. 244. 'Rifles can inflict the loss, but victory depends . . . on the bayonets.' Churchill, *London to Ladysmith*, pp. 244–5. See also Churchill's proud assertion in his mid-life autobiography that in the cavalry charge of the 21st Lancers at Omdurman, 'the British too fought with sword and lance as in the days of old'. Churchill, *Roving Commission*, p. 194. The eleventh edition of the *Encyclopaedia Britannica* informed its readers that 'losses in battle are . . . almost insignificant when compared with the fearful carnage wrought by sword and spear.' Manchester, *Last Lion*, p. 74.

28 Winston S. Churchill, *The World Crisis, 1915* (New York: Charles Scribner's Sons, 1928), p. 7.

29 Martin Gilbert, *Winston Churchill*, vol. IV: *The Stricken World. 1916–1922* (hereafter Gilbert, *WSC*, vol. IV) (Boston, MA: Houghton Mifflin, 1975), p. 521.

30 Churchill, *World Crisis, 1911–1914*, p. 3. See also Winston S. Churchill, *The World Crisis, 1916–1918*, Part I (London: Thornton Butterworth, 1927), p. 19.

31 Winston S. Churchill, *The Aftermath* (New York: Charles Scribner's Sons, 1929), p. 483.

32 Winston S. Churchill, *Thoughts and Adventures* (London: Odhams Press, 1949), pp. 112–13. See also Gilbert, *WSC*, vol. IV, p. 915, for the election speech notes used by Churchill in 1922 which began:
>What a disappointment the Twentieth Century has been
>How terrible & how melancholy
>is long series of disastrous events
>wh have darkened its first 20 years.

33 Churchill, *Thoughts and Adventures*, p. 201 and Churchill, *Aftermath*, p. 479.

34 Churchill, *Roving Commission*, p. 180. 'The scale on which events have shaped themselves, has dwarfed the episodes of the Victorian era. Its small wars . . . belong to a vanished period.' Churchill, *World Crisis, 1911–1914*, p. 20.

35 Churchill, *Thoughts and Adventures*, pp. 188–90. The article was published in *Nash's Pall Mall* magazine on 24 September 1924.

36 Quoted in Martin Gilbert, *Winston Churchill*, vol. V: *The Prophet of Truth, 1922–1939* (hereafter Gilbert, *WSC*, vol. V) (Boston, MA: Houghton, Mifflin, 1977), p. 443. In the article, Churchill referred to a 'German' who had recently told him that the next war would be fought with electricity. The German was Lindemann. Ibid., p. 51. Lindemann could hardly have been pleased by this reference, since he apparently had a lifelong grievance against his mother because she traveled from England to Baden-Baden shortly before he was born and gave birth to him on German territory. Jones, 'Churchill and Science', p. 430.

37 Quoted in Gilbert, *WSC*, vol. V, p. 421. In 1928, Churchill asked Lindemann to

work out the diameter of pipes and other data on the design and workings of fountains at Chartwell. Once these data were received and tried out, Churchill gratefully telegraphed the 'Prof.:' 'Water flowing beautifully according to your calculations.' Quoted in R. V. Jones, 'Winston Leonard Spencer Churchill, 1874–1965', *Biographical Memoirs of Fellows of the Royal Society*, vol. XII (London: Headley Brothers, 1966) p. 68. Churchill's youngest daughter later recalled that between 1925 until the outbreak of the Second World War, Lindemann signed the Chartwell Visitors' Book 112 times. Mary Soames, *Clementine Churchill: Biography of a Marriage* (Boston, MA: Houghton Mifflin, 1979), p. 229. On the personalities and relationship of Churchill and Lindemann, see C. P. Snow, *Science and Government* (Cambridge, MA: Harvard University Press, 1961), pp. 12 and 22–3; R. V. Jones, *Most Secret War* (London: Hamish Hamilton, 1978), p. 14; and John Colville, *The Churchillians* (London: Weidenfeld & Nicholson, 1981), p. 31.

38 The article appeared in *Strand Magazine*. See Churchill, *Thoughts and Adventures*, pp. 206 and 210. The only note of pessimism concerned what he called 'robotization', a condition in which man surrenders his freedom and ordering of life to a government of scientists and impersonal planners. He was influenced by Karel Čapek's play, *Rossum's Universal Robots (RUR)*, which he had seen a few years earlier. His views, of course, anticipated those in Huxley's *Ape and Essence* and Orwell's *1984*. As for the creations in *RUR*, Churchill concluded that 'Robots could be made to fit the grisly theories of Communism.' Ibid., p. 211. Tennyson's visionary future was also a favorite of President Truman, who wrote these lines on a scrap of paper that he carried with him for over 50 years. See John Hersey, *Life Sketches* (New York: Knopf, 1989), pp. 245–6.

39 Winston S. Churchill, *The Second World War*, vol. II: *Their Finest Hour* (hereafter Churchill, *Second World War*, vol. II) (Boston, MA: Houghton Mifflin, 1949), pp. 381–2.

40 Robert Rhodes James, ed., *Winston S. Churchill: His Complete Speeches, 1897–1963*, vol. VI: *1935–1942* (London: Chelsea House, 1974), p. 6238.

41 Ibid., vol. VII: *1943–1949*, p. 7246.

42 Ibid., p. 7920. The actual title of the speech was 'The Sinews of Peace'.

43 Ibid., vol. VIII: *1950–1963*, pp. 8629 and 8626. In the November 1953 debate concerning the H-bomb, Churchill expressed a similar thought: 'It may be that . . . when the advance of destructive weapons enables everyone to kill everybody else nobody will want to kill anyone at all.' Quoted in ibid., p. 8505. In terms of 'Fifty Years Hence', Churchill expressed the wish that 'the House will not reprove me for vanity or conceit if I repeat what I wrote a quarter of a century ago.' Quoted in ibid., p. 8625. See also Jones, *Biographical Memoirs of Fellows of the Royal Society*, pp. 98–100.

44 Quoted in Rhodes James, *Complete Speeches*, vol. VII: *1943–1949*, p. 7244.

45 Quoted in Jones, *Biographical Memoirs of Fellows of the Royal Society*, p. 100.

46 Quoted in Rhodes James, *Complete Speeches*, vol. VIII: *1950–1963*, p. 8705.

47 Ibid., p. 8706.

48 Quoted in Gilbert, *WSC*, vol. IV, p. 8, and Churchill, *World Crisis, 1916–1918*, Part II, p. 305. 'In nearly every great war there is some new mechanical feature introduced the early understanding of which confers important advantages,' Churchill noted after the war in his study of his great ancestor. Winston S. Churchill, *Marlborough His Life and Times*, vol. III. *1702–1704*. (New York: Charles Scribner's Sons, 1935), p. 107. See also Ashley, *Churchill as Historian*, p. 101.

49 Churchill, *World Crisis, 1915*, p. 80. On the origin of the term 'tank', see Ernest D. Swinton, *Eyewitness: Being Personal Reminiscences of Certain Phases of the Great War, Including the Genesis of the Tank* (Garden City, NY: Doubleday, Doran, 1933), p. 161.

50 Churchill, *World Crisis, 1916–1918*, Part 1, p. 185.

51 Churchill, *World Crisis, 1915*, p. 82.

52 Churchill, *World Crisis, 1916–1918*, Part 2, p. 567.

53 Winston S. Churchill, *The Unknown War* (New York: Charles Scribner's Sons, 1931, p. 311.

54 Churchill, *World Crisis, 1916–1918*, Part 2, p. 345. Churchill later commented: 'Accusing as I do without exception all the great allied offensives of 1915, 1916, and 1917, as needless and wrongly conceived operations of infinite cost, I am bound in reply to the question, What else could be done? And I answer it, pointing to the Battle of Cambrai, "This could have been done." This in many variants, this in larger and better forms ought to have been done, and would have been done if only the Generals had not been content to fight machine-gun bullets with the breasts of gallant men, and think that that was waging war.' Ibid., p. 348.

55 Prior to the beginning of the Somme Campaign on 1 July 1916, a British barrage had lashed the German trenches for a week. 'Thus', Churchill noted mournfully, 'there was no chance of surprise.' Ibid., Part 1, p. 172. See also H. G. Martin, 'Churchill and the Army', in Eade, ed., *Churchill by His Contemporaries*, p. 23.

56 Churchill, *World Crisis, 1916–1918*, Part 2, pp. 504–5 and 507. Churchill knew Sir Henry Rawlinson from Omdurman where the future general had been on Kitchener's staff. In the First World War, they had watched together from a haystack the battle around Soissons in September 1914. Later, Rawlinson had arrived at Antwerp to take over command from Churchill before the evacuation of that city.

57 Ibid., pp. 517–18.

58 Quoted in Jones, *Biographical Memoirs of Fellows of the Royal Society*, p. 84; Alfred Stanford, *Force Mulberry* (New York: William Morrow, 1951), p. 39; and Guy Hartcup, *Code Name Mulberry: The Planning, Building and Operation of the Normandy Harbors* (New York: Hippocrene Books, 1977), p. 28. For D-Day, the requirements were to land, supply and reinforce 185,000 men and 20,000 vehicles. Robin Higham, 'Technology and D-Day', Eisenhower Foundation, ed., *D-Day: The Normandy Invasion in Retrospect*, (Lawrence, KS: University of Kansas Press, 1971), p. 22. For the July 1917 memorandum dealing with the creation of '*a torpedo – and weather-proof harbour*', see Churchill, *Second World War*, vol. II, p. 245. (Original emphasis.) Churchill did not print the memorandum in *The World Crisis* for reasons of space – a fortuitous choice, as he later noted, since 'the Germans certainly read my war books with attention'. Ibid., p. 246.

59 Handel, *War, Strategy and Intelligence*, p. 144.

60 Hartcup, *Code Name Mulberry*, p. 141.

61 Churchill, *World Crisis, 1915*, p. 65.

62 Ibid., p. 300.

63 Ibid., Part 2, p. 564.

64 Quoted in Gilbert, *WSC*, vol. VI, p. 97. The de-magnetization process became known because of the publicity given the subject when Queen Elizabeth arrived in New York. Winston S. Churchill *The Second World War: vol. I: The Gathering Storm* (hereafter Churchill, *Second World War*, vol. I) (Boston, MA: Houghton, Mifflin, 1948), p. 711.

65 Gilbert, *WSC*, vol. VI, pp. 102 and 283, and Jones, *Most Secret War*, pp. 92–5.
66 Quoted in Gilbert, *WSC*, vol. VI, p. 583.
67 Churchill, *Second World War*, vol. II, p. 387.
68 Ibid. See also Gilbert, *WSC*, vol. VI, p. 1082, for the very successful beam bend on 8 May 1941 in which German bombers dropped 235 bombs on empty fields many miles distant from their actual target at the Rolls-Royce works in Derby. Churchill later told Jones that Knickebein worried him 'for a few minutes more than any other in 1940'. In Jones, *Biographical Memoirs of Fellows of the Royal Society*, p. 73.
69 Quoted in Jones, *Most Secret War*, p. 297. Window was first used during the 24 July 1943 night attack on Hamburg to great effect. It was unanticipated by the Germans and for some time reduced British bomber losses by half. 'On the whole', Churchill concluded, 'it may be claimed that we released it about the right time.' Winston S. Churchill, *The Second World War*, vol. IV: *The Hinge of Fate* (hereafter Churchill, *Second World War*, vol. IV) (Boston, MA: Houghton, Mifflin, 1950), p. 289. The Germans were surprised by the metallic chaff because of the timing. They had tested devices similar to Window (*Duppel*), but, with what Michael Handel called 'ostrich-like' irrationality, deliberately elected not to develop counter-measures, fearing that the British might learn from their experiments and devise a similar counter-measure. Handel, *War, Strategy and Intelligence*, p. 135.
70 Michael Handel, 'Introduction: Strategic and Operational Deception in Historical Perspective', in idem., ed., *Strategic and Operational Deception in the Second World War* (London: Frank Cass, 1987), pp. 32 and 35. A series of incredible windfalls provided Britain with the three principal German naval codes, affording that country in Churchill's estimation, 'the incomparable advantage of reading the plans and orders of the enemy before they were executed'. Churchill, *World Crisis, 1916–1918*, Part I, pp. 118–19. See also ibid., *1911–1914*, p. 503, and Christopher Andrew, *Her Majesty's Secret Service* (New York: Viking, 1986), p. 89.
71 Patrick Beesly, *Room 40* (London: Hamish Hamilton, 1981), p. 16. Beesly observed that 'Excessively Secret' would have been a more accurate description.
72 Churchill, *World Crisis, 1915*, p. 51.
73 Ibid., p. 127. By noon, the next day, the battle was over; and although one of the four German battle cruisers had been sunk, there had been a combination of mixed signals and missed opportunities. For Churchill, this was just one more piece in a mosaic depicting how wide the gap could be between accurate, timely strategic intelligence and successful use of that intelligence for surprise at the operational level. 'Thus', he summed up the Dogger Bank action, 'when already in the jaws of destruction, the German Battle Cruiser Squadron escaped.' Ibid., p. 137.
74 Ronald Lewin, *Ultra Goes to War* (New York: McGraw-Hill, 1978), p. 183.
75 Ibid.
76 Without Churchill's support, Harold Deutsch pointed out, 'Bletchley Park would have been almost inconceivable.' Quoted in David Kahn, *Kahn on Codes* (London: Macmillan, 1983), p. 91. To the question why, if Ultra was so important, it had not ended the war earlier, Deutsch replied, 'It did end sooner.' Ibid.
77 Lewin, *Ultra Goes to War*, p. 127.
78 Latter, the cryptoanalyst recalled that 'almost from that day the rough ways began miraculously to be made smooth . . . and we were able to devote ourselves uninterruptedly to the business-at-hand'. Quoted in P. S. Milner-Barry, '"Action this

Day": The Letter from Bletchley Park Cryptoanalysts to the Prime Minister, 21 October 1941', *Intelligence and National Security*, vol. 1, No. 2 (May 1986), pp. 272–3. See also Appendix 3, in F. H. Hinsley *et al.*, *British Intelligence in the Second World War: Its Influence on Strategy and Operations*, vol. II (London: HMSO, 1981), pp. 655–7; Andrew Hodges, *Alan Turing: The Enigma* (New York: Simon & Schuster, 1983), pp. 219–21; and Gilbert, *WSC*, vol. VI, p. 1185.

79 Churchill, *World Crisis, 1911–1914*, pp. 122–3. The Admiralty yacht, *Enchantress*, became his office, 'almost my home', in the three years prior to the war. In all, Churchill spent eight months afloat in that period. Ibid. For Churchill's 1 July 1913 speech, in which he defended the use of the yacht, see Rhodes James, *Complete Speeches*, vol. II, *1908–1913*, pp. 2122–4. On one such trip, he and the Prime Minister went to sea to witness gunnery practice. Soon, one observer noted, Churchill was 'dancing about behind the guns, elevating, depressing, and sighting'. Quoted in Arthur J. Marder, *From the Dreadnought to Scapa Flow: The Royal Navy in the Fisher Era, 1904–1919*, vol. I: *The Road to War, 1904–1914* (London: Oxford University Press, 1961), p. 253. Lloyd George believed at the time that the Navy had become 'an obsession' with Churchill: 'You have become a water creature', he told him. 'You think we all live in the sea . . . You forget that most of us live on land.' Quoted in Randolph S. Churchill, *Winston S. Churchill*, vol. II, *1901–1914: Young Statesman* (hereafter Randolph Churchill, *WSC*, vol. II) (Boston, MA: Houghton Mifflin, 1967), p. 558.

80 Churchill, *World Crisis, 1911–1914*, p. 139.

81 In 1913, Churchill had read 'one of those nightmare novels', in which the Germans had fired on the British Fleet with an unheard-of 15-inch gun. 'There was real satisfaction', he noted after the successful British test of the gun, 'in feeling that anyhow this boot was on the other leg.' Ibid. Churchill entitled the entire chapter dealing with the new naval guns in his post-war memoirs, 'The Romance of Design.' Ibid., pp. 125–48.

82 Ibid., p. 136.

83 Marder, *Dreadnought to Scapa Flow*, pp. 270–1. 'To commit the Navy irrevocably to oil was indeed "to take arms against a sea of troubles".' Churchill, *World Crisis, 1911–1914*, p. 135. See Churchill's 17 March 1914 speech on 'Naval Estimates' for 1914–15 on the advantages of oil and the link to naval armament and speed. In Rhodes James, *Complete Speeches*, vol. III: *1914–1922*, pp. 2241 and 2250–2. The *Daily Telegraph*, not a friendly source, called it 'the most weighty and eloquent speech . . . during the present generation'. Quoted in ibid., p. 2233. Robert Rhodes James regards the speech 'as one of the finest he made during his tenure of the Admiralty'. Ibid.

84 Michael Howard, 'Churchill and the First World War', in Blake and Louis, eds, *Churchill*, p. 135.

85 Randolph Churchill, *WSC*, vol. II, p. 683. See also ibid., pp. 597 and 592–3 and Churchill, *World Crisis, 1911–1914*, p. 139. For Churchill's prescient forecast for expanded naval aviation roles, see his 17 March 1914, 'Navy Estimates for 1914–15' speech. In Rhodes-James, *Complete Speeches*, vol. III, *1914–1922*, pp. 2244–5. See also Norman Friedman, *British Carrier Airation: The Evolution of the Ships and Their Aircraft* (Annapolis, MD: Naval Institute Press, 1988), pp. 23 and 28, and Roger Chessman, *Aircraft Carriers of the World: 1914 to the Present: An Illustrated Encyclopedia* (Annapolis, MD: Naval Institute Press, 1984), p. 79.

86 Swinton, *Eyewitness*, p. 79, Churchill recalled that the design produced in October

1914 was for a caterpillar tractor. Churchill, *World Crisis, 1915*, p. 63. Swinton, however, pointed out that the design was for a wheeled tractor capable of crossing trenches by means of a portable bridge to be laid down in front and then hauled up after passage. Swinton, *Eyewitness*, p. 80. See also Howard, 'Churchill and the First World War', p. 136 and Jones, *Biographical Memoirs of Fellows of the Royal Society*, p. 57.

87 Swinton, *Eyewitness*, p. 80. The Admiralty and the War Office proceeded on two independent tracks, each unaware of the other's efforts. It was not until 30 May 1915 that a link was established concerning tank development between the two offices. 'This surely was a malicious prank of fate', Swinton concluded, 'for had we been able to collaborate in that autumn of 1914 – Mr Churchill bringing to the scheme his initiative, driving power, and all the weight attaching to his position as a Minister – it is possible that the benefit of this new weapon might have been bestowed on our arms many months earlier than was actually the case – with what saving of life God alone knows.' Ibid., p. 81.

88 Basil Liddell Hart, 'The Military Strategist', in Taylor, ed., *Churchill Revised*, p. 196. Nevertheless, Churchill never claimed primary advocacy. He acknowledged that a 1903 H. G. Wells article 'had practically exhausted the possibilities in this sphere'. Moreover, there was also Swinton and his small band of armor pioneers in the British Army. 'There never was a moment which it was possible to say that a tank had been "invented"', Churchill wrote later. 'There never was a person about whom it could be said "this man invented the tank".' Churchill, *World Crisis, 1915*, pp. 69–70. Swinton referred to himself as the 'originator' of the tank. Swinton, *Eyewitness*, p. x. But his own flowchart of the tank's development demonstrates the absolute criticality of the efforts by Churchill and the Admiralty in 1915 that resulted in the successful trial of 'Mother' on 2 February 1916. See the diagram in ibid., p. 326. Churchill's 3 December 1915 memorandum to the Army commander was entitled 'Variants of the Offensive', the first of which was 'The Attack by Armour'. Churchill, *World Crisis, 1915*, p. 78–81. See also Jones, *Biographical Memoirs of Fellows of the Royal Society*, p. 57, and Howard, 'Churchill and the First World War', p. 136. For Churchill's account of how he momentarily lost a copy of the 'Variants' memo on the front lines while commanding his battalion at 'Plugstreet', see Churchill, *Thoughts and Adventures*, pp. 79–85.

89 Churchill, *World Crisis, 1915*, p. 425.

90 Ibid., p. 71.

91 Ibid., *1916–1918*, Part 2, p. 564. This belief was reinforced by Churchill's experience with the Stokes gun, a hand-held mortar with a design based on the need for immediately responsive, short-range indirect fire to be used at close quarters in attacks on trenches. 'All the ideas on which this scheme rests', he wrote after the demonstration, 'have come from officers who have been themselves constantly engaged in trench warfare.' Churchill, *World Crisis, 1915*, p. 496. See also ibid., *1916–1918*, Part 2, pp. 139 and 553.

92 Churchill, *World Crisis, 1916–1918*, Part 2, p. 315. For examples of Churchill's continued interest in the effects of the tank on the battlefield, see ibid., pp. 297–303 and 13–18. Churchill was delighted as Minister of Munitions by the use of tanks when the British Army began its offensive in August 1918. 'Coming over here', he wrote from France in September, 'makes me thoroughly content with my office . . . I am content to be associated with the splendid machines of the British Army . . .'. Howard, 'Churchill and the First World War', pp. 142–3. Churchill continued

to press for mechanization as Chancellor of the Exchequer in the late 1920s. At the same time, however, he insisted that since mechanized units would be able to perform the same duties as a larger number of non-mechanized units, the process should result in a significant and almost immediate reduction in the army estimates. Ironically, the consequent lack of funding was a major obstacle to mechanization, even as Churchill continued to encourage the realization of that goal. See David French, 'The Mechanisation of the British Cavalry Between the Wars'. Unpublished paper.

93 Churchill, *World Crisis, 1916–1918*, Part 1, p. 199, and Churchill, *Thoughts and Adventures*, p. 109.

94 Churchill, *Great Contemporaries*, p. 118. See also Churchill, *World Crisis, 1916–1918*, Part 1, pp. 213–14.

95 Churchill, *Second World War*, vol. II, pp. 337–8. Churchill, 'saw himself mainly as a stimulus for the development of new and better technologies rather than as an expert in his own right'. Michael I. Handel, 'Leaders and Intelligence', in idem., ed., *Leaders and Intelligence* (London: Frank Cass, 1989), p. 8.

96 Herbert Goldhammer, *The Adviser* (New York: Elsevier, 1978), p. 89. 'The Lindemann–Churchill relation is the purest example possible of court politics.' Snow, *Science and Government*, p. 63. In his early days as grey eminence, Lindemann made his influence known by conducting interviews at 10 Downing Street. Ibid., p. 64.

97 Churchill, *Second World War*, II, pp. 337–8. See also Goldhammer, *Adviser*, p. 91, and Gilbert, *WSC*, vol. VI, p. 659. But see Churchill's tribute in his only novel to Savrola, a man 'whose business it was to know everything'. Winston S. Churchill, *Savrola: A Tale of the Revolution in Laurania* (New York: Random House, 1956), p. 41.

98 Snow, *Science and Government*, p. 63. Much of the criticism was based on Lindemann's lack of support for the development of radar in the inter-war years. 'How anyone could listen with anything but the deepest skepticism to an authority whose scientific opinion on a military matter of the first importance had proved so resoundingly wrong is not intelligible to an ordinary man. But Churchill was not an ordinary man.' Richard Ollard, 'Churchill and the Navy', in Blake and Louis, *Churchill*, p. 389.

99 As calculated by the noted scientist P. M. S. Blackett who noted that Whitehall, plagued by 'a certain allergy to arithmetic', did not listen to his warning. P. M. S. Blackett, *Studies of War: Nuclear and Conventional* (New York: Hill & Wang, 1962), p. 110. But Cherwell also instigated an investigation of the 7 November 1941 Bomber Command raid on Berlin which concluded that only about one-third of aircraft claiming to have reached the target actually did so. This so-called 'Butt Report' increased Churchill's skepticism concerning strategic bombing. 'You need not argue the value of bombing Germany', he wrote to the Air Staff in March 1942, 'because I have my own opinion about that, namely, that it is not decisive . . .'. Quoted in Gilbert, *WSC*, vol. VII, p. 75.

100 In May 1943, Lindemann considered the development of German rockets 'a remote contingency'. Hinsley *et al.*, *British Intelligence in the Second World War*, vol. III, Part I (London: HMSO, 1984), p. 373. The next month, he arranged for R. V. Jones to give a briefing on the rocket threat. After each of Jones' points, all in contradiction of Lindemann's, Churchill would turn to 'the Prof.' 'Hear that! Remember it was you who introduced him to me.' Quoted in Jones, *Biographical Memoirs of Fellows of the Royal Society*, p. 82.

101 John Keegan, 'Churchill's Strategy', in Blake and Louis, *Churchill*, p. 344.
102 Churchill, *World Crisis, 1916–1918*, Part 1, p. 193.
103 Jones, *Biographical Memoirs of Fellows of the Royal Society*, p. 75, and R. V. Jones, 'Intelligence and Command', in Handel, *Leaders and Intelligence*, pp. 290–1. Michael Handel concludes that 'Churchill's genius as a leader was in identifying men of good scientific judgement and knowing to whom he should listen.' Handel, 'Leaders and Intelligence', p. 8. In 1953, John Martin, Churchill's Private Secretary, wrote to Lindemann: 'Those without experience in the inner circle will never know the size of Winston's debt to you and how much stimulus and inspiration of ideas flowed from your office.' Quoted in Gilbert, *WSC*, vol. V, p. 50n.
104 Gilbert, *WSC*, VI, p. 615.
105 Ibid., p. 768.
106 Blackett, *Studies of War*, p. 238. See also, Churchill's exhortation to a similar committee in the previous war: 'Let every resource and invention be applied. Let the anti-submarine war claim priority and dominance over every other form of British effort.' Churchill, *World Crisis, 1916–1918*, Part 1, p. 254.
107 Frederick Winston Smith, *The Professor and the Prime Minister* (Boston, MA: Houghton, Mifflin, 1962), pp. 234–5; R. Stuart Macrae, *Winston Churchill's Toyshop* (New York: Walker, 1971), p. 96; and Lewin, *Churchill as Warlord*, p. 52.
108 Quoted in Macrae, *Winston Churchill's Toyshop*, pp. 125, 169 and 186. At weapon demonstrations, Churchill's bodyguard always carried a stengun for the Prime Minister's use on the nearest target whenever there were lulls in the proceedings. Ibid., p. 167.
109 Quoted in Gilbert, *WSC*, vol. VI, p. 684.
110 Churchill chose the code name from the biblical text: 'Behold ye among the heathen, and regard, and wonder marvelously: for I will work a work in your days which ye will not believe, though it be told you.' Quoted in ibid., vol. VII, p. 446.
111 Quoted in ibid., VI, p. 1296. 'We must just KBO', Churchill said on 11 December 1941, the day after the sinking of the two ships. (KBO, he explained, meant 'Keep Buggering On.') In ibid., p. 1273. 'They had been sent to these waters', Churchill wrote of the two ships, 'to exercise that kind of vague menace which capital ships of the highest quality whose whereabouts is unknown can impose upon all hostile naval calculations.' Churchill, *Second World War*, vol. III, pp. 615–16. 'In common with the prevailing Admiralty belief before the war, I did not sufficiently measure the danger to . . . British warships from air attack.' Churchill, *Second World War*, vol. I, p. 325. See also S. W. Roskill, *Churchill and the Admirals* (New York: William Morrow, 1978), pp. 196–201. Admiral Tom Phillips, who lost his life in the attacks, was so convinced that aircraft could not seriously damage great ships, that once during the Phoney War, a colleague rounded on the diminutive officer in exasperation: 'One day, Tom, you will be standing on a box on your bridge . . . and your ship will be smashed to pieces by bombers and torpedo aircraft. As she sinks, your last words will be, "That was a . . . great mine!"' Quoted in Hastings Lionel Ismay, *The Memoirs of General Lord Ismay* (New York: Viking Press, 1960), p. 240.
112 Churchill, *Second World War*, vol. II, p. 43. 'Not having had access to official information for so many years, I did not comprehend the violence of the revolution . . . I knew about it, but it had not altered my inward convictions as it should have done.' Ibid.
113 Quoted in Rhodes James, *Complete Speeches*, vol. VI, *1935–1942*, p. 6655. The humorist A. P. Herbert, an MP for Oxford University, was present at the time.

'The world seemed suddenly a better place', he recalled, 'Rommel a menace no more, and Churchill the only man.' A. P. Herbert, 'Churchill's Humor', in Eade, *Churchill by His Contemporaries*, p. 373. At the conclusion of the debate, only 25 members voted against Churchill, a consoling figure to the historically minded Prime Minister in more than one way, since it duplicated the number of votes against the younger Pitt in his conduct of the war in 1799. Equally important was a message from across the Atlantic. 'Good for you', Roosevelt telegraphed. 'Action of House of Commons today delighted me.' Gilbert, *WSC*, vol. VII, p. 140. See also Lewin, *Churchill as War Lord*, p. 51.

114 During the war, Churchill gave 56 broadcasts to British audiences, 49 as Prime Minister. These broadcasts varied in length from 84 seconds for the initial announcement in 1940 of the fall of France to the 48-minute May 1943 address to the US Congress. D. J. Wender, 'Churchill, Radio, and Cinema', in Blake and Louis, eds, *Churchill*, pp. 216 and 221. See also Richard Dimbleby, 'Churchill the Broadcaster', in Eade, *Churchill by His Contemporaries*, pp. 344–54.

115 Nevertheless, Churchill did not hoard the information for his own use, as Hitler and Stalin did with their intelligence, and made it available to the Chiefs of Staff, the Joint Intelligence Committee and the Commanders-in-Chief. With the information soaked into his prodigious memory, Churchill would still hector his military advisers, but would only act in the end after he had persuaded them or they, normally after Herculean efforts, had convinced him. Lewin, *Ultra Goes to War*, pp. 183–4. For examples of how oppressively Churchill could apply his Ultra knowledge in his communication with his operational commanders, see Gilbert, *WSC*, vol. VII, pp. 130, 213, 227, and 359 and Ralph Bennett, *Ultra in the West* (London: Hutchinson, 1979), p. 38.

116 Quoted in Blackett, *Studies of War*, p. 107.

117 Quoted in Snow, *Science and Government*, p. 45. The group was under the leadership of Sir Henry Tizard, the scientific adviser to the Air Ministry, and a chairman of the inter-war Air Defence Committee, in which he had been at odds with his former friend Lindemann. For complete details on the mission, see David Zimmerman, *Top Secret Exchange: The Tizard Mission and the Scientific War* (Montreal and Kingston: McGill-Queen's University Press, 1996).

118 Blackett, *Studies of War*, p. 108. See also Snow, *Science and Government*, p. 45. It was also an acknowledgment by Churchill that when British scientists made technological breakthroughs as with the cavity magnetron, the basis for short-range radar, British industry could not manufacture it in quantity and had to depend on reimportation from the United States to satisfy demand. Keegan, 'Churchill's Strategy', p. 344.

119 Churchill, *Thoughts and Adventures*, p. 213. See also Low, 'Churchill and Science', p. 387.

120 Quoted in Gilbert, *WSC*, vol. VII, p. 847.

121 Quoted in Gilbert, *WSC*, vol. VI, pp. 90–1. At the end of June 1940, as the invasion seemed imminent, Churchill approved a scheme to send five ships into German-held French ports to 'scatter burning all over the harbour, possibly with most pleasing results'. In ibid., p. 815. This was followed in August by 'Operation Razzle', the dropping of incendiary pellets into German forests. Ibid., p. 711. Neither operation was successful.

122 Quoted in Jones, *Biographical Memoirs of Fellows of the Royal Society*, p. 86. In August 1941, a report from the British MAUD Committee on the potential of the uranium bomb was sent to the United States. By June 1942, the collaboration

began to fray as the Americans became less forthcoming, operating on the principle that only atomic information helpful to winning the war should be released to Britain. On 10 August 1943, Roosevelt and Churchill signed an agreement in which all British rights in post-war atomic industrial and commercial developments were surrendered to the United States, Ibid., pp. 86–8.

123 Quoted in Gilbert, *WSC*, vol. VII, p. 776. For an exoneration of charges later made in a BBC broadcast that Churchill's intentions for the development of the N-bombs went beyond just deterrence, see Appendix 8, 'Churchill and Biological Warfare, 1944', in Julian Lewis, *Changing Direction: British Military Planning for Post-War Strategic Defence, 1942–1947* (London: Sherwood Press, 1988), pp. 388–405. In any event, judging by the protracted and heated arguments on 'Window', there would have been even more extreme debate before crossing the biological warfare threshold.

124 Quoted in Gilbert, *WSC*, vol. VII, pp. 840–1.

125 Quoted in ibid., p. 865. The subject of using poison gas either for technological surprise or as a deterrent was not raised again, even when the V-2 attacks began.

Index

For Product Safety Concerns and Information please contact our EU
representative GPSR@taylorandfrancis.com Taylor & Francis Verlag GmbH,
Kaufingerstraße 24, 80331 München, Germany

Batch number: 08153778

Printed by Printforce, the Netherlands